MANAGING ELECTRONIC RESOURCES

MANAGING ELECTRONIC RESOURCES

Prasidh Kumar Mishra

ISHA BOOKS

Managing Electronic Resources

ISBN: 978-81-8205-520-9

Published in 2011 in India by
Isha Books
B-69, New Gupta Colony
New DDA Market
New Delhi-110009

Laser Type Setting by: Shubhdeep Printers, Delhi
Printed at : Chawla Offset Printers, Delhi

CONTENTS

PREFACE

Every literate person are familiar with textbooks, as they are secondary information resources. They will provide you with a good general understanding of a topic. They will often cover many areas of one more general topic. Textbooks will provide you with a good overview and will interprete relevant primary material. To find textbooks on your topic search UCD Library's catalogue using the Keyword function. These are basically research-based articles written by subject experts and professional writers. Some are free online, while others can be purchased. Each journal title focuses on a specific area or discipline. They describe research - the generation of new knowledge - and focus on very specific topics.

If you are interested in digital library research and development, then D-lib magazine will solve your purpose. It is an online magazine. Current and past issues are available free of charge. The publication is financially supported by contributions from the D-Lib Alliance. Prior to April 2006, the magazine was sponsored by the Defense Advanced Research Project Agency (DARPA) on behalf of the Digital Libraries Initiative and by the National Science Foundation (NSF). It seems that the term "hybrid library" was first coined in 1998 by Chris Rusbridge in an article for D-Lib Magazine.

Change is the law of nature and everything changes with the passage of time. Change management wanted to ensure that standardised methods and procedures are used for efficient handling of all changes. A change is "an event that results in a new status of one or more configuration items (CIs)" approved by management, cost effective, enhances business process changes (fixes)—with a minimum risk to IT infrastructure.

CSI refers to aligning and realigning IT services to changing business needs because standstill implies decline. It aims to align and realign IT Services to changing business needs by identifying and implementing improvements to the IT services that support the Business Processes. The perspective of CSI on improvement is the business perspective of service quality, even though CSI aims to improve process effectiveness, efficiency and cost effectiveness of the IT processes through the whole lifecycle.

While writing this book, we searched many reference books, relevant articles, features and blogs and also surf many sites for upto date information and current scenario in Managing Electronic Resources. We are highly grateful to all these resources, without these the completion of this book wouldn't have possible. Suggestions for any improvements are always welcome.

—Author

CHAPTER–1

FACETS OF MANAGEMENT AND RESOURCES TYPES

The world has become a global village, where knowledge can be shared transmitted and explored. The arrival of internet has transformed the image of information technology. The management of vast knowledge is the big question before us. The goal of this essay is to suggest a framework for the design of the meta-information environments for DL's that takes advantage of digital technology and compensates for the loss of direct user-librarian interactions.

The information environment programme has included work on preservation, repositories, linked data, library systems, research management, developer communities etc. .

The widening interest in knowledge management by the IFLA community was confirmed by the approval of Knowledge Management as IFLA Section in December 2003.

With this growing interest in the implementation of Knowledge Management throughout the library and information environment, LIS professionals have expressed a desire for a deeper understanding of KM's multiple dimensions and its relevance to their work. The IFLA KM section endeavors to facilitate the application of KM in libraries by developing a program of activities that supports information professionals implement knowledge management in their own organizations.

WORKING DEFINITION OF KNOWLEDGE MANAGEMENT

Knowledge Management is a technique of creating, storing, sharing, applying and re-using organisational knowledge to enable an organisation to achieve its goals and objectives. The concept of knowledge is not limited to memory, storage and information. The term covers such areas as tacit knowledge (expertise), implicit knowledge, explicit knowledge and procedural knowledge.

DIMENSION OF ORGANISATIONAL MANAGEMENT

KM encompasses many dimensions of organisational management and the activities of the Section are intended to reflect this by providing a wide platform of integrated activities, through working cooperatively with other IFLA sections and divisions, and appropriate professional organisations.

The objectives of the Section are to:

(i) Support the implementation of KM culture in libraries and information environments;

(ii) to make an global platform for professional communication and understanding of the significance of KM for librarians and their institutions

(ii) follow the developments in KM and promote its practical implementation within the IFLA community

To facilitate librarians and to sharpen their skills in an fast changing work environment, the Section seeks to provide theoretical and practical knowledge in areas of KM such as:

(i) sharing of knowledge information;

(ii) improving performance;

(iii) being value-oriented rather than just service-oriented;

(iv) study the advantages and disadvantages of KM implementation;

(v) utilize interactive communication in information settings to enhance knowledge sharing;

(vi) using Information Technology for changing knowledge into information for use;

(vii) knowledge retention and preservation.

The Main Functions of Knowledge Management are :

(i) It aims to work cooperatively with other sections to develop sessions and programmes that focus on various aspects of KM and explore areas of mutual interest e.g., education and training; professional development; LIS theories and methodologies; intercultural communication; organisational development; IT and media.

(ii) To share best practice examples and case studies to make KM applicable to a wide range of information professionals in libraries and information centres, worldwide.

(iii) Study how professional associations influence and support the implementation of KM in libraries and information environments.

(iv) Maintaining a KM Section website as a repository of KM information, KM list-serve for communication and distribution of information relevant to section members and publishing a twice yearly newsletter.

Libraries are systematically arranged to facilitate access to controlled collections of information. Traditional libraries (TL's) have three organizational trait that, together, provide a basis for such access. These are :

(i) the organization of information into physical information objects (IO's) such as books;

(ii) the physical organization of the collections of IO's according to various attributes, such as subject matter and author;

(iii) an organized information environment that develops

direct access to the IO's based on such attributes as author, title, and subject matter, as well as a limited degree of indirect access to the information contained in the IO's.

The third trait involves multiple sources of information to support access, such as librarians, brochures, and the way in which the collections are made. As it involves information about information, one can term this trait the meta-information environment of a library.

Digital libraries (DL's) are libraries in which the controlled collections are in digital form and access to the information in the collections is based almost entirely on digital technology. From a user's point of view, digital technology changes the three organizational characteristics of TL's. First, the organization of information into physical information object is replaceable with a more flexible organization into logical information object. Second, the single physical organization of a collection of information object is replaceable with multiple logical organizations of IO's.

The most visible changes, however, occur in the meta-information environment of a library. Merits : Having the IO's in digital form permits the use of digital technology in extracting information from the IO's. The extracted information may satisfy a user's ultimate need for information. Digal librariesalso do the same purpose. In the latter case, this meta-information may be employed in providing access to the information encoded in the IO's. Demerits important interactions between librarians and users that occur in the meta-information environments of TL's may be lost with the near-automation of information access in DL's.

Later, book we briefly examine the use of the terms "metadata" and "meta-information". Further, we employ a simple scenario of library use in order to characterize the meta-information environment of a traditional libraries. We generalize this characterization to the meta-information environment of libraries in general. The environment is modeled in terms of a set of high-level services which are, in turn, supported by sets of lower level services, some of which are provided by an extensible set of "knowledge representation systems". Finally, we examine the implications of this general characterization in terms of a design for the meta-information environment of a digital library. In particular, we suggest a design that is implementable within a distributed object framework.

Concept of Metadata

As an example of its use in the context of TL's, the term "metadata" is sometimes used to describe the descriptive cataloging that is specified by the Anglo-American cataloging rules and the MARC interchange format. For example, the topics of papers at a recent conference on metadata ranged from metadata in data dictionaries and its use in controlling the operations of database management systems; to metadata used for describing scientific datasets and supporting data sharing among scientists; to metadata used in digital libraries to support user access to information.

The concept of metadata, when applied in the context of current libraries, digital or traditional, typically refers to information that

(i) It provides a (usually brief) characterization of the individual IO's in the collections of a library.

(ii) It is stored principally as the contents of library catalogs in TL's.

(iii) It is used principally in aiding users to access IO's of interest.

Such information constitutes a major component of the cataloging information in most TL's. As an example of its use in the context of DL's, the term "metadata" has been used to describe the information of the "Dublin Core" and the associated "Warwick Framework" which is intended to support access to information on the World Wide Web. The Core specifies the concrete syntax for a small set of meta-information elements, and the Framework specifies a container architecture for aggregating additional metadata objects for interchange.

As we have seen that it becomes apparent that the concept associated with the term "metadata" is the central focus of an emerging area of the information sciences whose objective is to discover appropriate methods for the modeling of various classes of IO's. Since a model of an IO is itself typically an IO, and since the concept that is generally associated with the term "data" is subsumed by the concept associated with the term "information object", it seems preferable to use the term "meta-information" and to define it as a model of an information object.

For the sake of concreteness, let us assume a user whose interest is in finding information on condor re-introduction programs in California. In order to access such information in a traditional library (TL), the user may engage in a variety of activities. The four most important activities include consulting a librarian; consulting available catalog and reference materials; browsing through the open collections of the library; and processing the information that has been accessed.

COGNITIVE MODEL

Let us assume that the user begins a search by consulting a librarian, and indicates an initial interest in discovering whether programs for re-introducing condors from captive breeding populations have been a success. Several important processes may co-occur during these interactions. First, the librarian may build a "cognitive model" of the user that is employed in helping the user. As an example, the librarian may note the user's level of knowledge about the use of a library, and discover that the user does not understand the value of subject heading catalogs in searching for references to information on the decline of the condors.

The librarian may build a cognitive model of the user's information requirements, or "query", typically in an iterative process during which the user may change the initial query. The librarian may discover, for example, that the user would like to know the locations of the release sites in order to visit them. Third, and depending on the context of the query, the librarian may also construct a model of the user's information processing requirements. These might include estimating the time to hike to the release sites.

In conjunction with these emerging models of the user's knowledge base and information needs, the librarian employs a cognitive model of the library's information resources to determine an appropriate set of actions that will lead to the satisfaction of the user's information needs. Three classes of activities are worthy of note. 1. The librarian may direct the user to meta-information, such as the subject catalog, that points directly to IO's of interest. 2. The librarian may guide the user to "general" meta-information that can be used in a less direct manner in finding IO's of interest.

For example, the user may be directed to a gazetteer in order to find the geographical coordinates of the release sites, whose names the librarian may happen to know. These coordinates may then be used in accessing the appropriate maps from the library's map collection. 3. The librarian may suggest that the user browse in the ornithology section of the library to look for books that may be relevant to the topic of condors. In so doing, the user may assess meta-information in the form of titles and tables of contents.

In the final step, the user may employ the relevant maps to calculated the time it would take to hike to the condor release areas.

Satisfying Information Needs

The preceding example, which is by no means artificial, emphasizes the fact that the meta-information accessed by users of TL's in satisfying their information needs is not restricted to the meta-information in the author, title and subject catalogs. In particular, the scenario was devised to emphasize that, during search, a user may conceivably employ as meta-information almost all the information sources in a library. Such sources range from the librarian's general knowledge of the world to information encoded in the IO's on the stacks.

The meta-information environment of a TL can be defined as "The set of all information services accessible to users of the library, together with all available means for co-ordinating the use of these services, that enable users to access, evaluate, and use any information that may be extracted from the total information resources of the library;

An analysis of the preceding and similar usage scenarios suggests that one may further characterize the meta-information environment of a library in terms of a simple model involving sets of services for;

SAMPLE MODEL

(i) coordinating user interactions with the meta-information environment, exemplified in the above scenario in terms of the user's interactions with the librarian;

(ii) constructing models of the user, the user's query, and the user's workspace requirements, exemplified in our scenario by interactions with the librarian;

(iii) providing access to models of IO's, exemplified in our scenario by use of the subject catalog and browsing among the stacks;

(iv) making matches between the model of user queries and models of IO's, exemplified in our scenario in part by actions of the librarian and in part by actions of the user in relation to such library resources as the subject catalog;

(v) extracting information from retrieved IO's, exemplified in our scenario by the computation from the maps of the time it would take the user to hike to the release sites.

(vi) creating models of IO's which, although an important service of the meta-information environment of libraries, is not exemplified in the preceding scenario.

The milieu emphasizes the key role played by librarians in providing services in the meta-information environment of many TL's. It has been understood that the vast use of the services of electronic catalogs in many TL's do not alter the significance of this emphasis for present purposes.

Useful Theoretical Framework

It is useful to introduce the concept of knowledge representation systems (KRS's). Concepts similar to the concept of a KRS that have been used by other researchers in relation to meta-information include formal systems with interpretations and semi-formal systems. We argue that an important component of the functionality of the six sets of meta-information services in TL's is provided by a diverse set of KRS's. This conceptualization in terms of KRS's provides a useful theoretical framework for the design and analysis of DL's.

A knowledge management system (KRS) may be defined as a system for representing and reasoning about the knowledge in some domain of discourse, and is generally comprised of:

(i) an underlying knowledge representation language (KRL), whose expressions are intended to represent knowledge about some domain of discourse;

(ii) a semantics that gives meaning to the expressions of the KRL in terms of the domain of discourse;

(iii) a set of reasoning rules that may be employed in inferring further useful expressions from a given set of expressions;

(iv) a body of knowledge about the domain of discourse expressed in terms of the KRL.

In general, we may view the KRS's of a library as providing a diverse set of services that are of particular value in the modeling of both IO's and user queries. They are, for example, of particular significance in supporting the modeling of IO's in terms of their content, since, in principle, the content of library materials may refer to any representable aspect of our knowledge.

The KRL of a thesaurus, is designed to possess a restricted syntax and semantics that permits the representation of restricted domains of discourse in an unambiguous manner. These restrictions result in the construction of many domain-specific thesauri, which in essence represents a "divide-and-conquer" approach to building unambiguous representations of a complex world.

In order to gain further insight into the nature and significance of KRS's, we provide examples of their use in supporting key sets of services in the meta-information environments of TL's.

Thesauri are an important class of KRS's that are employed in constructing models of the subject matter (or "content") of IO's for the catalog systems of TL's. The motivation for the use of thesauri is the difficulties that arise from using a KRS based on natural language (NL) in this context. These difficulties arise from the syntactic and semantic complexity and the high levels of ambiguity that are typically associated with general expressions in NL.

ANSI-NISO Standard for Theasuras

For the present purpose, we may use a highly-simplified view of a thesaurus that is abstracted from the ANSI-NISO standard for thesauri.

(i) The KRL of a thesaurus may be viewed as specifying the terms of a simple language and a few relations (or predicates) defined on the terms. These predicates include the three "broad term/narrow-term" predicates, the "related term" predicate, and the "synonymous term" predicate.

(ii) In relation to the semantics associated with its KRL, a term defined in a thesaurus is intended to denote a single concept. Typically, terms represent classes of entities, although class instances are permitted. Ambiguity arising from synonymous and homonymous terms is effectively removed. The mapping from terms to concepts is provided informally by the cognitive processing of the reader of the terms.

(iii) With respect to reasoning procedures, the use of the basic inference rules of logic (such as "if A and A implies B are both true, then B is true"), together with axioms involving the various predicates (such as "if A is a narrow term for B, and B is a narrow term for C, then A is a narrow term for C"), it is possible to carry out simple reasoning that is interpretable in terms of the concepts being represented in the KRL.

(iv) In terms of viewing a thesaurus as representing a body of knowledge about some aspect of the world, the terms and predicates of a thesaurus represent a set of concepts and their relations that model some aspect of the world.

Large numbers of thesauri are currently employed in library contexts. The representation of the content of IO's is typically achieved by choosing a relatively small number of terms from some domain-specific thesaurus.

CLASSES OF KRS

Other classes of KRS that are also employed in the modeling of IO's for the catalog systems of TL's include subject headings and descriptive cataloging systems. The Library of Congress Subject Headings now bear great apparent similarities to thesauri. They are different in the sense that single terms do not necessarily denote a single concept. The descriptive cataloging that is used to represent such contextual information about IO's as title and author, may also be interpreted in terms of KRS's. In particular, the KRL that is employed for most of the descriptive cataloging in TL's is specified by the Anglo-American cataloging rules (AACR2) and the MARC interchange format for exchanging such information between libraries.

KRS in the User, Query, and Workspace Modeling Component

In traditional libraries, there are a variety of KRS that may aid a user in expressing a query that is answerable in terms of the catalog. A gazetteer is a good example of such a KRS and is essentially a set of terms that represent classes of features on the surface of the Earth, such as rivers and towns, and a large set of named instances of such features, such "Brahamputra River". The spatial coordinates of the feature instances on the surface of the

Earth are provided as an essential component of a gazetteer. One may therefore view a gazetteer as a geographic thesaurus of limited extent, in which large numbers of class instances are given, and a function is defined on these instances that assigns geographic coordinates to the instances.

ELECTRONIC CATALOGS

In TL's with electronic catalogs, KRS's may be employed in representing user queries. A simple example is the use of the terms of the KRL of some thesaurus in order to represent the content that a user wishes to find in acceptable IO's. In the case of representing queries, the user is frequently permitted to define the content of IO's in terms of boolean expressions of the terms from acceptable thesauri. The reasoning procedures of the thesaurus may be used to expand the representation of the query by replacing, for example, one synonym with another, or a narrow term with a broad term.

It is not unreasonable to view a librarian as providing the services of a large set of KRS's, each focused on a specific domain of discourse. These KRS's are employed in the various roles played by the librarian in the meta-information environment of a library.

The meta-information environments of current DL's may be viewed as special cases of the preceding model. In terms of the testbed for the Alexandria Digital Library (ADL), for example, the system provides services that: support access to models of IO's in terms of USMARC and Federal Geographic Data Committee (FGDC) standards; support the construction of models of user queries in terms of regions of interest, defined in part by the services of a background map and in part by the services of a gazetteer, as well as models of IO's based USMARC/FGDC standards: support the computation of exact matches between query and IO models; and support a simple workspace involving a local cache in which users may save retrieved items.

It currently appears reasonable, therefore, to use the general model of the meta-information environment of a TL developed above as a basis for designing the meta-information environment of a DL.

Main Clusters of Services

(i) A first set of services provides support for the coordination of interactions between the user and the meta-information environment.

(ii) A second set of services is employed in modeling the user, the queries presented by the user, and the workspace requirements of the user. The services are intended to represent some of the functionality of a librarian in relation to similar services in TL's. In modeling a user, for example, there may be a service for determining a user's area of expertise and, on this basis, choosing a KRL in which the user's query may be expressed.

(iii) A third set of services supports storage of, and access to, models of the IO's available in the collections of the library, as well as other corresponding libraries. In general, the models of IO's may be interpreted in terms of various relations between some symbolic representation of the IO itself and representations of the characteristics of the IO. In particular, the representations of the IO itself may be provided in terms of access paths and the representations of the characteristics of the IO expressed in some KRL. As in the catalog of a traditional library, therefore, these services support direct access to IO's on the basis of the characteristics of the IO's. These services may be generalized to provide models of aggregates of IO's and even of whole libraries. Such aggregate representations are of value for realizing the efficiencies associated with hierarchical search.

(iv) A fourth set of services supports choosing and applying appropriate matching procedures between models of user queries and models of IO's. The goal of these services is to return appropriate IO's to the user. The matching services may involve, for example, query translation (since the models of IO's may be represented in languages that are different from the languages in which the user's query is represented); branching by search type, hierarchical search, and iterative search. Matching may employ different matching services depending on the nature of the query using, for example, standard information retrieval procedures for text information or a browsing-type search for images based on a relevance feedback algorithm. The process may proceed iteratively and hierarchically, by returning to the user information that allows the user to have input into the search process. The system may present, for example, generalized information about the content of various sub-collections in order to obtain information on the most appropriate sub-collections to search. There may also be services that support the distribution to other libraries of queries that cannot be satisfied.

(v) It supports access to, and application of, procedures that may be applied to retrieved IO's in order to extract useful information. Such services may, for example, include the modeling of procedures and the modeling of the results of applying procedures to IO's.

(vi) It provides support for librarians in creating models of IO's. These services may also support, for example, the automated creation of aggregate representations of collections of IO's and of whole libraries.

We note that this list of sets of services is not intended to be exhaustive.

High-level Services of a Digital Library

Digital technology makes it possible to construct relatively complete and complex models of queries and IO's. We envisage the high-level services of a digital library as being supported, in part, by other sets of services that are provided by various KRS's. The services of a given KRS may support several sets of high-level services, as in the case of the services of a thesaurus supporting the modeling of both queries and IO's. We now provide a few examples of classes of KRS's that may be of value in supporting the high-level services of the meta-information environment of a DL.

Services of particular importance in the meta-information environment of a DL are those supporting the construction of models of both user queries and the IO's of the library. Important categories of characteristics of IO's, for example, that may be modeled by meta-information include the access path of the IO; the type of the IO (such as book, map, or video); the logical structure of the IO including such structural components as title page, preface, chapters, and index if it is a book; the representation of the IO, including its form (html file, or postscript file, or gif file); and its language (English, or French, or Arabic); the context of the IO (including such information as author, publisher, lineage); the content of the IO; the terms and conditions of access to, and use of, the IO; evaluative information about of the IO, particularly with respect to its value in various applications; the relations of the IO to other IO's.

An example of a characteristic of an aggregate of IO's that may be modeled by meta-information is the number of items in the aggregate that possess specified values for a given characteristic of the individual IO's.

The services of an extensible set of KRS's may be employed in constructing models of queries and IO's in terms of such categories of meta-information. These KRS include digital versions of some of the KRS mentioned in the context of TL's, such as thesauri, subject headings, and gazetteers. Digital technology, however, makes it possible to support a wide variety of other KRS. We briefly discuss a few of these possibilities.

(i) As the power and efficiency of NL processing increases, it is likely that partial modeling of IO's in terms of NL as the KRL of choice will become important. It is reasonable to assume, for example, that NL representations of the abstracts of text documents will be used as partial models of IO's.

(ii) There is widespread current interest in using ontologies as a basis for modeling IO's. An ontology may be generally defined as a linguistic representation of a conceptualization of some domain of knowledge. Hence an ontology may be viewed as a KRS. In general, ontologies specify fairly general languages, and typically include specifications of classes, relations, functions, and other objects. They differ from the representation schemes provided by thesauri, for example, insofar as the semantic relations defined over the terms are not necessarily strictly hierarchical. In the general case, the KRL's of ontologies are equivalent to first order predicate calculus.

(iii) An advantage of such KRS's is that predicate calculus is well-understood, particularly in terms of the inferential mechanisms associated with this logic. There is also a growing interest in KRS whose KRL's are graphical in nature. Conceptual Structures, for example, represent a class of KRS's for which the KRL's have an expressive power equivalent to that of the predicate calculus, and whose expressions have a graphical form. It is also possible to employ KRS with iconic KRL's, in which there is a natural relationship between the form of the expressions and their meaning. An example of such a KRL for modeling image IO's would be reduced resolution images.

(iv) There are variety of special KRS's that have been developed for the purpose of modeling specific classes of IO's. One such class of KRS's are various metadata content standards, such as the FGDC metadata content standard, which was designed specifically to model digitized maps and images. In particular, we note that the FGDC specification permits the use of iconic terms.

It is important that designs for the meta-information environment allow the easy addition of new KRS's and removal of old KRS's. This is facilitated by distributed object technology. A related research issue of some interest concerns whether it is best to use a large number of relatively small KRS's, or a small number of relatively large KRS's.

The research issue concerns the construction of semantic mappings between the KRL's of different KRS's. It is possible to employ different sets of KRS's for modeling user queries and for modeling IO's. There is therefore a need for translation during the application of matching services. One approach to constructing such mappings involves the use of human experts working in a top-down manner, which is likely to be a time-consuming and controversial process. An approach that is promising in terms of automation involves bottom-up techniques based on empirical analyses of the use of language.

The meta-information environment of a library is the aspect of library structure that is likely to be most affected by DL technology. It is important to design meta-information environments for DL's that simultaneously compensate for the loss of many of the services of librarians and take advantage of the ability to apply digital processing to information objects in the collection of DL's. In particular, the essay suggests the importance of a top-down component that takes the perspective of the user in the process of designing such environments.

The approach to design suggested in the essay involves the implementation of a meta-information environment in terms of six basic sets of services that are, at least in part, supported by services from a variety of knowledge representation systems. Such an environment is probably best implemented within a distributed object framework.

We need different resources for different information needs. Wecan't get all the information under one roof. It is upto you which resource you think is the best possible option for the information you need. Information in its most restricted technical sense is an ordered sequence of symbols that record or transmit a message. It can be recorded as signs, or conveyed as signals by waves.

Information is a vast field and it has multiple meanings. Nowadays, every corporate sector have a information officer who give information and solve the query of prespective clients.

IMPORTANCE OF INPUTS

Information is seen as a type of input of an organism or system inputs that influences the formation or transformation of other. In this sense, there is no need for a conscious mind to perceive, much less appreciate, the pattern. Consider, for example, DNA. The sequence of nucleotides is a pattern that influences the formation and development of an organism without any need for a conscious mind. Inputs are of two types. Some inputs are important to the function of the organism (for example, food) or system (energy) by themselves. In his book *Sensory Ecology*, Dusenbery called these as causal inputs. Other inputs (information) are important only because they are associated with causal inputs and can be used to predict the occurrence of a causal input at a later time (and perhaps another place). Some information vitual as of association with other information but eventually there must be a link to a causal input.

Information is generally carried by weak stimuli that must be detected by specialized sensory systems and amplified by energy inputs before they can be functional to the organism or system. For example, light is often a causal input to plants but provides information to animals. The colored light reflected from a flower is too less to do much photosynthetic work but the visual system of the bee detects it and the bee's nervous system uses the information to guide the bee to the flower, where the bee often finds nectar or pollen, which are causal inputs, serving a nutritional function.

Primary Information

Original material that has not been interpreted or analysied.

Statistics, Research articles, Blogs, Websites

Secondary Material

Created from primary material, interpretating original material.

Texbooks, Review articles

Tertiary Material

Acts as a tool in understanding and locating information

Databases, Subject Gateways, Dictionaries, Bibliographies

Primary Sources

Research, Statistics and Interviews

Conscious Mind

Sigmund Frevd was a word renowned sociologist who wrote on human relationships and psychoanalytic theory of personality. He states that conscious mind is vast which includes everything that touches awareness. Conscious mind guide and motivate us to think and act in a pragmatic way. The conscious mind carries such things as the sensations, perceptions, memories, feeling and fantasies inside of our current awareness. Closely allied with the conscious mind is the preconscious, which includes the things that we are not thinking of at the moment but which we can easily draw into conscious awareness.

System Theory

It is the transdisciplinary study of systems in general, with the goal of elucidating principles that can be applied to all kinds of systems in all fields of research. The term does not yet have a well-established, precise meaning, but systems theory can reasonably be considered a specialization of systems thinking and a generalization of systems science. The term originates from Bertalanffy's General System Theory (GST) and is used in later efforts in other fields, such as the action theory of Talcott Parsons and the system-theory of Niklas Luhmann.

Gregory Bateson defines "information" as a "difference that makes a difference". Systems theory at times seems to refer to information in this sense, assuming information does not necessarily involve any conscious mind, and patterns circulating (due to feedback) in the system can be called information. In other words, it can be said that information in this sense is something potentially perceived as representation, though not created or presented for that purpose.

If, however, the premise of "influence" implies that information has been perceived by a conscious mind and also interpreted by it, the specific context associated with this interpretation may cause the transformation of the information into knowledge.

Both "information" and "knowledge" make such semantic and logical analysis difficult, but the condition of "transformation" is an important point in the study of information as it relates to knowledge, especially in the business discipline of knowledge management. In this practice, tools and processes are used to assist a knowledge worker in performing research and making decisions, including the following steps are :

1. reviewing information in order to effectively derive value and meaning;
2. referencing metadata if any is available;
3. establishing a relevant context, often selecting from many possible contexts;
4. deriving new knowledge from the information;
5. making decisions or recommendations from the resulting knowledge.

Transformation of Information

Stewart (2001) opines that the transformation of information into knowledge is a critical one, lying at the core of value creation and competitive advantage for the modern enterprise.

The Danish Dictionary of Information Terms argues that information only provides an answer to a posed question. Whether the answer provides knowledge depends on the informed person.

So a generalized definition of the concept should be: "Information"is an answer to a specific question".

When Marshall McLuhan speaks of media and their effects on human cultures, he refers to the structure of artifacts that in turn shape our behaviors and mindsets. Also, pheromones are often said to be "information" in this sense.

INFORMATION RESOURCES

The world of information is vast and so are the resources. Technology advantage have added new dimensions to the information resources. Sometimes back, we have only books, journals, newspapers, magazines as resources for information. Now, the internet, search engines and websites have totally revolutionized the information industry.

Reference

Reference is generally for research scholars looking for detail and deep infomation. Reference material includes dictionaries, enclyopedias and bibliographies. UCD library provides access to a wide range of online reference material.

Textbooks

Every literate person are familiar with textbooks, as they are secondary information resources. They will provide you with a good general understanding of a topic. They will often cover many areas of one more general topic. Textbooks will provide you with a good overview and will interprete relevant primary material. To find textbooks on your topic search UCD Library's catalogue using the Keyword function.

Journal Articles

These are basically research-based articles written by subject experts and professional writers. Some are free online, while others can be purchased. Each journal title focuses on a specific area or discipline. They describe research - the generation of new knowledge - and focus on very specific topics.

Databases

These are tertiary sources information. Which allow us to search across a range of journal articles from different journals.

Don't forget to see the 'scope' or 'about' feature of a database to see what years it covers.

Newspapers

Newspapers are cheapest and convenient source of information about politics, world affairs, crime, development report etc. UCD Library provides access to both print and electronic versions of daily newspapers.

Conference Proceedings

These are primary sources of information and record papers presented at conferences.

Websites

A website of any company or organisations gives the detail information on a topic or company profile.

Subject Gateways

it provide a useful starting point when searching for information on the Internet. They provide access to relevant and reliable webistes. UCD Library Subject Portals are subject gateways.

Statistics

Statistics are primary information. They can be very useful for looking at patterns and trends.

Search Engines

These are tools to search information on Internet. There are especially two kinds of specialized search engines news searchs engines and blogs search engines.

PHYSICAL INFORMATION

In 2003, J. D. Bekenstein claimed there is a growing trend in physics to define the physical world as being made of information itself (and thus information is defined in this way). Information has a well-defined meaning in physics. Examples of this include the phenomenon of quantum entanglement where particles can interact without reference to their separation or the speed of light.

Information is transmitted fastly from source to various persons. This could lead to the fact that all attempts at physically observing a particle with an "entangled" relationship to another are slowed down, even though the particles are not connected in any other way other than by the information they carry. In Maxwell's demon experiment, a direct relationship between information and another physical property, entropy, is demonstrated.

A consequence is that it is impossible to destroy information without increasing the entropy of a system; in practical terms this often means generating heat. Another, more philosophical, outcome is that information could be thought of as interchangeable with energy. Thus, in the study of logic gates, the theoretical lower bound of thermal energy released by an and gate is higher than for the NOT gate (because information is destroyed in an AND gate and simply converted in a NOT gate). Physical information is of peculiar importance in the theory of quantum computers.

Records : Means of Information

The international standard on records management, ISO 15489, defines records as "information created, received, and maintained as evidence and information by an organization or person, in pursuance of legal obligations or in the transaction of business". Records are an important form of information. Essentially, records are information produced consciously or as by-products of business activities or transactions and retained because of their value. Primarily their value is as evidence of the activities of the organization but they may also be retained for their informational value. Sound records management ensures that the integrity of records is preserved for as long as they are required.

The International Committee on Archives (ICA) Committee on electronic records defined a record as, "a specific piece of recorded information generated, collected or received in the initiation, conduct or completion of an activity and that comprises sufficient content, context and structure to provide proof or evidence of that activity".

According to management guru Willis to meet legal, fiscal and accountability requirements of any organization, records should be maintained. "...six key requirements for good corporate governance...transparency; accountability; due process; compliance; meeting statutory and common law requirements; and security of personal and corporate information."

MULTI-FACETED CONCEPT OF INFORMATION

Beynon-Davies explains the multi-faceted concept of information in terms of signs and signal-sign systems. Signs themselves can be considered in terms of four inter-dependent levels, layers or branches of semiotics: pragmatics, semantics, syntax and empirics. These four layers serve to connect the social world on the one hand with the physical or technical world on the other...

Pragmatics is basically concerned with the purpose of communication and links the issue of signs with the context within which signs are used. The focus of pragmatics is on the intentions of living agents underlying communicative behaviour. In other words, pragmatics link language to action.

Semantics is concerned with content of communication and with the meaning of a signs and message conveyed in a communicative act. Semantics is the study of the meaning of signs-the association between signs and behaviour. It can be considered as the study of the link between symbols and their referents or concepts; particularly the way in which signs relate to human behaviour.

Syntax explores the form of communication in terms of the logic and grammar of sign systems. Syntax is devoted to the study of the form rather than the content of signs and sign-systems. It is mainly concerned with the formalism used to represent a message.

Empirics is the study of the signals used to carry a message; and of communication. Empirics is devoted to the study of communication channels and their characteristics, e.g., sound, light, electronic transmission etc..

Concept of Lexicographic Information Costs

Information is the amount of the data after data compression. Nielsen (2008) studied the relationship between semiotics and information in relation to dictionaries. The concept of lexicographic information costs is introduced and refers to the efforts users of dictionaries need to make in order to, first, find the data sought and, secondly, understand the data so that they can generate information.

Generally communication exists within the context some social situation or enviornment. The social situation sets the context for the intentions conveyed (pragmatics) and the form in which communication takes place. In a communicative situation, intentions are expressed through messages which comprise collections of inter-related signs taken from a language which is mutually understood by the agents involved in the communication.

Mutual understanding implies that agents involved understand the chosen language in terms of its agreed syntax (syntactics) and semantics. The sender codes the message in the language and sends the message as signals along some communication channel (empirics). The chosen communication channel will have inherent properties which determine outcomes such as the speed with which communication can take place and over what distance.

Combined Online Information System

It is a HM Treasury's detailed analysis of departmental spending under thousands of category headings. The database contains around 24 million lines of data. The database has codes for more than 1,700 public bodies in the United Kingdom including central government departments, local authorities, NHS trusts and public corporations. COINS is used by the Office of National Statistics for statistical purposes.

The database describes a by treasury as “a web based multi-dimensional database used by HM Treasury to collect financial information”.Data from the COINS database is used to prepare the National Accounts. The Combined Online Information System or COINS database is one of the biggest datasets in government. COINS uses a database called Camelot. The system is supplied by Descisys.

During British rule, there were Public Expenditure System (PES), Government Online Data System (GOLD) and General Expenditure Monitoring System (GEMS). But COINS replaced these systems.

The Treasury turned down requests under the Freedom of Information Act 2000 for data contained in COINS prior to the 2010 General Election. However, after promises during the election campaign to publish the database if elected, the coalition government has made available all 120GB of COINS data in a raw format as of 4 June 2010. The hope in doing so is that this will spur third party organisations to find innovative ways to present this information to the public.

Understanding Silo Busting

We are familiar of the fact that systems atrophy when they divide their work into silos. Silos entrench difference and prevent learning across sectors whether we are talking about departments in an organization, or a social system like health care or child and family services.

It have ephemereal life. They divide work into manageable chunks. But in general they create reductionist responses to systemic problems and they pose a massive challenge to people working for change. If we first have to bust the silos, and only then can we address the problems, how do we know we’ll have energy left for the real work?

Silos arethe reality of any organizaton. Seventy-five percent of the 440 organizations in the Global Intranet Trends survey say that their main silos are those represented by employee functions such as HR, communications and IT. Silos are behind much of the difficulty in achieving a coherent digital workplace from an employee viewpoint. Different stakeholders have different sites and approaches; lack of overall coordination is not unusual.

Automated customization of the common entry point into the digital workplace correlates to fewer silos in the enterprise.

- The "employee support silos" drops from 75 percent to 58 percent when half or more of the content on the common entry page is customized in an automated way.
- The "collaborative space silos" drops from 43 percent to 30 percent.

Obviously, the question is: do the "less silo'ed" enterprises also have more automated customization? Or does customization somehow help breakdown the silos? I have run workshops in many complex, multi-stakeholder organizations where the objective was to define a customization strategy for the entry page. The workshops are sometimes tough going because, in many cases, they trigger conversations between employee support functions that have never before worked together on a shared project.

Need of Individual Personalization

Need of correlates with a drop in employee support silos, but increases for collaborative space silos to 47 %, slightly higher than the survey average.

In spite of the general belief that people do not use it, the leaders enable it more than the others. 14 % enable it for half or more of the content compared to 8 % of the others.

HYBRID LIBRARY

Can traditional books and magazines can be juxtapose with electronic-based material like e-books, electronic journals etc. The answer is "Hybrid Library." It is a mix of traditional and digital library. Majority of the libraries in these days are hybrid libraries. The libraries own and subscribe to different resources in different formats. Some of the common formats are e-journals, serials, print monographs, CD and DVD. The main components of digital library framework are user interfaces, repository, handles system, and search system. A proposed model of the hybrid library was developed and was shown to the eLib hybrid library projects. Reactions to the model were obtained. In addition, the paper reports the results of details discussions with the project staff regarding how the hybrid library will evolve. It is clear that the development of the hybrid library depends more upon cultural shift than technological development.

Academic Library

The emergence of the hybrid library has put a new emphasis on copyright issues for many libraries. The complicated and changing copyright laws in both the United States and the European Union have made it a challenge for many libraries to make sure their patrons are using the digital items lawfully.

Hybrid libraries are the new norm for many archivists as well. Digitization has changed the way archivists have gone about preserving historical items. Archivists are now using digital technology to preserve items that were once only preserved by things like microfiche. Archivists now use things like digital imaging which make it possible for researchers to see historical items online. Academic library usually cater the propose of graduate and postgraduate students and also research materials for thesis work. These libraries serve two complementary purposes: to support the school's curriculum, and to support the research of the university faculty and students. The support of teaching requires material for class readings and for student papers. In the past, the material for class readings, intended to supplement lectures as prescribed by the instructor, has been called reserves. In the period before electronic resources became available, the reserves were supplied as actual books or as photocopies of appropriate journal articles.

Traditionally, one copy of a book was made available for each ten students — this is practical for large classes only if paperback copies are available, and the books reused from term to term.

Academic libraries must decide what focus they take in collecting materials since no single library can supply everything. When there are particular areas of specialization in academic libraries these are often referred to as niche collections. These collections are often the basis of a special collection department and may include original papers, artwork, and artifacts written or created by a single author or about a specific subject.

If you are interested in digital library research and development, then D-lib magazine will solve your purpose. It is an online magazine. Current and past issues are available free of charge. The publication is financially supported by contributions from the D-Lib Alliance. Prior to April 2006, the magazine was sponsored by the Defense Advanced Research Project Agency (DARPA) on behalf of the Digital Libraries Initiative and by the National Science Foundation (NSF). It seems that the term "hybrid library" was first coined in 1998 by Chris Rusbridge in an article for D-Lib Magazine. Hybrid libraries evolved in the 1990s when electronic resources became more easily available for libraries to acquire for public use. Initially these electronic resources were typically access to material distributed on media such as CD-ROM or searches of specialised databases. OCLC helped push libraries towards acquiring digital resources by providing a centralized technology resource for participating libraries.Now, with the widespread availability of digital content, it includes Internet resources and documents which are online, such as eprints.

Hybrid libraries need staff that are trained in helping patrons navigate the vast amount of information available in the digital age. Librarians working in hybrid libraries have training in electronic media as well as the traditional print forms.

The problems hybrid libraries facing are the digital divide, interoperability, collection development, ownership of electronic resources and preservation of digital media. Any advancement in information technology will be useful only when you know how to use it. The term digital divide is used to describe the gap between those with information technology knowledge and those who do not.

The handle system and search system are the main components that should be designed with interoperability features to search across different repositories owned by different vendors. The user interface should be designed in a generic way that it helps library patrons develop a common knowledge to do advanced searches across all repositories.

Challenge

Hybrid library is facing an another challange which is, collection development. The process of collection management in a hybrid library is similar to that of a traditional library. Hybrid libraries follow the same policies and procedures followed in traditional library collection development.

Ownership of Electronic Resources

There are no clear policies about the ownership of electronic materials once the subscription is cancelled or expired. It is another issue facing the hybrid libraries. Ownership of electronic materials is virtual and not physical. Libraries have to pay attention to the legal contracts from the database vendors. If the libraries plan on archiving the electronic resources, then there are legal issues related to it. The most prominent legal issues are intellectual property and authenticity of digital information.

Preservation of Digital Media

Whether it's traditional way of storage or digital technology, durability of stored information is the pre-requisite any librarian. To make the preservation of digital media cost effective, standardization of different media format is required.

Technology preservation is not an easy task as it requires both hardware and software preservation which needs to be upgraded at regular period of time.

In emulation, some emulator software programs will mimic the hardware and software of the original data and display in the original format. In migration, digital information is converted to a standard media with standard format.

INFORMATION TECHNOLOGY INFRASTRUCTURE IN HYBRID LIBRARY (ITIL)

ITIL was built on the basis of process-model based view of controlling and managing operations designed by W. Edwards Deming and his plan-do-check-act (PDCA) cycle. It is contains Information Technology Services Management (ITSM), Information Technology (IT) development and IT operations. It gives detailed descriptions of a number of important IT practices and provides comprehensive checklists, tasks and procedures that any IT organization can tailor to its needs. ITIL is published in a series of books, each of which covers an IT management topic. The names ITIL and IT Infrastructure Library are registered trademarks of the United Kingdom's Office of Government Commerce (OGC).

After the initial publication in 1989–1996, the number of books quickly grew within ITIL v1 to over 30 volumes. In 2000/2001, to make ITIL more accessible (and affordable), ITIL v2 consolidated the publications into 8 logical "sets" that grouped related process-guidelines to match different aspects of IT management, applications, and services. However, the main focus was known as the Service Management sets (Service Support and Service Delivery) which were by far the most widely used, circulated, and understood of ITIL v2 publications.

In April 2001, the CCTA was merged into the Office of Government Commerce (OGC), an office of the UK Treasury. In 2006, the ITIL v2 glossary was published. In May 2007, this organisation issued the version 3 of ITIL (also known as the ITIL Refresh Project) consisting of 26 processes and functions, now grouped under only five volumes, arranged around the concept of Service lifecycle structure. In 2009, the OGC officially announced that ITIL v2 certification would be withdrawn and launched a major consultation as per how to proceed.

It focuses on the user of the ICT services and is primarily concerned with ensuring that they have access to the appropriate services to support the business functions.

To a business, customers and users are the entry point to the process model. They get involved in service support by the following points : Asking for changes, Needing communication, updates, Having difficulties, queries and Real process delivery.

The single contact-point for end-users' incidents is functions by the service desk. Its first function is always to "create" an incident. If there is a direct solution, it attempts to resolve the incident at the first level. If the service desk cannot solve the incident then it is passed to a 2nd/3rd level group within the incident management system.

Incidents can initiate a chain of processes: Incident Management, Problem Management, Change Management, Release Management and Configuration Management. This chain of processes is tracked using the Configuration Management Database (CMDB), which records each process, and creates output documents for traceability (Quality Management).

Handling Incidents and Requests

Tasks include handling incidents and requests, and providing an interface for other ITSM processes. The following features include :

1. single point of contact.
2. single point of entry and exit.
3. Customers friendly.
4. Data integrity
5. Smooth communication channel.

The main functions of the Service Desk include:

(a) incident control: life-cycle management of all service requests

(b) communication: keeping the customer informed of progress and advising on workarounds

The Service Desk function can have various names, there the following names.

(a) Call Center: main emphasis on professionally handling large call volumes of telephone-based transactions

(b) Help Desk: manage, co-ordinate and resolve incidents as quickly as possible at primary support level

(c) Service Desk: not only handles incidents, problems and questions but also provides an interface for other activities such as change requests, maintenance contracts, software licenses, service-level management, configuration management, availability management, financial management and IT services continuity management

The three types of structure for consideration are:

1. Local Service Desk: To meet local business needs - practical only until multiple locations requiring support services are involved
2. Central Service Desk: For organizations having multiple locations - reduces operational costs and improves usage of available resources
3. Virtual Service Desk: For organizations having multi-country locations - can be situated and accessed from anywhere in the world due to advances in network performance and telecommunications, reducing operational costs and improving usage of available resources

INCIDENT MANAGEMENT

Incident Management can be defined as an 'Incident' is any event which is not part of the standard operation of the service and which causes, or may cause, an interruption or a reduction of the quality of the service.

This is target to restore normal service operation as quickly as possible and minimise the adverse effect on business operations, thus ensuring that the best possible levels of service-quality and -availability are maintained. 'Normal service operation' is defined here as service operation within Service Level Agreement (SLA) limits.

The main aim is to restore normal operations as quickly as possible with the least possible impact on either the business or the user, at a cost-effective price.

PROBLEM MANAGEMENT

The principal purpose of problem management is to find and resolve the main cause of a problem and thus prevent further incidents. The aim of incident management is to return the service to normal level as soon as possible, with smallest possible business impact.

A 'problem' is an unknown underlying cause of one or more incidents, and a 'known error' is a problem that is successfully diagnosed and for which either a work-around or a permanent resolution has been identified.

It wanted to resolve the main cause of incidents and thus to minimise the adverse impact of incidents and problems on business that are caused by errors within the IT infrastructure, and to prevent recurrence of incidents related to these errors. The CCTA(Central Computer and Telecommunications Agency) defines problems and th following are the known errers :

A problem is a condition often identified as a result of multiple incidents that exhibit common symptoms. Problems can also be identified from a single significant incident, indicative of a single error, for which the cause is unknown, but for which the impact is significant.

A known error is a condition identified by successful diagnosis of the root cause of a problem, and the subsequent development of a work-around.

Problem Management is Totally Different from Incident Management

The problem-management process is intended to reduce the number and severity of incidents and problems on the business, and report it in documentation to be available for the first-line and second line of the help desk. The proactive process identifies and resolves problems before incidents occur. The following processes include:

1. Analysis of Trend;
2. Targeting support action;
3. Alert the organisation or company before any mishop or error is likely to strike.

The Error Control Process iteratively diagnoses known errors until they are eliminated by the successful implementation of a change under the control of the Change Management process.

The Problem Control Process aims to handle problems in an efficient way. Problem control identifies the main cause of incidents and reports it to the service desk. Other activities are:

1. Problem identification and recording;
2. Problem classification; and
3. Problem investigation and diagnosis.

The main task is to dig out the root cause of a problem Every problem has a solution. A technique for identifying the root cause of a problem is to use an Ishikawa diagram, also referred to as a cause-and-effect diagram, tree diagram, or fishbone diagram. Alternatively, a formal Root Cause Analysis method such as Apollo Root Cause Analysis can be implemented and used to identify causes and solutions. An effective root cause analysis method and/or tool will provide the most effective/efficient solutions to address problems in the Problem Management process.

CHANGE MANAGEMENT

Change is the law of nature and everything changes with the passage of time. Change management wanted to ensure that standardised methods and procedures are used for efficient handling of all changes,

A change is "an event that results in a new status of one or more configuration items (CIs)" approved by management, cost effective, enhances business process changes (fixes)—with a minimum risk to IT infrastructure.

The main purpose of Change Management include:

1. Minimal disruption of services
2. Reduction in back-out activities
3. Economic utilization of resources involved in the change

Change Management Terminology

- Change: the addition, modification or removal of CIs
- Request for Change (RFC) or in older terminology Change Request (CR): form used to record details of a request for a change and is sent as an input to Change Management by the Change Requestor
- Forward Schedule of Changes (FSC): schedule that contains details of all forthcoming Changes.

RELEASE MANAGEMENT

Quality control during the development and implementation of new hardware and software is the responsibility of Release Management. It is only used by software migration team for platform-independent and automated distribution of software and hardware, including license controls across the entire IT infrastructure. Proper software and hardware control ensures the availability of licensed, tested, and version-certified software and hardware, which functions as intended when introduced into existing infrastructure. This guarantees that all software meets the demands of the business processes.

CONFIGURATION MANAGEMENT

It is the management and traceability of every aspect of a configuration from initial to last and it includes the following key process areas under its umbrella : Identification, Planning, Change Control, Change Management, Release Management, Maintenance, process that tracks all individual Configuration Items (CI) generated by applying all of the key process areas in a system.

The service delivery discipline concerntrates on the proactive services the ICT must deliver to provide adequate support to business users. It focuses on the business as the customer of the ICT services. The discipline consists of the following processes:

Service Level Management

The service level management process is in close relation with the operational processes to control their activities. It provides for continual identification, monitoring and review of the levels of IT services specified in the Service Level Agreements (SLAs). It ensures that arrangements are in place with internal IT Support-Providers and external suppliers in the form of Operational Level Agreements (OLAs) and Underpinning Contracts (UCs), respectively.

The process involves assessing the impact of change upon service quality and SLAs. The central role of Service Level Management makes it the natural place for metrics to be established and monitored against a benchmark.

Service Level Management is the primary interface with the customer as opposed to the user serviced by the Service Desk. Service Level Management is responsible for:

(i) ensuring that the agreed IT services are delivered when and where they are supposed to be;

(ii) liaising with Availability Management, Capacity Management, Incident Management and Problem Management to ensure that the required levels and quality of service are achieved within the resources agreed with Financial Management;

(iii) producing and maintaining a Service Catalog (a list of standard IT service options and agreements made available to customers);

(iv) ensuring that appropriate IT Service Continuity plans exist to support the business and its continuity requirements;

The Service Level Manager relies on the other areas of the Service Delivery process to provide the necessary support which ensures the agreed services are provided in a cost-effective, secure and efficient manner.

Capacity Management

It supports the optimum and cost-effective provision of IT services by helping organisations match their IT resources to business demands. The high-level activities include:

- Application Sizing
- Workload Management
- Demand Management
- Modelling
- Capacity Planning
- Resource Management
- Performance Management

IT SERVICE CONTINUITY MANAGEMENT

It explores the processes by which plans are implemented and managed to ensure that IT Services can recover and continue even after a serious incident occurs. It is not just about reactive measures, but also about proactive measures -reducing the risk of a disaster in the first instance.

Few years back, many businesses practice the much further-reaching process of Business Continuity Planning (BCP), to ensure that the whole end-to-end business process can continue should a serious incident occur (at primary support level).

It contains the following steps and they are given below :

1. Prioritizing the activities to be recovered by conducting a Business Impact Analysis (BIA)
2. Analyzing a Risk Assessment (aka risk analysis) for each of the IT Services to identify the assets, threats, vulnerabilities and countermeasures for each service.
3. Evaluating the options for recovery
4. Testing, reviewing, and revising the plan on a regular basis.

AVAILABILITY MANAGEMENT

It targets allowing organisations to sustain the IT service-availability to support the business at a reasonable cost. The high-level activities are Realise Availability Requirements, Compile Availability Plan, Monitor Availability, and Monitor Maintenance Obligations.

Availability Management addresses the ability of an IT component to perform at an agreed level over a period of time.

1. *Reliability*: Ability of an IT component to perform at an agreed level at described conditions.
2. *Maintainability*: The ability of an IT component to remain in, or be restored to an operational state.
3. *Serviceability*: The ability for an external supplier to maintain the availability of component or function under a third-party contract.
4. *Resilience*: A measure of freedom from operational failure and a method of keeping services reliable. One popular method of resilience is redundancy.

5. *Security*: A service may have associated data. Security refers to the confidentiality, integrity, and availability of that data. Availability gives a clear overview of the end-to-end availability of the system.

IT Financial Management comprises the discipline of ensuring that the IT infrastructure is obtained at the most effective price which does not necessarily mean cheapest and calculating the cost of providing IT services so that an organisation can understand the costs of its IT services. These costs may then be recovered from the customer of the service. This is the second component of service delivery process.

ICT INFRASTRUCTURE MANAGEMENT

ICT Infrastructure Management processes recommend best practice for requirements analysis, planning, design, deployment and ongoing operations management and technical support of an ICT Infrastructure.

It describe those processes within ITIL that directly relate to the ICT equipment and software that is involved in providing ICT services to customers.

1. Design and Planning
2. Deployment
3. Operations
4. Technical Support

These disciplines are less well understood than those of Service Management and therefore often some of their content is believed to be covered 'by implication' in Service Management disciplines.

ICT Design and Planning provide a framework and approach for the Strategic and Technical Design and Planning of ICT infrastructures. It includes the necessary combination of business (and overall IS) strategy, with technical design and architecture. ICT Design and Planning drives both the Procurement of new ICT solutions through the production of Statements of Requirement ("SOR") and Invitations to Tender ("ITT") and is responsible for the initiation and management of ICT Programmes for strategic business change. Main Outputs from Design and Planning. They are given below:

1. ICT Strategies, Policies and Plans
2. The ICT Overall Architecture & Management Architecture
3. Feasibility Studies, ITTs and SORs
4. Business Cases

ICT Deployment provides a framework for the successful management of design, build, test and roll-out (deploy) projects within an overall ICT programme. It includes many project management disciplines in common with PRINCE2, but has a broader focus to include the necessary integration of Release Management and both functional and non functional testing.

ICT Operations Management provides the day-to-day technical supervision of the ICT infrastructure. Often confused with the role of Incident Management from Service Support, Operations has a more technical bias and is concerned not solely with Incidents reported by users, but with Events generated by or recorded by the Infrastructure. ICT Operations may often work closely alongside Incident Management and the Service Desk, which are not-necessarily technical, to provide an 'Operations Bridge'.

Operations should primarily work from documented processes and procedures and should be concerned with a number of specific sub-processes, such as: Output Management, Job Scheduling, Backup and Restore, Network Monitoring/Management, System Monitoring/Management, Database Monitoring/Management Storage Monitoring/Management. Operations are responsible for the following points are given below :

1. A stable, secure ICT infrastructure
2. A current, up to date Operational Documentation Library ("ODL")

3. A log of all operational Events
4. Maintenance of operational monitoring and management tools.
5. Operational Scripts
6. Operational Procedures

LEVELS OF SUPPORT

It is the most specialist technical function for information with in ICT. Primarily as a support to other processes, both in Infrastructure Management and Service Management, Technical Support provides a number of specialist functions: Research and Evaluation, Market Intelligence (particularly for Design and Planning and Capacity Management), Proof of Concept and Pilot engineering, specialist technical expertise (particularly to Operations and Problem Management), creation of documentation (perhaps for the Operational Documentation Library or Known Error Database). There are different levels of support under the ITIL structure, these being primary support level, secondary support level and tertiary support level, higher-level administrators being responsible for support at primary level.

SECURITY MANAGEMENT

This tight is to ensure information security. The objective of information security, in turn, is to protect information assets against risks, and thus to maintain their value to the organisation. The ITIL-process Security Management describes the structured fitting of information security in the management organisation. ITIL Security Management is based on the code of practice for information security management now known as ISO/IEC 27002.

Mounting pressure for many organisations to structure their Information Security Management Systems in accordance with ISO/IEC 27001 requires revision of the ITIL v2 Security Management volume, and indeed a v3 release is in the works.

Software Asset Management (SAM)

It is the combined practice of integrating people, processes and technology to allow software licenses and usage to be systematically tracked, evaluated and managed. The purpose of this management is to less IT expenditures, human resource overhead and risks inherent in owning and managing software assets the following points :

SAM practices include:

1. Maintaining software license compliance
2. Tracking inventory and software asset use
3. Maintaining standard policies and procedures surrounding definition, deployment, configuration, use, and retirement of software assets and the Definitive Software Library.

Softwar Management (SAM) represents the software component of IT asset management. This includes hardware asset management because effective hardware inventory controls are critical to efforts to control software. This means overseeing software and hardware that comprise an organisation's computers and network.

MANAGING E-RESOURCES FOR USERS

Not many e-resources librarians live among the folks in reference and instruction – link resolvers, proxy servers, A-Z lists, COUNTER compliance, and ERMs usually keep us pretty close to our colleagues in acquisitions, serials and IT. Public services librarians, who spend their days building relationships with teaching faculty, performing classroom instruction, and juggling reference questions don't have time to worry about the circuitous, detailed process involved in e-resources acquisitions and maintenance.

Early job ads for e-resources librarians emphasized public services skills like reference and instruction (Fisher 2003: "the position title of Electronic Resources Librarian has been pre-empted by the public service sector of the profession"); over the years, these changed to emphasize more specialized technical skills –

licensing, web development and customization (Albitz & Shelburne 2007).

For someone in a public services e-resources position, tracking information about e-resources and the issues that affect every stage of their lifecycles (from technology developments to budget pressures, staff changes, and trends in user behavior) was an important, if not the most important, part of my work. This is supported by Joan Conger & Bonnie Tijerina's assessment of e-resources management in "Collaborative Library-wide Partnerships: Managing Electronic Resources Through Learning and Adaptation" (in Collins & Carr 2008).

The dynamic process of managing e-resources "requires effective incorporation of information from a rich array of sources," they write (97). The information it is important to pursue is most often stored in experiences – of vendors, library professionals, and patrons. To get to this contextual information, they say, librarians must keep current, particularly with users. They suggest "usability tests, library advisory groups, focus groups, direct observation," as well as informal assessment to learn new things about user behavior (99). They also remind their readers that it is important to communicate what you learn.

Interfacing between the user experience and the information required to improve it proved to be the part of my job best suited to my location in public services, and in my first year at Bowling Green I focused on user issues. I participated in web and OPAC redesign projects, resource re-description, customization, usability testing, and training. I also made an effort to stay informed: I read (*Don't Make Me Think!, Studying Students, Online Catalogs: What Users and Librarians Want)*, I talked to vendors, I attended conferences and sat in on webinars. But no matter how much e mail I sent, how many meetings I attended, or how many blogs and wikis I used, I couldn't seem to find a way to merge the information I had together with the information from my colleagues so that together we could make our management of e-resources more effective for users.

I discovered, during this period, that it's not enough to recognize that lots of people are involved in making e-resources available; it's also about having a seat at the right tables so you can advocate for these materials and their users, and, in my library at least, I was sitting at the wrong table.

After a retirement incentive program was completed last fiscal year, our technical services department found itself down five people, two of them faculty librarians. Library-wide, we discussed reorganization, and a number of staff changed locations, but I was the only one who actually changed departments: officially, my position is now split, and I am now 51% technical services – no longer with reference and instruction, for the first time in my career.

I'm excited about this change – everyone involved thought it would be best for the library and collections. Many of my new tech services colleagues started their careers in reference, so a focus on the patron is embedded in all of their approaches to processing, cataloging and collection management. But I also feel a little like I've given up a good fight. Why did I have to move to technical services? I know the answer is because that's where a lot of e-resources work is still located. The model we had been trying, while I am convinced it is viable and know it worked at my previous job, wasn't scalable for a large academic library with broadly distributed functions. Not yet. However, while my location has changed, it's promising that my job description retains many of my public services functions. I will still work reference, teach, work on public web interfaces, and participate in usability efforts. These things may officially only be 49% of my job now, but I still want everything I do to be for users, 100%.

ELECTRONIC RESOURCE MANAGEMENT

Electronic resource management (ERM) is the practices and software systems used by libraries to keep track of important information about electronic information resources, especially internet-based resources such as electronic journals, databases, and electronic books. The development of ERM became necessary in the early 2000s as it became clear that traditional library catalogs and integrated library systems were not designed to handle metadata for resources as mutable as many online products are.

The idea of developing electronic resource management systems emerged in 2001-2002, growing out of research by Tim Jewell at the University of Washington. The Digital Library Federation and NISO began work in May 2002 to develop standards for ERM data.[1] These standards were published in the 2004 as *Electronic Resource Management: Report of the DLF ERM Initiative*.[2] Since the publication of the report, several vendors of integrated library systems have released ERM products.

The features of some ERM systems include: Supporting acquisition and management of licensed e-resources

- May be integrated into other library system modules or may be a standalone system
- May have a public interface, either separate or integrated into the OPAC
- Providing descriptions of resources at the package (database) level and relate package contents (e.g. e-journals) to the package record
- Encoding and perhaps publicly displaying licensed rights such as e-reserves, coursepacks, and interlibrary loan
- Tracking electronic resources from point of order through licensing and final access
- Providing information about the data providers, consortial arrangements, access platform
- Providing contact information for all content providers
- Logging problems with resources and providers
- Providing customizable e-mail alerting systems (e.g. notices to managers when actions are expected or required)
- Linking license documents to resource records
- Supports retrieval of SUSHI usage statistics

ERM Products

Several library automation companies have developed ERM products, including several with generic-sounding names for specific commercial products. Some open-source ERM systems also exist.

An online database is a database accessible from a network, including from the Internet.

It differs from a local database, held in an individual computer or its attached storage, such as a CD.

- For the system or software designed to manage a database, see Database management systems (DBMS)
- For information on the structure of a database itself, see Database
- For information on the programs for searching a database, see Search engines

Currently, there are several database products designed specifically as hosted databases delivered as Software as a Service products. These differ from typical traditional databases such as Oracle, Microsoft SQL Server, Sybase, etc. Some of the differences are:

- These online databases are delivered primarily via a web browser
- They are often purchased by a monthly subscription
- They embed common collaboration features such as sharing, email notifications, etc.

PROCESSES AND APPROACHES (ITIL)

The ITIL discipline - Planning to Implement Service Management attempts to provide practitioners with a framework for the alignment of business needs and IT provision requirements. The processes and approaches incorporated within the guidelines suggest the development of a Continuous Service Improvement Program (CSIP) as the basis for implementing other ITIL disciplines as projects within a controlled program of work. Planning to

Implement Service Management focuses mainly on the Service Management processes, but also applies generically to other ITIL disciplines. The following Components include:

1. creating vision.
2. analyzing organisation.
3. setting goals.
4. implementing IT service management.

Small-Scale Implementation

Small-Scale Implement provides an approach to ITIL framework implementation for smaller IT units or departments. It is primarily an auxiliary work that covers many of the same best practice guidelines as Planning to Implement Service Management, Service Support, and Service Delivery but provides additional guidance on the combination of roles and responsibilities, and avoiding conflict between ITIL priorities.

Service Strategy

As the center and origin point of the ITIL Service Lifecycle, the ITIL Service Strategy volume provides guidance on clarification and prioritisation of service-provider investments in services. More generally, Service Strategy focuses on helping IT organisations improve and develop over the long term. In both cases, Service Strategy relies largely upon a market-driven approach. Main topics covered include service value definition, business-case development, service assets, market analysis, and service provider types. List of covered processes are :

1. Service Portfolio Management
2. Demand Management
3. IT Financial Management

Design of IT Services

IT provides good-practice guidance on the design of IT services, processes and other aspects of the service management effort. Significantly, design within ITIL is understood to encompass all elements relevant to technology service delivery, rather than focusing solely on design of the technology itself.

As such, Service Design addresses how a planned service solution interacts with the larger business and technical environments, service management systems required to support the service, processes which interact with the service, technology, and architecture required to support the service, and the supply chain required to support the planned service.

Within ITIL v2, design work for an IT service is aggregated into a single Service Design Package (SDP). Service Design Packages, along with other information about services, are managed within the service catalogues. List of covered processes are :

1. Service Catalogue Management
2. Service Level Management
3. Risk Management
4. Capacity Management
5. Availability Management
6. IT Service Continuity Management
7. Information Security Management
8. Compliance Management
9. IT Architecture Management
10. Supplier Management

Service Transition

As described by the ITIL Service Transition volume, it relates to the delivery of services required by a business into live/operational use, and often encompasses the "project" side of IT rather than "BAU" (Business as usual). This area also covers topics such as managing changes to the "BAU" environment.

List of processes are :

1. Service Asset and Configuration Management

2. Service Validation and Testing
3. Evaluation
4. Release Management
5. Change Management
6. Knowledge Management

Service Operation

Service operation, as described in the ITIL Service Operation volume, is the part of the lifecycle where the services and value is actually directly delivered. Also the monitoring of problems and balance between service reliability and cost etc. are considered. The functions include technical management, application management, operations management and Service Desk as well as, responsibilities for staff engaging in Service Operation. Best practice for achieving the delivery of agreed levels of services both to end-users and the customers (where "customers" refer to those individuals who pay for the service and negotiate the SLAs).

The following is list of processes:

1. Event Management
2. Incident Management
3. Problem Management
4. Request Fulfilment
5. Access Management

CONTINUAL SERVICE IMPROVEMENT (CSI)

CSI refers to Aligning and realigning IT services to changing business needs (because standstill implies decline).

It aims to align and realign IT Services to changing business needs by identifying and implementing improvements to the IT services that support the Business Processes. The perspective of CSI on improvement is the business perspective of service quality, even though CSI aims to improve process effectiveness, efficiency and cost effectiveness of the IT processes through the whole lifecycle.

To manage improvement, CSI should clearly define what should be controlled and measured. CSI needs to be treated just like any other service practice.There needs to be upfront planning, training and awareness, ongoing scheduling, roles created, ownership assigned,and activities identified to be successful. CSI must be planned and scheduled as process with defined activities, inputs, outputs, roles and reporting.

The following is the list of processes:

1. Service Level Management
2. Service Measurement and Reporting
3. Continual Service Improvement

Criticisms

ITIL has been criticised on several for the following points.

CIO Magazine columnist Dean Meyer has presented some cautionary views of ITIL, including five pitfalls such as "becoming a slave to outdated definitions" and "Letting ITIL become religion." As he notes, "...it doesn't describe the complete range of processes needed to be world class. It's focused on ... managing ongoing services."

The books are not affordable for non-commercial users. Accusations that many ITIL advocates think ITIL is "a holistic, all-encompassing framework for IT governance". Accusations that proponents of ITIL indoctrinate the methodology with 'religious zeal'at the expense of pragmatism. Implementation and credentialing requires specific training. Debate over ITIL falling under BSM or ITSM frameworks.

Rob England (also known as "IT Skeptic") has criticised the protected and proprietary nature of ITIL . He urges the publisher, OGC, to release ITIL under the the Open Government Licence (OGL).

In a 2004 survey designed by Noel Bruton (author of "How to Manage the IT Helpdesk" and "Managing the IT Services Process"), organisations adopting ITIL were asked to relate their actual experiences in having implemented ITIL. Seventy-seven percent of survey respondents either agreed or strongly agreed that "ITIL does not have all the answers". ITIL exponents accept this, citing ITIL's stated intention to be non-prescriptive, expecting organisations to engage ITIL processes with existing process models. Bruton notes that the claim to non-prescriptiveness must be, at best, one of scale rather than absolute intention, for the very description of a certain set of processes is in itself a form of prescription.

While ITIL addresses in depth the various aspects of Service Management, it does not address enterprise architecture in such depth. Many of the shortcomings in the implementation of ITIL do not necessarily come about because of flaws in the design or implementation of the Service Management aspects of the business, but rather the wider architectural framework in which the business is situated. Because of its primary focus on Service Management, ITIL has limited utility in managing poorly designed enterprise architectures, or how to feed back into the design of the enterprise architecture.

Closely related to the Architectural criticism, ITIL does not directly address the business applications which run on the IT infrastructure; nor does it facilitate a more collaborative working relationship between development and operations teams. The trend toward a closer working relationship between development and operations is termed: DevOps. This trend is related to increased application release rates and the adoption of Agile software development methodologies. Traditional service management processes have struggled to support increased application release rates - due to lack of automation - and/or highly complex enterprise architecture. Some researchers group ITIL with Lean, Six Sigma and Agile IT operations management.

ENGINEERING APPROACH

Applying Six Sigma techniques to ITIL brings the engineering approach to ITIL's framework. Applying Lean techniques promotes continuous improvement of the ITIL's best practices. However, ITIL itself is not a transformation method, nor does it offer one. Readers are required to find and associate such a method. Some vendors have also included the term Lean when discussing ITIL implementations, for example Lean-ITIL. The initial consequences of an ITIL initiative tend to add cost with benefits promised as a future deliverable. ITIL does not provide usable methods "out of the box" to identify and target waste, or document the customer value stream as required by Lean, and measure customer satisfaction.

The Microsoft Operations Framework (MOF) is based on ITILv2. While ITIL deliberately aims to be platform agnostic, MOF is designed by Microsoft to provide a common management framework for its products. Microsoft has mapped MOF to ITIL as part of their documentation of the framework.

The British Educational Communications and Technology Agency (BECTA) used ITIL as the basis for their development of Framework for ICT Technical Support (FITS). Their aim was to develop a framework appropriate for British schools which often have very small IT departments. FITS became independent from BECTA in 2009.

Frameworks and Supporting Toolset

ITIL is generally equivalent to the scope of the ISO/IEC 20000 standard (previously BS 15000).. While it is not possible for an organization to be certified as being ITIL compliant, certification of an organisation is available for ISO20000.

COBIT is an IT governance framework and supporting toolset developed by ISACA. ISACA view ITIL as being complimentary to COBIT. They see COBIT as providing a governance and assurance role while ITIL providing guidance for service management.

The enhanced Telecom Operations Map eTOM published by the TeleManagement Forum offers a framework aimed at telecommunications service providers. In a joined effort, TM Forum and itSMF developed an Application Note to eTOM (GB921) that shows how the two frameworks can be mapped to each other. It addresses how eTom process elements and flows can be used to support the processes identified in ITIL. IBM Tivoli Unified Process (ITUP) is aligned with ITIL, but is presented as a complete, integrated process model compatible with IBM's products.

References

1. Beynon-Davies P. (2002). Information Systems: an introduction to informatics in Organisations. Palgrave, Basingstoke, UK. ISBN 0-333-96390-3
2. Beynon-Davies P. (2009). Business Information Systems. Palgrave, Basingstoke. ISBN 978-0-230-20368-6
3. David Clifford, Jan van Bon (2008). Implementing ISO/IEC 20000 Certification: The Roadmap. ITSM Library. Van Haren Publishing. ISBN 908753082X.
4. Office of Government Commerce (UK)CCTA and OGC. Retrieved May 5, 2005.
5. Office of Government Commerce (UK). Retrieved August 19, 2009.
6. Office of Government Commerce (2000). Service Support. The Stationery Office. ISBN 0113300158.
7. Office of Government Commerce (2001). Service Delivery. IT Infrastructure Library. The Stationery Office. ISBN 0113300174.
8. Office of Government Commerce (2002). ICT Infrastructure Management. The Stationery Office. ISBN 0113308655.
9. Cazemier, Jacques A.; Overbeek, Paul L.; Peters, Louk M. (2000). Security Management. The Stationery Office. ISBN 011330014X.

10. Office of Government Commerce (2002). Application Management. The Stationery Office. ISBN 0113308663.
11. Office of Government Commerce (2002). Planning to Implement Service Management. The Stationery Office. ISBN 0113308779.
12. Office of Government Commerce (2005). ITIL Small Scale Implementation. The Stationery Office. ISBN 0113309805.
13. Majid Iqbal and Michael Nieves (2007). ITIL Service Strategy. The Stationery Office. ISBN 9780113310456.
14. Vernon Lloyd and Colin Rudd (2007). ITIL Service Design. The Stationery Office. ISBN 9780113310470.
15. Shirley Lacy and Ivor Macfarlane (2007). ITIL Service Transition. The Stationery Office. ISBN 9780113310487.
16. David Cannon and David Wheeldon (2007). ITIL Service Operation. The Stationery Office. ISBN 9780113310463.
17. George Spalding and Gary Case (2007). ITIL Continual Service Improvement. The Stationery Office. ISBN 9780113310494.
18. Meyer, Dean, 2005. "Beneath the Buzz: ITIL", CIO Magazine, March 31, 2005
19. Survey: "The ITIL Experience - Has It Been Worth It", author Bruton Consultancy 2004, published by Helpdesk Institute Europe, The Helpdesk and IT Support Show, and Hornbill Software.
20. Microsoft Operations Framework; Cross Reference ITIL V3 and MOF 4.0. Microsoft Corporation. May 2009. http://go.microsoft.com/fwlink/?LinkId=151991.
21. Van Bon, Jan; Verheijen, Tieneke (2006), Frameworks for IT Management, Van Haren Publishing, ISBN 9789077212905, http://books.google.com/books?id=RV3jQ16F1_cC

22. ISACA (2008), COBIT Mapping: Mapping of ITIL V3 With COBIT 4.1, ITGI, ISBN 9781604200355, http://www.isaca.org/Knowledge-Center/Research/ResearchDeliverables/Pages/COBIT-Mapping-Mapping-of-ITIL-V3-With-COBIT-4-1.aspx

23. Brooks, Peter (2006), Metrics for IT Service Management, Van Haren Publishing, pp. 76–77, ISBN 9789077212691, http://books.google.com/books?id=UeWDivqKcm0C

24. Morreale, Patricia A.; Terplan, Kornel (2009), "3.6.10.2 Matching ITIL to eTOM", CRC Handbook of Modern Telecommunications, Second Edition (2 ed.), CRC Press, ISBN 9781420078008, http://books:google.com/books?id=VEp0aMmH3iQC

25. APMG (2008). "ITIL Service Management Practices: V3 Qualifications Scheme". http://www.itil-officialsite.com/nmsruntime/saveasdialog.asp?lID=572&sID=86. Retrieved 24 February 2009.

26. Chris Rusbridge: "Toward the Hybrid Library", D-Lib Magazine, July/August 1998.

27. Malinconico, S. Michael: "Digital Preservation Technologies and Hybrid Libraries," Information Services and Use, 159(74): 173, 2002

28. Malinconico, S. Michael: "Digital Preservation Technologies and Hybrid Libraries," Information Services and Use, 159(74): 162, 2002

29. Oppenheim, Charles: "Copyright Issues in Digitisation and the Hybrid Library," Information Services and Use, 203(7): 204.[when?]

30. Choemprayong, S.: Closing Digital Divides: The United States' Policies, 2006.[where?]

31. Arms, W. Y., Blanchi, C., & Overly, E. A.: "An Architecture for Information in Digital Libraries". D-Lib Magazine, February 1997.

32. Chowdhury, G. & Chowdhury, S.: Introduction to Digital Libraries. London: Facet Publication, 2003.

33. "http://en.wikipedia.org/wiki/Hybrid_library"

CHAPTER–2

CHANGING FACE OF LIBRARY WITH MODERN AGE

In a technical term, a library catalogue is a file or register of all the bibliographic items found in a library or group of libraries. A bibliographic item can be any information entity (e.g., books, computer files, graphics, realia, cartographic materials, etc.) that is considered library material (e.g., a single novel in an anthology), or a group of library materials (e.g., a trilogy), or linked from the catalog (e.g., a webpage) as far as it is relevant to the catalog and to the users (patrons) of the library.

A catalogue is the real picture of any publication house. A catalogue tellsus about the total no. of books published, book's title, author information, ISBN no. along with price and other details. In the same mannerevery library has its own catalogue but now it has been effectively replaced by the online public access catalog (OPAC). Some still refer to the online catalog as a "card catalog". Some libraries with OPAC access still have card catalogs on site, but these are now strictly a secondary resource and are seldom updated. Many of the libraries that have retained their physical card catalog post a sign advising the last year that the card catalog was updated. Some libraries have eliminated their card catalog in favour of the OPAC for the purpose of saving space for other use, such as additional shelving. Federated searching products allow simultaneous searching of multiple collections and resources through a single interface.

The software packages often rely on z39.50 connections, XML gateways, SR/W to search for information, then merge, de-duplicate, sort and rank results. Fans of federated searching point to their timesaving metasearch capabilities, while critics argue that dumbing down the search interfaces can ruin quality.

ONLINE PUBLIC ACCESS CATALOG

OPAC (Online Public Access Catalogue) allows users to search all materials (such as Books, Journals, Magazines, Digital material etc.) available in the library collection. Only Library Members can access Full text and Digital material by using their User ID and Password.

Library is an information-enriched center that assists its users throughout their learning process and always works towards fulfilling its user's information needs. We aim to develop a comprehensive collection of e-publication information resources and prints that are useful for studying, references, teaching, research, and other curricular and co-curricular research needs of the students and faculty of the Institute for achieving excellence in their chosen disciplines. An Online Public Access Catalog (OPAC) is e-Library website which is part of Integrated Library System (ILS), also known as a Library Management System (LMS), and managed by a library or group of libraries.

Online Public Access Catalogues (OPAC)

International

- Library of Congress
- National Library of Australia
- National Library of Medicine

India

- American Center Information Resource Centers in India
- Auroville Library

- Bangalore University.com
- British Council Libraries in India
- Calcutta Library Network
- Cochin University of Science and Technology Library
- Goa University Libraries Network
- Gokhale Institute of Politics and Economics Library, Pune
- Health Education Library for People
- Indian Institute of Science Library, Bangalore
- Indian Institute of Technology Library, Mumbai
- Indian Statistical Institute Library, Delhi
- Indian Statistical Institute Library, Kolkata
- Indira Gandhi Institute of Development Research Library, Mumbai
- Institute for Studies in Industrial Development
- International Crops Research Institute for the Semi-Arid Tropics (ICRISAT)
- NAL Information Centre for Aerospace Science and Technology, Bangalore
- National Institute of Bank Management Library, Pune
- National Law School Library, Bangalore
- National Science Library, New Delhi
- Osmania University Libraries Network
- Rajiv Gandhi University of Health Sciences, Bangalore
- Tata Institute of Fundamental Research Library, Mumbai
- Tata Institute of Social Sciences Library, Mumbai
- Vishal Information Technologies

Stagnation and Dissatisfaction

The 1990s saw a relative stagnation in the development of online catalogs. Although the earlier character-based interfaces were replaced with ones for the web, both the design and the underlying search technology of most systems did not advance much beyond that developed in the late 1980s.

At the same time, organizations outside of libraries began developing more sophisticated information retrieval systems. Web search engines like Google and popular e-commerce websites such as Amazon.com provided simpler to use (yet more powerful) systems that could provide relevancy ranked search results using probabilistic and vector-based queries.

Prior to the widespread use of the Internet, the online catalog was often the first information retrieval system library users ever encountered. Now accustomed to web search engines, newer generations of library users have grown increasingly dissatisfied with the complex (and often arcane) search mechanisms of older online catalog systems.

This has, in turn, led to vocal criticisms of these systems within the library community itself, and in recent years to the development of newer (often termed 'next-generation') catalogs.

Next-generation Catalogs

The newest generation of library catalog systems are distinguished from earlier OPACs by their use of more sophisticated search technologies, including relevancy ranking and faceted search, as well as features aimed at greater user interaction and participation with the system, including tagging and reviews.

These modern systems are almost always independent of the library's integrated library system, instead providing drivers that allow for the synchronization of data between the two systems. While older online catalog systems were almost exclusively built by ILS vendors, libraries are increasingly turning to next generation catalog systems built by enterprise search companies and open source projects, often led by libraries themselves. The costs associated with these new systems, however, have slowed their adoption, particularly at smaller institutions.

Union Catalogs

Although library catalogs typically reflect the holdings of a single library, they can also contain the holdings of a group or consortium of libraries. These systems, known as union catalogs, are usually designed to aid the borrowing of books and other materials among the member institutions via interlibrary loan. The largest such union catalog is WorldCat, which includes the holdings of over 70,000 libraries worldwide. There are a number of systems that share much in common with library catalogs, but have traditionally been distinguished from them. Libraries utilize these systems to search for items not traditionally covered by a library catalog.

These include bibliographic databases — such as Medline, ERIC, PsycINFO, and many others — which index journal articles and other research data. There are also a number of applications aimed at managing documents, photographs, and other digitized or born-digital items. Particularly in academic libraries, these systems (often known as digital library systems or institutional repository systems) assist with efforts to preserve documents created by faculty and students.

FEDERATED SEARCH : DEEPWEB SEARCH

The federated search is the deepweb search. It is an information retrieval technology that allows the simultaneous search of multiple searchable resources. A user makes a single query request which is distributed to the search engines participating in the federation. The federated search then aggregates the results that are received from the search engines for presentation to the user.

Federated content is digital media content that is designed to be self-managing to support reporting and rights management in a peer-to-peer (P2P) network. Ex: Audio stored in a digital rights management (DRM) file format. In one query we can search multiple database at one time and arrange the informations in useful form and it returns the results to the user.

Today's kid cann't think of living without a computer. Imagine, what would happen if computer is separated from their life for few days. Boffins have found that taking a kid's computer technology away for a day gives them similar symptoms as going cold turkey. The study was carried out by the University of Maryland. It found that 79 percent of students subjected to a complete media blackout for just one day reported adverse reactions ranging from distress to confusion and isolation. One of the things the kids spoke about was having overwhelming cravings while others reported symptoms such as 'itching'.

The study conducted on students aged between 17 and 23 in ten countries. Researchers banned them from using phones, social networking sites, the internet and TV for 24 hours.

The kids could use landline phones or read books and were asked to keep a diary.

One in five reported feelings of withdrawal like an addiction while eleven percent said they were confused. Over 19 percent said they were distressed and eleven percent felt isolated. Some students even reported stress from simply not being able to touch their phone.

- Cengage Learning: General OneFile - A meta-search management system with overview and tour.
- Central Search - Serials Solutions' product site.
- CrossRef - Information on the reference linking service using Digital Object Identifiers (DOI).
- ENCompass - Provides integrated access. News and information from Endeavor Information Systems.
- Federated Search Engines and Link Resolvers - A weblog with progress reports, from the University of Pretoria.
- MetaLib - The Ex Libris library portal. Includes features list and other resources.
- MuseGlobal - Java-enabled, hub-based, metasearch engine by Peter and Kate Noerr. Demonstrations and background information.

- WebFeat - Information on WebFeat Prism, news, and contact information.
- ZPortal - Product information on the Z39.50 search engine from OCLC PICA.
- In Defense of Stupid Users - Article on federated search engines by Todd Miller, president of WebFeat. [Library Journal] (March 15, 2005)
- Cross database searching: Information literacy for the 'real world'? - John Terrell, RMIT University Library, examines the process of cross database searching in the light of the Information Literacy Framework and supporting student development. [PDF] (July 07, 2004)
- The Truth About Federated Searching - Reviews five common misconceptions about federated searching services. [Information Today]
- Trumping Google? Metasearching's Promise - Discussion of federated searching models, with selected links. [Library Journal]
- List of Portal Application Functionalities for the Library of Congress - Requirements list for federated searching products, similar to a RFP (request for proposal) vendor format. From the Library of Congress Portals Applications Issues Group (LCPAIG). [PDF] (July 15, 2003)
- The Right Solution: Federated Search Tools - Library Journal Digital column by Roy Tennant, providing an introduction to the benefits of federated searching. (June 15, 2003)

Federated Searching

As described by Peter Jacso (2004), federated searching consists of (a) transforming a query and broadcasting it to a group of disparate databases or other web resources, with the appropriate syntax, (b) merging the results collected from the databases, (c) presenting them in a succinct and unified format with minimal duplication, and (d) providing a means, performed either automatically or by the portal user, to sort the merged result set.

Federated search portals, either commercial or open access, generally search public access bibliographic databases, public access Web-based library catalogues (OPACs), Web-based search engines like Google and/or open-access, government-operated or corporate data collections. These individual information sources send back to the portal's interface a list of results from the search query. The user can review this hit list. Some portals will merely screen scrape the actual database results and not directly allow a user to enter the information source's application. More sophisticated ones will de-dupe the results list by merging and removing duplicates. There are additional features available in many portals, but the basic idea is the same: to improve the accuracy and relevance of individual searches as well as less the amount of time required to search for resources.

This process allows federated search some key advantages when compared with existing crawler-based search engines. Federated search need not place any requirements or burdens on owners of the individual information sources, other than handling increased traffic. Federated searches are inherently as current as the individual information sources, as they are searched in real time.

What is Deep Web?

One application of federated searching is the metasearch engine; however, this is not a complete solution as many documents are not currently indexed. These documents are on what is known as the deep Web, or invisible Web. Many more information sources are not yet stored in electronic form. Google Scholar is one example of many projects trying to address this.

When the search vocabulary or data model of the search system is different from the data model of one or more of the foreign target systems the query must be translated into each of the foreign target systems. This can be done using simple data-element translation or may require semantic translation.

A challenge faced in the implementation of federated search engines is scalability, in other words, the performance of the site as the number of information sources comprising the federated search engine increase. One federated search engine that has begun to address this issue is WorldWideScience, hosted by the U.S. Department of Energy's Office of Scientific and Technical Information.

WorldWideScience is composed of more than 40 information sources, several of which are federated search portals themselves. One such portal is Science.gov which itself federates more than 30 information sources representing most of the R&D output of the U.S. Federal government. Science.gov returns its highest ranked results to WorldWideScience, which then merges and ranks these results with the search returned by the other information sources that comprise WorldWideScience.This approach of cascaded federated search enables large number of information sources to be searched via a single query.

Another application Sesam running in both Norway and Sweden has been built on top of an open sourced platform specialised for federated search solutions. Sesat,an acronym for Sesam Search Application Toolkit, is a platform that provides much of the framework and functionality required for handling parallel and pipelined searches and displaying them elegantly in a user interface, allowing engineers to focus on the index/database configuration tuning.

Challenges

When federated search is performed against secure data sources, the users' credentials must be passed on to each underlying search engine, so that appropriate security is maintained. If the user has different login credentials for different systems, there must be a means to map their login ID to each search engine's security domain.

Another challenge is mapping results list navigators into a common form. Suppose two university sites are searched, each provides a list of hyperlinked college names to click on, to see matches only in each college. Ideally these facets would be combined into one set, but that presents additional technical challenges. The system also needs to understand "next page" links if it's going to allow the user to page through the combined results.

Gone are the days when one has to stand in long space age, we can pick up books requesting online, which is indeed a hassle-free process.

Following a call by (PM Manmohan Singh) The Union Ministry of culture is funding the digitisation project, estimated at Rs 100 million, which houses more than 50 lakh rare books published before 1860 on its 30-acre campus in Alipore's Belvedere Estate.

"The Prime Minister's Office has given us six months to complete the work. We have approached some software companies but nothing has been finalised. The contract will be awarded after the necessary formalities," said the official.

The main objective is to make the library more user-friendly. Online access to the library's collection has been a long-standing demand of the readers.

Once the digitisation project is completed, people would be able to download membership forms from the library's website and submit them online. Readers would also be allowed to email queries regarding borrowing of books to the authorities, according to library officials.

DIGITISATION OF LIBRARY CATALOGUES.

ETH Zürich has worked in cooperation with the Zentralbibliothek Zürich on a project to digitise the complete central catalogue of the library and to make it available through an electronic text retrieval system. The Alphabetischer Zentralkatalog (AZK) consists of about 2.2 million paper cards referring to 1.7 million documents. The AZK is an important catalogue because 1.58 million of the libary's documents (93%) are only accessible through this catalogue. The AZK includes entries in six main European languages plus other languages like Russian, Arabic, Turkish and Latin.

This aspect of the catalogue presents difficulties for Optical Character Recognition (OCR), since these languages contain many accented characters and also make it impossible to do automatic correction of OCR errors, since the automatic recognition of language for lexicon lookup is infeasible. This is further complicated by the large number of proper nouns and abbreviations in the collection. A typical index card of the AZK\ contains, on the average, 23 words. An example index card from the catalogue is shown below. In a pilot study of the problem of digitising the catalogue we focused on a sample of 8,500 index cards. The index cards were scanned at 300dpi and processed through a commercial OCR system (OmniPage Professional) to produce OCR text. The OCR process resulted in a word accuracy of 67%, which means that one of every three words in the catalogue sample was incorrectly recognised.

A central objective of our study was to establish the extent to which it was feasible to deliver effective search and retrieval facilities over the digitised catalogue with minimal manual intervention in the digitisation process. We therefore proposed a probabilistic approach to retrieval, taking into account the error probabilities associated with the OCR process.

Objectives

Charles Ammi Cutter made the first explicit statement regarding the objectives of a bibliographic system in his Rules for a Printed Dictionary Catalog in 1876. According to Cutter, those objectives were :

1. to enable a person to find a book of which either (Identifying objective)
   - the author
   - the title
   - the subject
   - the category

   is known.

2. to show what the library has (Collocating objective)
   - by a given author
   - on a given subject
   - in a given kind of literature
3. to assist in the choice of a book (Evaluating objective)
   - as to its edition (bibliographically)
   - as to its character (literary or topical)

These objectives can still be recognized in more modern definitions formulated throughout the 20th century. 1960/61 Cutter's objectives were revised by Lubetzky and Lubetzky and the Conference on Cataloging Principles (CCP) in Paris. The latest attempt to describe a library catalog's goals and functions was made in 1998 with Functional Requirements for Bibliographic Records (FRBR) which defines four user tasks: find, identify, select, and obtain.

Types

The following types catalogaue given below.

1. Author card: a formal catalog, sorted alphabetically according to the authors' or editors' names of the entries.
2. Title catalog: a formal catalog, sorted alphabetically according to the title of the entries.
3. Dictionary catalog: a catalog in which all entries (author, title, subject, series) are interfiled in a single alphabetical order. This was the primary form of card catalog in North American libraries just prior to the introduction of the computer-based catalog.
4. Keyword catalog: a subject catalog, sorted alphabetically according to some system of keywords.
5. Mixed alphabetic catalog forms: sometimes, one finds a mixed author / title, or an author / title / keyword catalog.
6. Systematic catalog: a subject catalog, sorted according to some systematic subdivision of subjects. Also called a Classified catalog.

7. Shelf list catalog: a formal catalog with entries sorted in the same order as bibliographic items are shelved. This catalog may also serve as the primary inventory for the library.

Library catalogs originated as manuscript lists, arranged by format (folio, quarto, etc.) or in a rough alphabetical arrangement by author. Printed catalogs, sometimes called dictionary catalogs enabled scholars outside a library to gain an idea of its contents. These would sometimes be interleaved with blank leaves on which additions could be recorded, or bound as guardbooks in which slips of paper were bound in for new entries.

Slips could also be kept loose in cardboard or tin boxes, stored on shelves. The first card catalogs appeared in the nineteenth century, enabling much more flexibility, and towards the end of the twentieth century the OPAC was developed.

1. c. 245 BC: Callimachus is considered the first bibliographer and is the one that organized the library by authors and subjects. The Pinakes (Ancient Greek: Ðßíáêåŏ "tables") was the first ever library catalogue.Variations on this system were used in libraries until the late 1800s when Melvil Dewey developed the Dewey Decimal Classification in 1876, which is still in use today.
2. c. 800: Library catalogues are introduced in the House of Wisdom and other medieval Islamic libraries where books are organized into specific genres and categories.
3. 1595: Nomenclator of Leiden University Library appears, the first printed catalog of an institutional library.
4. 1674: Thomas Hyde's catalog for the Bodleian Library.

More about the early history of library catalogs has been collected in 1956 by Strout.

Consistent Cataloging

It have been defined to allow for consistent cataloging of different library materials across several persons of a cataloging team and across time. Users can use them to clarify how to find an entry and how to interpret the data in an entry. Cataloging rule. The larger a collection, the more elaborate cataloging rules are needed. Users cannot and do not want to examine hundreds of catalog entries or even dozens of library items to find the one item they need.

These rules organize the bibliographic description of an item in the following areas: title and statement of responsibility (author or editor), edition, material specific details(for example, the scale of a map), publication and distribution, physical description (for example, number of pages), series, notes, and standard number (ISBN). The most commonly used set of cataloging rules in the English speaking world are the Anglo-American Cataloguing Rules, 2nd Edition, or AACR2 for short. In the German-speaking world there exists the Regeln für die alphabetische Katalogisierung, abbreviated RAK. AACR2 has been translated into many languages, however, for use around the world. AACR2 provides rules for descriptive cataloging only and does not touch upon subject cataloging.

Library items that are written in a foreign script are, in some cases, transliterated to the script of the catalog.

Cataloging Terms

Generally refers to the first author named on the item. Additional authors are added as "added entries." In cases where no clear author is named, the title of the work is considered the main entry.

Sorting

In a title catalog, one can distinguish two sort orders:

- Grammatical sort order (it is used mainly in older catalogs), the most important word of the title is the first sort term. The importance of a word is measured by grammatical rules; for example, the first noun may be defined to be the most important word.
- Mechanical sort order, the first word of the title is the first sort term. Most new catalogs use this scheme, but

still include a trace of the grammatical sort order: they neglect an article (The, A, etc.) at the beginning of the title.

The grammatical sort order has the advantage that often, the most important word of the title is also a good keyword (question 3), and it is the word most users remember first when their memory is incomplete. However, it has the disadvantage that many elaborate grammatical rules are needed, so that only expert users may be able to search the catalog without help from a librarian.

The name of the person is always (cataloged and) sorted in a standard form, even if it appears differently in the library material in some catalogs. This standardization is achieved by a process called authority control. An advantage of the authority control is that it is easier to answer question 2 (which works of some author does the library have?). On the other hand, it may be more difficult to answer question 1 (does the library have some specific material?) if the material spells the author in a peculiar variant. For the cataloguer, it may incur (too) much work to check whether Smith, J. is Smith, John or Smith, Jack.

For some works, even the title can be standardized. The technical term for this is uniform title. For example, translations and reeditions are sometimes sorted under their original title. In many catalogs, parts of the Geeta are sorted under the standard name of the book(s) they contain. The plays of William Shakespeare are another frequently cited example of the role played by a uniform title in the library catalog.

For alphabetic order, there are many complications :

1. Sorting conventions differ from country to country, and one which may be applicable to one country, may not be applicable to another country. For example, some Dutch catalogs sort IJ as Y. Should an English catalog follow this suit? And should a Dutch catalog sort non-Dutch words the same way?
2. Some titles contain numbers, for example 2001: A Space Odyssey. Should they be sorted as numbers, or spelled out as Two thousand and one?

3. de Balzac, Honoré or Balzac, Honoré de? Ortega y Gasset, José or Gasset, José Ortega y?

In a subject catalog, he cataloguer will select appropriate subject headings for the bibliographic item and a unique classification number (sometimes known as a "call number") which is used not only for identification but also for the purposes of shelving, placing items with similar subjects near one another, which aids in browsing by library users, who are thus often able to take advantage of serendipity in their search process. Here one has to decide on which classification system to use.

Online Catalogs

Online cataloging has greatly enhanced the usability of catalogs, thanks to the advancement of Machine Readable Cataloging = MARC standards in the 1960s. Rules governing the creation of catalog MARC records include not only formal cataloging rules like AACR2 but also special rules specific to MARC, available from the Library of Congress and also OCLC. MARC was originally used to automate the creation of physical catalog cards. Now the MARC computer files are accessed directly in the search process. OPACs have enhanced usability over traditional card formats because:

1. The online catalog does not need to be sorted statically; the user can choose author, title, keyword, or systematic order dynamically.
2. Most online catalogs offer a search facility for any word of the title; the goal of the grammatic word order (provide an entry on the word that most users would look for) is reached even better.
3. Many online catalogs allow links between several variants of an author name. So, authors can be found both under the original and the standardised name (if entered properly by the cataloguer).
4. The elimination of paper cards has made the information more accessible to many people with disabilities, such

as the visually impaired, wheelchair users, and those who suffer from mold allergies.

Social Networking

Social Networking is the new craze among new generation. It's the most popular and visited sites. On social networking via Facebook or twitter, one can share their thoughts, pictures, video albums, songs etc. On networking sites, one can meet people of all hues and sizes living thousands of miles away from us. The internet is filled with millions of net surfers who are looking to meet other people, to gather and share first-hand information and experiences about travelling, trekking, developing friendships or professional alliances, finding employment, business-to-business marketing and even groups sharing information about the dooms day and the Great Shift to arrive December 21-2012. The topics and interests are as varied and rich as the stars on the sky.

The use of online social networks by libraries is also an increasingly prevalent and growing tool that is being used to communicate with more potential library users, as well as extending the services provided by individual libraries.

A final rise in social network use is being driven by college students using the services to network with professionals for internship and job opportunities. Many studies have been done on the effectiveness of networking online in a college setting, and one notable one is by Phipps Arabie and Yoram Wind published in Advances in Social Network Analysis.

Early social networking on the World Wide Web began in the form of generalized online communities such as Theglobe.com (1995), Geocities (1994) and Tripod.com (1995). These online communities created a single platform on bringing people together to interact with each other through chatrooms, and encouraged users to share personal information and ideas via personal webpages by providing easy-to-use publishing tools and free or inexpensive webspace. Some communities - such as Classmates.com - took a different approach by simply having people link to each other via email addresses. In the late 1990s, user profiles became a central feature of social networking sites, allowing users to compile lists of "friends" and search for other users with similar interests. New social networking methods were developed by the end of the 1990s, and many sites began to develop more advanced features for users to find and manage friends. The 21st century generation of social networking sites began to flourish with the emergence of Makeoutclub in 2000, followed by Friendster in 2002, and soon became part of the Internet mainstream. Friendster was followed by MySpace and LinkedIn a year later, and finally, Bebo. Attesting to the rapid increase in social networking sites' popularity, by 2005, MySpace was reportedly getting more page views than Google.

Facebook, launched in 2004, has become the most popular social networking site in the world. Today, it is estimated that there are now over 200 active sites using a wide variety of social networking models. When it comes to online social networking, websites are commonly used. These websites are known as social sites. Social networking websites function like an online community of internet users. Depending on the website in question, many of these online community members share common interests in hobbies, religion, or politics. Once you are granted access to a social networking website you can begin to socialize. This socialization may include reading the profile pages of other members and possibly even contacting them.

We can make friends all over the world on social networking sites, and also understand the lifestyle and living standards of other peoples of the country. This means that although you are in the United States, you could develop an online friendship with someone in Australia, England or Switzerland.

The potential for computer networking to facilitate new forms of computer-mediated social interaction was suggested early on. Efforts to support social networks via computer-mediated communication were made in many early online services, including Usenet, ARPANET, LISTSERV, and bulletin board services (BBS). Many prototypical features of social networking sites were also present in online services such as America Online, Prodigy, and CompuServe.

TYPICAL STRUCTURE

Basics

One can create profile on social networking sites and also update it from time to time. Users can often upload pictures of themselves to their profiles, post blog entries for others to read, search for other users with similar interests, and compile and share lists of contacts. In addition, user profiles often have a section dedicated to comments from friends and other users. To protect user privacy, social networks usually have controls that allow users to choose who can view their profile, contact them, add them to their list of contacts, and so on.

Recently, it has also become platform for an array of organizations to create profiles to advertise products and services.

Additional Features

Some social networks have some additional features, such as the availability of to create groups that share common interests or affiliations, upload or stream live videos, and hold discussions in forums. Geosocial networking co-opts internet mapping services to organize user participation around geographic features and their attributes.

There is also a trend for more interoperability between social networks led by technologies such as Open ID and OpenSocial.

Lately, mobile social networking has become popular.In most mobile communities, mobile phone users can now create their own profiles, make friends, participate in chat rooms, create chat rooms, hold private conversations, share photos and videos, and share blogs by using their mobile phone. Some companies provide wireless services which allow their customers to build their own mobile community and brand it, but one of the most popular wireless services for social networking in North America is Facebook Mobile.

Emerging Trends in Social Networking

With each passing day, the number of social networkers users is increasing, as Internet has become economical and easily accessible.

In todays business, one popular use for this technology is social networking Companies have found that social networking sites such as Facebook and Twitter are great ways to build their brand image. According to Jody Nimetz, author of Marketing Jive, there are five major uses for businesses and social media: to create brand awareness, as an online reputation management tool, for recruiting, to learn about new technologies and competitors, and as a lead gen tool to intercept potential prospects. These companies are able to drive traffic to their own online sites while encouraging their consumers and clients to have discussions on how to improve or change products or services.

Twitter set the trend for "real time" services, where users can broadcast to the world what they are doing, or what is on their minds within a 140 character limit. Facebook followed suit with their "Live Feed" where users' activities are streamed as soon as it happens.While Twitter focuses on words, Clixtr, another real time service, focuses on group photo sharing where users can update their photo streams with photos while at an event. Friends and nearby users can contribute their own photos and comments to that event stream, thus contributing to the "real time" aspect of broadcasting photos and comments as it is being uploaded. In the location based social networking space, Foursquare gained popularity as it allowed for users to "check-in" to places that they are frequenting at that moment. Gowalla is another such service which functions in much the same way that Foursquare does, leveraging the GPS in phones to create a location-based user experience. Clixtr, though in the real time space, is also a location based social networking site since events created by users are automatically geotagged, and users can view events occurring nearby through the Clixtr iPhone application Recently, Yelp announced its entrance into the location based social networking space through check-ins with their mobile app; whether or not this becomes detrimental to Foursquare or Gowalla is yet to be seen as it is still considered a new space in the internet technology industry.

One other use that is being discussed is the use of Social Networks in the Science communities. Julia Porter Liebeskind et al. have published a study on how New Biotechnology Firms are using social networking sites to share exchanges in scientific knowledge. They state in their study that by sharing information and knowledge with one another, they are able to "increase both their learning and their flexibility in ways that would not be possible within a self-contained hierarchical organization." Social networking is helping scientists to expand their knowledge base and share scientific views, and without these new means of communicating their theories might become "isolated and irrelevant".

USE AS A COMMUNITION TOOL

Social networks are also being used by teachers and students as a communication tool. Because many students are already using a wide-range of social networking sites, teachers have begun to familiarize themselves with this trend and are now using it to their advantage. Teachers and professors are doing everything from creating chat-room forums and groups to extend classroom discussion to posting assignments, tests and quizzes, to assisting with homework outside of the classroom setting. Social networks are also being used to foster teacher-parent communication. These sites make it possible and more convenient for parents to ask questions and voice concerns without having to meet face-to-face.

Social networks are being used by social workers as a means of low-cost grassroots organizing. Extensive use of an array of social networking sites enabled organizers of the 2009 National Equality March to mobilize an estimated 200,000 participants to march on Washington with a cost savings of up to 85% per participant over previous methods.

Social Network Hosting Service

A social network hosting service is a web hosting service that specifically hosts the user creation of web-based social networking services, alongside related applications. Such services are also known as vertical social networks due to the creation of SNSes which cater to specific user interests and niches; like larger, interest-agnostic SNSes, such niche networking services may also possess the ability to create increasingly niche groups of users.

Business Model

Some social networking site change money for membership. In part, this may be because social networking is a relatively new service, and the value of using them has not been firmly established in customers' minds.Companies such as MySpace and Facebook sell online advertising on their site. Their business model is based upon large membership count, and charging for membership would be counterproductive. Some believe that the deeper information that the sites have on each user will allow much better targeted advertising than any other site can currently provide.

Social networks operate under an autonomous business model, in which a social network's members serve dual roles as both the suppliers and the consumers of content. This is in contrast to a traditional business model, where the suppliers and consumers are distinct agents. Revenue is typically gained in the autonomous business model via advertisements, but subscription-based revenue is possible when membership and content levels are sufficiently high.

Social Networking Websites

Social networking often involves grouping specific individuals or organizations together. While there are a number of social networking websites that focus on particular interests, there are others that do not. The websites without a main focus are often referred to as "traditional" social networking websites and usually have open memberships. This means that anyone can become a member, no matter what their hobbies, beliefs, or views are. However, once you are inside this online community, you can begin to create your own network of friends and eliminate members that do not share common interests or goals.

As I'm sure you're aware, there are dangers associated with social networking including data theft and viruses, which are on the rise. The most prevalent danger though often involves online predators or individuals who claim to be someone that they are not. Although danger does exist with networking online, it also exists in the real world, too. Just like you're advised when meeting strangers at clubs and bars, school, or work — you are also adv.sed to proceed with caution online. By being aware of your cyber-surroundings and who you are talking to, you should be able to safely enjoy social networking online. It will take many phone conversations to get to know someone, but you really won't be able to make a clear judgment until you can meet each other in person. Just use common sense and listen to your inner voice; it will tell you when something doesn't feel right about the online conversations taking place.

Once you are know everything about the internet, you can begin your search from hundreds of networking communities to join. This can easily be done by performing a standard internet search. Your search will likely return a number of results, including MySpace, FriendWise, FriendFinder, Yahoo! 360, Facebook, Orkut, and Classmates.

ELECTRONIC RESOURCE MANAGEMENT

Electronic resource management (ERM) is the practices and software systems used by libraries to keep track of important information about electronic information resources, especially internet-based resources such as electronic journals, databases, and electronic books. The development of ERM became necessary in the early 2000s as it became clear that traditional library catalogs and integrated library systems were not designed to handle metadata for resources as mutable as many online products are.

The idea of developing electronic resource management systems emerged in 2001-2002, growing out of research by Tim Jewell at the University of Washington. The Digital Library

Federation and NISO began work in May 2002 to develop standards for ERM data.These standards were published in the 2004 as Electronic Resource Management: Report of the DLF ERM Initiative.Since the publication of the report, several vendors of integrated library systems have released ERM products.

The following features of ERM system are given below :

1. Supporting acquisition and management of licensed e-resources
2. May be integrated into other library system modules or may be a standalone system
3. May have a public interface, either separate or integrated into the OPAC
4. Providing descriptions of resources at the package (database) level and relate package contents (e.g. e-journals) to the package record
5. Encoding and perhaps publicly displaying licensed rights such as e-reserves, coursepacks, and interlibrary loan
6. Tracking electronic resources from point of order through licensing and final access
7. Providing information about the data providers, consortial arrangements, access platform
8. Providing contact information for all content providers
9. Logging problems with resources and providers
10. Providing customizable e-mail alerting systems (e.g. notices to managers when actions are expected or required)
11. Linking license documents to resource records
12. Supports retrieval of SUSHI usage statistics

Several library automation companies have developed ERM products, including several with generic-sounding names for specific commercial products. Some open-source ERM systems also exist.

CITATION MANAGEMENT SOFTWARE AND CITATION MANAGEMENT

This software allows a users to see and collet information, such as citations for books, articles, and Websites, by interfacing with library databases. The citation manager then works with word-processing software to insert properly formatted footnotes or citations into a paper and create a properly formatted bibliography.

Reference management software, citation management software or personal bibliographic management software is software for scholars and authors to use for recording and utilising bibliographic citations (references). Once a citation has been recorded, it can be used time and again in generating bibliographies, such as lists of references in scholarly books, articles and essays. The development of reference management packages has been driven by the rapid expansion of scientific literature.

These software packages normally consist of a database in which full bibliographic references can be entered, plus a system for generating selective lists of articles in the different formats required by publishers and scholarly journals. Modern reference management packages can usually be integrated with word processors so that a reference list in the appropriate format is produced automatically as an article is written, reducing the risk that a cited source is not included in the reference list. This will also be beneficial for the author while making or preparing bibliography.

Reference management software does not do the same job as bibliographic database, bibliographic database, which tries to list all articles published in a particular discipline or group of disciplines; examples are those provided by Ovid Technologies (e.g. Medline), the Institute for Scientific Information (e.g. Web of Knowledge) or monodisciplinary learned societies e.g. the American Psychological Association (PsycINFO). These databases are large and have to be housed on major server installations. Reference management software collects a much smaller database, of the publications that have been used or are likely to be used by a particular author or group, and such a database can easily be housed on an individual's personal computer.

Apart from managing references, most reference management software also enables users to search references from online libraries. These online libraries are usually based on Z39.50 public protocol. Users just need to specify the IP address, database name and keywords to start a Z39.50 search. It is quicker and more efficient than a web browser. However, Z39.50 is a little out of date. Some popular scientific websites, such as Google Scholar, IEEE Xplore and arXiv, do not support the Z39.50 protocol.

Reference software is software which emulates and expands upon print reference forms including the dictionary, translation dictionary, encyclopedia, thesaurus, and atlas. Like print references, reference software can either be general or specific to a domain, and often includes maps and illustrations, as well as bibliography and statistics. Reference software may include multimedia content including animations, audio, and video, which further illustrate a concept. Well designed reference software improves upon the navigability of print references, through the use of search functionality and hyperlinks. Many dictionaries and encyclopedias rushed into CD-ROM editions soon after the widespread introduction of the CD-ROM to home computers. A second major development occurred as the internet also became widely available in homes, with reference works becoming available online as well. The conversion of previously print-only reference materials to electronic format marked a major change to the marketing and accessibility of such works.

A striking case study is that of the venerable Encyclopedia Britannica, which was previously only available at prices of USD 1500 and higher, restricting it to the better libraries and the wealthy. Today, the Encyclopedia Britannica and World Book Encyclopedia retail in electronic format for around 50 USD, with cheaper OEM versions sometimes bundled with new computers. Such dramatic changes brought conventionally restricted knowledge repositories to the fingertips of an almost universal audience in a period of less than 11 years. The opportunities brought by new media enticed new competitors into the reference software market. One of the earliest and most well-known was Microsoft Encarta, first introduced on CD-ROM and then also moving online along with other major reference works. In the dictionaries market, one of the more prolific brands was Merriam-Webster, which released CD-ROM and then online versions of English dictionaries, thesauri and foreign language dictionaries.

A long list of online dictionaries is maintained under "dictionaries". Wikipedia and its offspins (such as Wiktionary) marked a new departure in educational reference software. Previous encyclopedias and dictionaries had compiled their contents on the basis of invited and closed teams of specialists. The Wiki concept allowed anyone and everyone to join in creating and editing an online set of reference works.

DOCUMENT DELIVERY PATRON SERVICES

Recalling a book that is charged out is a service available only to UConn faculty, students, emeritus retirees, staff and affiliates of the University. To avoid a $5.00 per day fine, return recalled books promptly. Borrowers who are temporarily unable to respond to recall notices should contact iDesk staff at (860) 486-2518 to make prior arrangements and avoid overdue charges.

Procedures for placing RECALLS online are as follows:

From a HOMER book title record, click on the Recall This Item button at the top of the screen.

From the NetID/Single-Sign-On page, click on the blue box.

Enter your NetID and Password.

Click on Login.

Click on OK to select Recall.

Click Submit Request at bottom of screen.

If the Recall was completed the following message will appear: Your Patron Initiated Request was successful.

For any other messages or complications call 860-486-2518 or email Askcirc@uconn.edu

Holds

Any borrower may request that a circulating item be held for patron pick up when it is returned to the main iDesk on the Plaza Level of the Library.

Retrievals

Traveling from a long distance? See an item from the circulating collections that you would like? Call us at (860) 486-2518 to see if the item you want is on the shelf BEFORE you leave home. We will be happy to retrieve it for you. Please note that only items from the circulating collections are eligible for retrievals.

Searches

For items that cannot be located in the collection, one can visit the Library's iDesk on the Plaza Level to submit a Search request. The item will be searched for nearly two months. The patron will be notified of its availability when found. If the item is urgently needed, it is recommended that one place an ILL request.

InterCampus Express (ICE)

The Intercampus Express (Ice) Program is a Service of Document Delivery/Interlibrary Loan Services.

Books or videos that are located at any of the Regional Campus Libraries are available for loan through the Document Delivery/Interlibrary Loan Services. Members of the University community may request to have those books or videos delivered to the Homer Babbidge Library for pick-up and check-out.

To initiate requests for books or videos located at any of the Regional Campus Libraries: Request via HOMER, by searching for the title in HOMER and then placing the order by clicking on Request From Another UConn Campus.

If the Regional Campus Library book is currently charged-out, you can process a Recall on that item.

Boston Library Consortium Card Program

The University of Connecticut Libraries is a member of the Boston Library Consortium (BLC). As a member, the University community is offered privileges associated with the Boston Library Consortium Card Program.

Eligibility —University of Connecticut (Health Center and Law School communities excluded) faculty, staff, visiting scholars, graduate and undergraduate students, and retirees are eligible for a BLC Card. Applicants must have an active unblocked patron record in the University of Connecticut Library's (UCL) patron file.

Registration —Applicants may register for the BLC Card at the Babbidge Library iDesk or at any of the Circulation Desks at any of the Regional Campus Libraries. BLC Cards are issued to faculty, staff, visiting scholars, graduate students, and retirees with an expiration date of August 31st of the current year. BLC Cards are issued to undergraduate students with an expiration date of the current semester. Cards may be renewed as long as the applicant still meets eligibility criteria. Consortium Cards are non-transferable.

Borrowing Privileges and Borrower Responsibilities — Borrowing privileges vary at each member institution. There are different loan periods and fine structures at each library. Cardholders are responsible for any charges accrued. Failure to abide by lending library rules may result in the loss of library privileges at all BLC libraries. Borrowers should return materials to the home library.

Member Libraries —See the BLC User Guide on the BLC website http://www.blc.org for a list of member libraries and information on individual library policy, library fees, as well as hours and directions.

Proxy Patron Program

Faculty, University administrators and staff may employ students (both graduate and undergraduate) to serve as research assistants. Duties of these research assistants include locating items in the library and subsequently checking them out on behalf of the employer (aka Proxy Grantor.) These students are registered as Proxy Patrons at the iDesk.

Any items charged out of the library on behalf of the Proxy Grantor will be charged to the Proxy Grantor's record. The students must show iDesk staff their own UCONN photo ID when registering and checking out items.

Use the Proxy Borrower Permission form in order to set up privileges as a Proxy Patron. The Proxy Grantor must sign the form in order for it to be valid. The form should be brought to the iDesk by the research assistant/Proxy Patron for processing.

Honors Students

Undergraduate students participating in the Honors Students Program receive graduate student/faculty borrowing privileges for books at the Babbidge Library and the regional campuses libraries. These enhanced borrowing privileges provide Honors Students with extended access to resources for their academic courses, thesis work, and undergraduate research.

The privileges are as follows:

180-day loan period for books

Five 180 -day renewals that can be conducted on-line

Books may be recalled by other users, and would have to be brought back to the library after a student receives a recall notice

Books may be borrowed beyond the 5th 180-day renewal period if they are brought back to the library for discharge and inspection and have not been requested by other patrons.

Role of Patron Services Supervisor

The Schaffner Patron Services Supervisor oversees front line patron services at the Schaffner Library Circulation desk, including circulation, reserve, interlibrary loan, and patron access. Trains, schedules and monitors four students assistants, and also trains four library school interns on circulation procedures. Monitors activities and prepares reports on circulation activities.

Assists in delivery of information, instruction services and collection management. Works closely with Schaffner Librarians, Operations Manager, and Head of Reference to maintain high quality public services. Actively participates in Schaffner Library, Reference Department, Public Services Division, and Library meetings, forums, and planning activities.

Responsibilities

1. Directs the daily operations of the Circulation Desk at the Schaffner Library (Chicago Campus) including training, scheduling and supervising student assistants and library school interns. Develops and maintains training manual and material. Works collaboratively with Schaffner Librarians, Operations Manager and Head of Reference to maintain high quality services, including service and facilities planning and review, and policy and procedures development. Monitors schedule for Writing and Math Place. Oversees closing of the library on weekdays. Primary contact for safety and security in the evenings. Maintains relations with Campus Police. 2. Performs full range of circulation functions including ILL, document delivery and reserve, fines processing, materials checkout search.

Manages patron access including library privileges and guest IDs. Supports the information, instruction and collection management work of the department by performing bibliographic searches, preparing orders, assisting in surveys of collections, and processing materials added to or weeded from the collection. Assists with preparation and dissemination of handouts, guides and web pages. 3. Ensures current and accurate records/information in the Voyager (Circulation, Acquisitions, Catalog modules) system and OCLC's PRISM ILL module. Oversees delivery of electronic and print materials and transfer of materials between schaffner Library and Main Library. 4. Works with Reference Department and other Library staff on the Evanston Campus. Occasionally attends Circulation Services Committee meetings on the Evanston Campus as back up to Branch Operations Manager. Other duties as asigned.

Required Qualifications

1. High school diploma or equivalent in experience and education. 2. Strong computer literacy skills. 3. Ability to handle multiple tasks simultaneously. 4. Must be able to push and pull carts of books weighing in range of 50-75 pounds. —Minimum Competencies: 1. Ability to work effectively in an environment in which the parameters may change daily and to adjust behavior to meet the needs of different people and situations; Successfully uses multiple software programs independently including Microsoft Office applications such as PowerPoint, Word, Excel, and Access, email, web browsers, and PeopleSoft; Demonstrated ability to communicate effectively one-to-one, in small groups and in public speaking contexts; Ability to write precise, well-organized emails, letters and proposals while using appropriate vocabulary and grammar; Regularly monitors customer satisfaction and provides suggestions to improve quality and value to the customer; Effectively performs duties and responsibilities with attention to detail and support for organizational policies; Demonstrated ability to work on multiple projects simultaneously; Demonstrated ability to formulate realistic plans and contingencies and establish appropriate measurements of anticipated results; Demonstrated ability to work on multiple projects simultaneously; Demonstrated ability to formulate realistic plans and contingencies and establish appropriate measurements of anticipated results; Ability to build collaboration by encouraging trust, mutual respect and shared purpose among various participants in an engagement.

Preferred Qualifications:

1. A bachelor's degree or the equivalent combination of education, training and experience from which comparable skills can be acquired; 2. Previous library work experience; 3. Previous supervisory experience; 4. Familiarity with NU applications and web browsers.

Proxy Server

Server that sites between a client application, such as a Web browser, and a real server. It intercepts all requests to the real server to see if it can fulfill the requests itself. If not, it forwards the request to the real server. A client connects to the proxy server, requesting some service, such as a file, connection, web page, or other resource, available from a different server. The proxy server evaluates the request according to its filtering rules. For example, it may filter traffic by IP address or protocol.

If the request is validated by the filter, the proxy provides the resource by connecting to the relevant server and requesting the service on behalf of the client. A proxy server may optionally alter the client's request or the server's response, and sometimes it may serve the request without contacting the specified server. In this case, it 'caches' responses from the remote server, and returns subsequent requests for the same content directly.

Most proxies are a web proxy, allowing access to content on the World Wide Web(WWW).

A proxy server has a large variety of potential purposes, including:

1. To keep machines behind it anonymous (mainly for security).
2. To speed up access to resources (using caching). Web proxies are commonly used to cache web pages from a web server.
3. To apply access policy to network services or content, e.g. to block undesired sites.

4. To log/audit usage, i.e. to provide company employee Internet usage reporting.
5. To bypass security/ parental controls.
6. To scan transmitted content for malware before delivery.
7. To scan outbound content, e.g., for data leak protection.
8. To circumvent regional restrictions.

A proxy server that passes requests and replies unmodified is usually called a gateway or sometimes tunneling proxy. A proxy server can be placed in the user's local computer or at various points between the user and the destination servers on the Internet. A reverse proxy is (usually) an Internet-facing proxy used as a front-end to control and protect access to a server on a private network, commonly also performing tasks such as load-balancing, authentication, decryption or caching. Forward proxies are proxies where the client server names the target server to connect to. Forward proxies are able to retrieve from a wide range of sources (in most cases anywhere on the Internet).

The terms "forward proxy" and "forwarding proxy" are a general description of behaviour (forwarding traffic) and thus ambiguous. Except for Reverse proxy, the types of proxies described on this article are more specialized sub-types of the general forward proxy concept.

The two main purpose of proxy servers are given below :

1. Improve Performance: Proxy servers can dramatically improve performance for groups of users. This is because it saves the results of all requests for a certain amount of time. Consider the case where both user X and user Y access the World Wide Web through a proxy server. First user X requests a certain Web page, which we'll call Page 1.

   Sometime later, user Y requests the same page. Instead of forwarding the request to the Web server where Page 1 resides, which can be a time-consuming operation, the proxy server simply returns the Page 1 that it already fetched for user X. Since the proxy server is often on the same network as the user, this is a much faster operation. Real proxy servers support hundreds or thousands of users. The major online services such as America Online, MSN and Yahoo, for example, employ an array of proxy servers.

2. Filter Requests: Proxy servers can also be used to filter requests. For example, a company might use a proxy server to prevent its employees from accessing a specific set of Web sites.

Open Proxies

An open proxy is a forward proxy server that is accessible by any Internet user. Gordon Lyon estimates there are "hundreds of thousands" of open proxies on the Internet.An anonymous open proxy allows users to conceal their IP address while browsing the Web or using other Internet services.

Reverse Proxies

A reverse proxy is s server that appears to clients to be an normal and ordinary server. Requests are forwarded to one or more origin servers which handle the request. The response is returned as if it came directly from the proxy server.

Reverse proxies are installed in the neighborhood of one or more web servers. All traffic coming from the Internet and with a destination of one of the web servers goes through the proxy server. The use of "reverse" originates in its counterpart "forward proxy" since the reverse proxy sits closer to the web server and serves only a restricted set of websites.

The several reasons for using reverse proxy server, are given below :

1. Encryption / SSL acceleration: when secure web sites are created, the SSL encryption is often not done by the web server itself, but by a reverse proxy that is equipped with SSL acceleration hardware. See Secure Sockets Layer. Furthermore, a host can provide a single "SSL

proxy" to provide SSL encryption for an arbitrary number of hosts; removing the need for a separate SSL Server Certificate for each host, with the downside that all hosts behind the SSL proxy have to share a common DNS name or IP address for SSL connections. This problem can partly be overcome by using the SubjectAltName feature of X.509 certificates.

2. Load balancing: the reverse proxy can distribute the load to several web servers, each web server serving its own application area. In such a case, the reverse proxy may need to rewrite the URLs in each web page (translation from externally known URLs to the internal locations).
3. Serve/cache static content: A reverse proxy can offload the web servers by caching static content like pictures and other static graphical content.
4. Compression: the proxy server can optimize and compress the content to speed up the load time.
5. Spoon feeding: reduces resource usage caused by slow clients on the web servers by caching the content the web server sent and slowly "spoon feeding" it to the client. This especially benefits dynamically generated pages.
6. Security: the proxy server is an additional layer of defense and can protect against some OS and WebServer specific attacks. However, it does not provide any protection to attacks against the web application or service itself, which is generally considered the larger threat.
7. Extranet Publishing: a reverse proxy server facing the Internet can be used to communicate to a firewalled server internal to an organization, providing extranet access to some functions while keeping the servers behind the firewalls. If used in this way, security measures should be considered to protect the rest of your infrastructure in case this server is compromised, as its web application is exposed to attack from the Internet.

USES OF PROXY SERVERS

Filtering

A content-filtering web proxy server provides administrative control over the content that may be relayed through the proxy. It is commonly used in both commercial and non-commercial organizations (especially schools) to ensure that Internet usage conforms to acceptable use policy. In some cases users can circumvent the proxy, since there are services designed to proxy information from a filtered website through a non-filtered site to allow it through the user's proxy.

A content filtering proxy will support user authentication to control web access. It also usually produces logs, either to give detailed information about the URLs accessed by specific users, or to monitor bandwidth usage statistics. It may also communicate to daemon-based and/or ICAP-based antivirus software to provide security against virus and other malware by scanning incoming content in real time before it enters the network.

Many workplaces, schools, and colleges restrict the web sites and online services that are made available in their buildings. This is done either with a specialized proxy, called a content filter (both commercial and free products are available), or by using a cache-extension protocol such as ICAP, that allows plug-in extensions to an open caching architecture.

Some common methods used for content filtering include: URL or DNS blacklists, URL regex filtering, MIME filtering, or content keyword filtering. Some products have been known to employ content analysis techniques to look for traits commonly used by certain types of content providers.

Requests made to the open internet must first pass through an outbound proxy filter. The web-filtering company provides a database of URL patterns (regular expressions) with associated content attributes. This database is updated weekly by site-wide subscription, much like a virus filter subscription. The administrator instructs the web filter to ban broad classes of content (such as sports, pornography, online shopping, gambling, or social networking). Requests that match a banned URL pattern are rejected immediately. Assuming the requested URL is acceptable, the content is then fetched by the proxy. At this point a dynamic filter may be applied on the return path. For example, JPEG files could be blocked based on fleshtone matches, or language filters could dynamically detect unwanted language. If the content is rejected then an HTTP fetch error is returned and nothing is cached.

Mostly web-filtering companies are internet wide crawling robot the assesses the likelihood that a content is a certain type (e.g. "This content is 70% chance of porn, 40% chance of sports, and 30% chance of news" could be the outcome for one web page). The resultant database is then corrected by manual labor based on complaints or known flaws in the content-matching algorithms.

Web filtering proxies are not able to peer inside secure sockets HTTP transactions, assuming the chain-of-trust of SSL/TLS has not been tampered with. As a result, users wanting to bypass web filtering will typically search the internet for an open and anonymous HTTPS transparent proxy. They will then program their browser to proxy all requests through the web filter to this anonymous proxy. Those requests will be encrypted with https. The web filter cannot distinguish these transactions from, say, a legitimate access to a financial website. Thus, content filters are only effective against unsophisticated users.

As mentioned above, the SSL/TLS chain-of-trust does rely on trusted root certificate authorities; in a workplace setting where the client is managed by the organization, trust might be granted to a root certificate whose private key is known to the proxy. Concretely, a root certificate generated by the proxy is installed into the browser CA list by IT staff. In such scenarios, proxy analysis of the contents of a SSL/TLS transaction becomes possible. The proxy is effectively operating a man-in-the-middle attack, allowed by the client's trust of a root certificate the proxy owns.

A special case of web proxies is “CGI proxies”. These are web sites that allow a user to access a site through them. They generally use PHP or CGI to implement the proxy functionality. These types of proxies are frequently used to gain access to web sites blocked by corporate or school proxies. Since they also hide the user’s own IP address from the web sites they access through the proxy, they are sometimes also used to gain a degree of anonymity, called “Proxy Avoidance”.

Caching

A caching proxy server accelerates service requests by retrieving content saved from a previous request made by the same client or even other clients. Caching proxies keep local copies of frequently requested resources, allowing large organizations to significantly reduce their upstream bandwidth usage and costs, while significantly increasing performance. Most ISPs and large businesses have a caching proxy. Caching proxies were the first kind of proxy server.

Some poorly-implemented caching proxies have had downsides (e.g., an inability to use user authentication). Some problems are described in RFC 3143 (Known HTTP Proxy/Caching Problems).

Another important use of the proxy server is to reduce the hardware cost. An organization may have many systems on the same network or under control of a single server, prohibiting the possibility of an individual connection to the Internet for each system. In such a case, the individual systems can be connected to one proxy server, and the proxy server connected to the main server.

Bypassing Filters and Censorship

If the destination server filters content based on the origin of the request, the use of a proxy can remove this filter. For example, a server using IP-based geolocation to restrict its service to a certain country can be accessed using a proxy located in that country to access the service.

Likewise, a badly configured proxy can provide access to a network otherwise isolated from the Internet.

Logging and Eavesdropping

Proxies can be used or installed in order to eavesdrop upon the data-flow between client machines and the web. All content sent or accessed – including passwords submitted and cookies used – can be captured and analyzed by the proxy operator. For this reason, passwords to online services (such as webmail and banking) should always be exchanged over a cryptographically secured connection, such as SSL.

By chaining proxies which do not reveal data about the original requester, it is possible to obfuscate activities from the eyes of the user's destination. However, more traces will be left on the intermediate hops, which could be used or offered up to trace the user's activities. If the policies and administrators of these other proxies are unknown, the user may fall victim to a false sense of security just because those details are out of sight and mind.

In what is more of an inconvenience than a risk, proxy users may find themselves being blocked from certain Web sites, as numerous forums and Web sites block IP addresses from proxies known to have spammed or trolled the site. Proxy bouncing can be used to maintain your privacy.

Gateways to Private Networks

Proxy servers can perform a role similar to a network switch in linking two networks.

Accessing Services Anonymously

An anonymous proxy server (sometimes called a web proxy) generally attempts to anonymize web surfing. There are different varieties of anonymizers. The destination server (the server that ultimately satisfies the web request) receives requests from the anonymizing proxy server, and thus does not receive information about the end user's address.

However, the requests are not anonymous to the anonymizing proxy server, and so a degree of trust is present between the proxy server and the user. Many of them are funded through a continued advertising link to the user.

Access control: Some proxy servers implement a logon requirement. In large organizations, authorized users must log on to gain access to the web. The organization can thereby track usage to individuals.

Some anonymizing proxy servers may forward data packets with header lines such as HTTP_VIA, HTTP_X_FORWARDED_FOR, or HTTP_FORWARDED, which may reveal the IP address of the client. Other anonymizing proxy servers, known as elite or high anonymity proxies, only include the REMOTE_ADDR header with the IP address of the proxy server, making it appear that the proxy server is the client. A website could still suspect a proxy is being used if the client sends packets which include a cookie from a previous visit that did not use the high anonymity proxy server. Clearing cookies, and possibly the cache, would solve this problem.

Implementations of Proxies

Web Proxy

A proxy that effects of focuses on world wide web traffic is called a "web proxy". The most common use of a web proxy is to serve as a web cache. Most proxy programs provide a means to deny access to URLs specified in a blacklist, thus providing content filtering. This is often used in a corporate, educational, or library environment, and anywhere else where content filtering is desired. Some web proxies reformat web pages for a specific purpose or audience, such as for cell phones and PDAs.

Suffix Proxies

A suffix proxy server allows a user to access web content by appending the name of the proxy server to the URL of the requested content (e.g. "en.wikipedia.org.example.com"). Suffix proxy servers are easier to use than regular proxy servers.

Transparent Proxies

An intercepting proxy server with a gateway or router (commonly with NAT capabilities). Connections made by client browsers through the gateway are diverted to the proxy without client-side configuration (or often knowledge). Connections may also be diverted from a SOCKS server or other circuit-level proxies.

RFC 2616 (Hypertext Transfer Protocol—HTTP/1.1) offers standard definitions:

1. "A 'transparent proxy' is a proxy that does not modify the request or response beyond what is required for proxy authentication and identification".
2. "A 'non-transparent proxy' is a proxy that modifies the request or response in order to provide some added service to the user agent, such as group annotation services, media type transformation, protocol reduction, or anonymity filtering".

A security flaw in the way that transparent proxies operate was published by Robert Auger in 2009 and advisory by the Computer Emergency Response Team was issued listing dozens of affected transparent, and intercepting proxy servers.

Purpose

Intercepting proxies are normally used in businesses to prevent avoidance of acceptable use policy, and to ease administrative burden, since no client browser configuration is required. This second reason however is mitigated by features such as Active Directory group policy, or DHCP and automatic proxy detection.

Intercepting proxies are also commonly used by ISPs in some countries to save upstream bandwidth and improve customer response times by caching. This is more common in countries where bandwidth is more limited (e.g. island nations) or must be paid for.

Issues

Interception of a TCP connection creates some issuse. Firstly the original destination IP and port must somehow be communicated to the proxy. This is not always possible (e.g. where the gateway and proxy reside on different hosts). There is a class of cross site attacks which depend on certain behaviour of intercepting proxies that do not check or have access to information about the original (intercepted) destination. This problem can be resolved by using an integrated packet-level and application level appliance or software which is then able to communicate this information between the packet handler and the proxy.

Intercepting also creates problems for HTTP authentication, especially connection-oriented authentication such as NTLM, since the client browser believes it is talking to a server rather than a proxy. This can cause problems where an intercepting proxy requires authentication, then the user connects to a site which also requires authentication.

Finally intercepting connections can cause problems for HTTP caches, since some requests and responses become uncacheble by a shared cache.

Therefore intercepting connections is generally discouraged. However due to the simplicity of deploying such systems, they are in widespread use.

IMPLEMENTATION METHODS

Interception can be performed using Cisco's WCCP (Web Cache Control Protocol). This proprietary protocol resides on the router and is configured from the cache, allowing the cache to determine what ports and traffic is sent to it via transparent redirection from the router. This redirection can occur in one of two ways: GRE Tunneling (OSI Layer 3) or MAC rewrites (OSI Layer 2).

Once traffic reaches the proxy machine itself interception is commonly performed with NAT (Network Address Translation). Such setups are invisible to the client browser, but leave the proxy visible to the web server and other devices on the Internet side of the proxy. Recent releases of Linux and some BSD provide TPROXY (Transparent Proxy) which performs IP-level (OSI Layer 3) transparent interception and Spoofing of outbound traffic. Hiding the proxy IP address from other network devices.

Detection

There are several methods which can be used to detect the presence of an intercepting proxy sever are given below :

1. By comparing the client's external IP address to the address seen by an external web server, or sometimes by examining the HTTP headers received by a server. A number of sites have been created to address this issue, by reporting the user's IP address as seen by the site back to the user in a web page.
2. By comparing the sequence of network hops reported by a tool such as traceroute for a proxied protocol such as http (port 80) with that for a non proxied protocol such as SMTP (port 25).
3. By attempting to make a connection to an IP address at which there is known to be no server. The proxy will accept the connection and then attempt to proxy it on. When the proxy finds no server to accept the connection it may return an error message or simply close the connection to the client. This difference in behaviour is simple to detect. For example most web browsers will generate a browser created error page in the case where they cannot connect to an HTTP server but will return a different error in the case where the connection is accepted and then closed.

Tor Onion Proxy Software

It's a system aiming at on online anonymity. Tor is an implementation of onion routing. It works by relaying communications through a network of systems run by volunteers in various locations. By keeping some of the network entry points hidden, Tor is also able to evade internet censorship. Tor is intended to protect users' personal freedom, privacy, and ability to conduct confidential business.

Users of a Tor network run an onion proxy software on their computer. The Tor software periodically negotiates a virtual circuit through the Tor network. At the same time, the onion proxy software presents a SOCKS interface to its clients or users. SOCKS-ifying applications like Polipo may be linked with the Tor onion proxy software, which then multiplexes the traffic through a Tor virtual circuit.The software is open-source and the network is free of charge to use. Vidalia is a cross-platform controller GUI for Tor.

I2P Anonymous Proxy

The I2P anonymous network ('I2P') is a proxy network aiming at online anonymity. It implements garlic routing, which is an enhancement of Tor's onion routing. I2P is fully distributed and works by encrypting all communications in various layers and relaying them through a network of routers run by volunteers in various locations. By keeping the source of the information hidden, I2P offers censorship resistance. The goals of I2P are to protect users' personal freedom, privacy, and ability to conduct confidential business.

Each user of I2P runs an I2P router on their computer (node). The I2P router takes care of finding other peers and building anonymizing tunnels through them. I2P provides proxies for all protocols.The software is free and open-source, and the network is free of charge to use.

Information Retrieval Process

Information retrieval is the area of study concerned with searching for documents, for information within documents, and for metadata about documents, as well as that of searching relational databases and the World Wide Web. There is overlap in the usage of the terms data retrieval, document retrieval, information retrieval, and text retrieval, but each also has its own body of literature, theory, praxis, and technologies. IR is interdisciplinary, based on computer science, mathematics, library science, information science, information architecture, cognitive psychology, linguistics, and statistics.

Automated information retrieval systems are used to reduce what has been called "information overload". Many universities and public libraries use IR systems to provide access to books, journals and other documents. Web search engines are the most visible IR applications.

An information retrieval process begins when a user enters a query into the system. Queries are formal statements of information needs, for example search strings in web search engines. In information retrieval a query does not uniquely identify a single object in the collection. Instead, several objects may match the query, perhaps with different degrees of relevancy. An object is an entity that is represented by information in a database. User queries are matched against the database information. Depending on the application the data objects may be, for example, text documents, images, audio, mind maps or videos. Often the documents themselves are not kept or stored directly in the IR system, but are instead represented in the system by document surrogates or metadata.

Most IR systems compute a numeric score on how well each object in the database match the query, and rank the objects according to this value. The top ranking objects are then shown to the user. The process may then be iterated if the user wishes to refine the query.

Performance Measures

Many different measures for evaluating the performance of information retrieval systems have been proposed. The measures require a collection of documents and a query. All common measures described here assume a ground truth notion of relevancy: every document is known to be either relevant or non-relevant to a particular query. In practice queries may be ill-posed and there may be different shades of relevancy.

Precision

Precision is the fraction of the documents retrieved that are relevant to the user's information need.

$$\text{precision} = \frac{|\{\text{relevant documents}\} \cap \{\text{retrieved documents}\}|}{|\{\text{retrieved documents}\}|}$$

In binary classification, precision is analogous to positive predictive value. Precision takes all retrieved documents into account. It can also be evaluated at a given cut-off rank, considering only the topmost results returned by the system. This measure is called precision at n or P@n.

Note that the meaning and usage of "precision" in the field of Information Retrieval differs from the definition of accuracy and precision within other branches of science and technology.

Recall

Recall is the fraction of the documents that are relevant to the query that are successfully retrieved.

$$\text{recall} = \frac{|\{\text{relevant documents}\} \cap \{\text{retrieved documents}\}|}{|\{\text{relevant documents}\}|}$$

In binary classification, recall is called sensitivity. So it can be looked at as the probability that a relevant document is retrieved by the query.

It is trivial to achieve recall of 100% by returning all documents in response to any query. Therefore recall alone is not enough but one needs to measure the number of non-relevant documents also, for example by computing the precision.

Fall-Out

The proportion of non-relevant documents that are retrieved, out of all non-relevant documents available:

$$\text{fall-out} = \frac{|\{\text{non-relevant documents}\} \cap \{\text{retrieved documents}\}|}{|\{\text{non-relevant documents}\}|}$$

In binary classification, fall-out is closely related to specificity (1 " specificity). It can be looked at as the probability that a non-relevant document is retrieved by the query.

It is trivial to achieve fall-out of 0% by returning zero documents in response to any query.

F-Measure

The weighted harmonic mean of precision and recall, the traditional F-measure or balanced F-score is:

$$F = \frac{2 \cdot \mathrm{precision} \cdot \mathrm{recall}}{(\mathrm{precision} + \mathrm{recall})}.$$

This is also known as the F_1 measure, because recall and precision are evenly weighted.

The general formula for non-negative real â is:

$$F_\beta = \frac{(1 + \beta^2) \cdot (\mathrm{precision} \cdot \mathrm{recall})}{(\beta^2 \cdot \mathrm{precision} + \mathrm{recall})}.$$

Two other commonly used F measures are the F_2 measure, which weights recall twice as much as precision, and the F_{05} measure, which weights precision twice as much as recall.

The F-measure was derived by van Rijsbergen (1979) so that $F_{â}$ "measures the effectiveness of retrieval with respect to a user who attaches â times as much importance to recall as precision". It is based on van Rijsbergen's effectiveness measure E = 1 " (1 / (á / P + (1 " á) / R)). Their relationship is $F_{â}$ = 1 " E where á = 1 / (â² + 1).

Average precision

Precision and recall are single-value metrics based on the whole list of documents returned by the system. For systems that return a ranked sequence of documents, it is desirable to also consider the order in which the returned documents are presented. Average precision emphasizes ranking relevant documents higher. It is the average of precisions computed at the point of each of the relevant documents in the ranked sequence:

$$\mathrm{AveP} = \frac{\sum_{r=1}^{N} (P(r) \times \mathrm{rel}(r))}{\mathrm{number\ of\ relevant\ documents}}$$

where r is the rank, N the number retrieved, rel() a binary function on the relevance of a given rank, and P(r) precision at a given cut-off rank:

$$\mathrm{P(r)} = \frac{|\{\text{relevant retrieved documents of rank r or less}\}|}{r}$$

This metric is also sometimes referred to geometrically as the area under the Precision-Recall curve.

Note that the denominator (number of relevant documents) is the number of relevant documents in the entire collection, so that the metric reflects performance over all relevant documents, regardless of a retrieval cutoff. See:.

R-Precision

Precision at rank R. Where R is the total number of relevant documents. This measure is highly correlated to Average Precision.

Mean average precision

Mean average precision for a set of queries is the mean of the average precision scores for each query.

$$\mathrm{MAP} = \frac{\sum_{q=1}^{Q} \mathrm{AveP(q)}}{Q}$$

where Q is the number of queries.

Discounted cumulative gain

DCG uses a graded relevance scale of documents from the result set to evaluate the usefulness, or gain, of a document based on its position in the result list. The premise of DCG is that highly relevant documents appearing lower in a search result list should be penalized as the graded relevance value is reduced logarithmically proportional to the position of the result.

The DCG accumulated at a particular rank position p is defined as:

$$\mathrm{DCG_p} = rel_1 + \sum_{i=2}^{p} \frac{rel_i}{\log_2 i}.$$

Since result set may vary in size among different queries or systems, to compare performances the normalised version of DCG uses an ideal DCG. To this end, it sorts documents of a result list by relevance, producing an ideal DCG at position p ($IDCG_p$), which normalizes the score:

$$\mathrm{nDCG_p} = \frac{DCG_p}{IDCGp}.$$

The nDCG values for all queries can be averaged to obtain a measure of the average performance of a ranking algorithm. Note that in a perfect ranking algorithm, the DCG_p will be the same as the $IDCG_p$ producing an nDCG of 1.0. All nDCG calculations are then relative values on the interval 0.0 to 1.0 and so are cross-query comparable.

Other Measures

- Mean reciprocal rank
- Spearman's rank correlation coefficient

Model types

Categorization of IR-models (translated from German entry, original source Dominik Kuropka).

For the information retrieval to be efficient, the documents are typically transformed into a suitable representation. There are several representations. The picture on the right illustrates the relationship of some common models. In the picture, the models are categorized according to two dimensions: the mathematical basis and the properties of the model.

1. First dimension: mathematical basis

- Set-theoretic models represent documents as sets of words or phrases. Similarities are usually derived from set-theoretic operations on those sets. Common models are:
    - Standard Boolean model
    - Extended Boolean model

  - Fuzzy retrieval
- Algebraic models represent documents and queries usually as vectors, matrices, or tuples. The similarity of the query vector and document vector is represented as a scalar value.
  - Vector space model
  - Generalized vector space model
  - (Enhanced) Topic-based Vector Space Model
  - Extended Boolean model
  - Latent semantic indexing aka latent semantic analysis
- Probabilistic models treat the process of document retrieval as a probabilistic inference. Similarities are computed as probabilities that a document is relevant for a given query. Probabilistic theorems like the Bayes' theorem are often used in these models.
  - Binary Independence Model
  - Probabilistic relevance model on which is based the okapi (BM25) relevance function
  - Uncertain inference
  - Language models
  - Divergence-from-randomness model
  - Latent Dirichlet allocation
- Feature-based retrieval models view documents as vectors of values of feature functions (or just features) and seek the best way to combine these features into a single relevance score, typically by learning to rank methods. Feature functions are arbitrary functions of document and query, and as such can easily incorporate almost any other retrieval model as just a yet anoth feature.

2. Second dimension: properties of the model

- Models without term-interdependencies treat different terms/words as independent. This fact is usually represented in vector space models by the orthogonality assumption of term vectors or in probabilistic models by an independency assumption for term variables.
- Models with immanent term interdependencies allow a representation of interdependencies between terms. However the degree of the interdependency between two terms is defined by the model itself. It is usually directly or indirectly derived (e.g. by dimensional reduction) from the co-occurrence of those terms in the whole set of documents.
- Models with transcendent term interdependencies allow a representation of interdependencies between terms, but they do not allege how the interdependency between two terms is defined. They relay an external source for the degree of interdependency between two terms. (For example a human or sophisticated algorithms.)

References

1. "DLF Electronic Resource Management Initiative". Digital Library Federation. 2004. http://www.diglib.org/standards/dlf-erm02.htm. Retrieved 2008-11-11.
2. Jewell,, Tim, et al. (2004). "Electronic Resource Management: Report of the DLF ERM Initiative". Digital Library Federation. http://www.diglib.org/pubs/dlf102/. Retrieved 2008-11-11.
3. Feather, Celeste (2007-03-22). "ERM Systems: What Are They and What Do They Do?". Columbus Metropolitan Library, Columbus, OH: OhioNET.

1. Singhal, Amit (2001). "Modern Information Retrieval: A Brief Overview". Bulletin of the IEEE Computer Society Technical Committee on Data Engineering 24 (4): 35–43. http://singhal.info/ieee2001.pdf.

2. Doyle, Lauren; Becker, Joseph (1975). Information Retrieval and Processing. Melville. pp. 410 pp.. ISBN 0471221511.
3. Maron, Melvin E. (2008). "An Historical Note on the Origins of Probabilistic Indexing". Information Processing and Management 44: 971–972. doi:10.1016/j.ipm.2007.02.012. http://yunus.hacettepe.edu.tr/~tonta/courses/spring2008/bby703/maron-on-probabilistic%20indexing-2008.pdf.
4. Korfhage, Robert R. (1997). Information Storage and Retrieval. Wiley. pp. 368 pp.. ISBN 978-0-471-14338-3. http://www.wiley.com/WileyCDA/WileyTitle/productCd-0471143383,descCd-authorInfo.html.
5. Goodrum, Abby A. (2000). "Image Information Retrieval: An Overview of Current Research". Informing Science, 3(2)
6. Foote, Jonathan (1999). "An overview of audio information retrieval". Multimedia Systems. Springer
7. Beel, Jöran; Gipp, Bela; Stiller, Jan-Olaf (2009). "Information Retrieval On Mind Maps - What Could It Be Good For?". Proceedings of the 5th International Conference on Collaborative Computing: Networking, Applications and Worksharing (CollaborateCom'09). Washington: IEEE. http://www.sciplore.org/publications_en.php
8. Frakes, William B. (1992). Information Retrieval Data Structures & Algorithms. Prentice-Hall, Inc.. ISBN 0-13-463837-9. http://www.scribd.com/doc/13742235/Information-Retrieval-Data-Structures-Algorithms-William-B-Frakes.
9. Turpin, Andrew; Scholer, Falk (2006). "User performance versus precision measures for simple search tasks". Proceedings of the 29th Annual international ACM SIGIR Conference on Research and Development in information Retrieval (Seattle, Washington, USA, August 06-11, 2006)

(New York, NY: ACM): 11–18. doi:10.1145/1148170.1148176.

10. "How-to". Linux.org. http://www.linux.org/docs/ldp/howto/Firewall-HOWTO-11.html#ss11.4. "The proxy server is, above all, a security device."
11. Thomas, Keir (2006). Beginning Ubuntu Linux: From Novice to Professional. Apress. "A proxy server helps speed up Internet access by storing frequently accessed pages"
12. "Forward and Reverse Proxies". httpd mod_proxy. Apache. http://httpd.apache.org/docs/2.0/mod/mod_proxy.html#forwardreverse. Retrieved 20 December 2010.
13. Lyon, Gordon (2008). Nmap network scanning. US: Insecure. p. 270. ISBN 9780979958717.
14. An intercepting proxy combines a proxy server with a gateway or router (commonly with NAT capabilities). Connections made by client browsers through the gateway are diverted to the proxy without client-side configuration (or often knowledge). Connections may also be diverted from a SOCKS server or other circuit-level proxies. Intercepting proxies are also commonly referred to as transparent proxies, or forced proxies, presumably because the existence of the proxy is transparent to the user, or the user is forced to use the proxy regardless of local settings. Become EC-Council ECSS certified.
15. "Socket Capable Browser Plugins Result In Transparent Proxy Abuse". The Security Practice. 2009-03-09. http://www.thesecuritypractice.com/the_security_practice/2009/03/socket-capable-browser-plugins-result-in-transparent-proxy-abuse.html. Retrieved 2010-08-14.
16. "US-CERT Vulnerability Note VU#435052". Kb.cert.org. http://www.kb.cert.org/vuls/id/435052. Retrieved 2010-08-14.

17. Wessels, Duane (2004). Squid The Definitive Guide. O'Reilly. pp. 130. 978-0-596-00162-9.

18. Jonathan Glater, "Privacy for People Who Don't Show Their Navels", The New York Times, 25 January 2006.

19. Tor: Bridges. "Tor: Bridges". http://www.torproject.org/bridges. Retrieved 2010-08-30.

20. The Tor Project. "Tor: anonymity online". http://www.torproject.org/. Retrieved 2010-08-30.

CHAPTER–3

MANAGING ELECTRONIC CONTENT PRODUCTS

By surfing on Internet, any one can get information about news, articles and features. Wikipedia is one ahead, as it compiles important information on the same subject or topic, from the different sources. Google scholar also indexes many materials which are not free on the web, but gives them a fairly solid reference, and also provides a live link to local subscription journals. One of the greatest strengths of Google Scholar is its ability to gather a listing of nearly everything that an author has written. For mainstream topics, however, standard databases such as Sociological Abstracts and SocIndex are more useful in finding materials in a focused way without burying the searcher in "everything including the kitchen stove" searching.

DATABASE INDEX

In simple words, the data base index is a data structure which minimises the speed of data retrieval operation on a database at the cost of slower writes and increased storage space. One can create index by created using one or more columns of a database table, providing the basis for both rapid random lookups and efficient access of ordered records. The disk space required to store the index is typically less than that required by the table (since indices usually contain only the key-fields according to which the table is to be arranged, and exclude all the other details in the table), yielding the possibility to store indices in memory for a table whose data is too large to store in memory.

An index is a copy of one part of a table in a relational database. Some databases extend the power of indexing by allowing indices to be created on functions or expressions. For example, an index could be created on upper(last_name), which would only store the upper case versions of the last_name field in the index. Another option sometimes supported is the use of "filtered" indices , where index entries are created only for those records that satisfy some conditional expression. A further aspect of flexibility is to permit indexing on user-defined functions, as well as expressions formed from an assortment of built-in functions.

There are two kinds of indixes: unique and non-unique A unique index acts as a constraint on the table by preventing duplicate entries in the index and thus the backing table.

Index architectures can be classified in 2 categories (i) Non-clustred (ii) Clustered

1. *Non-clustered* : The data is present in random order, but the logical ordering is specified by the index. The data rows may be randomly spread throughout the table. The non-clustered index tree contains the index keys in sorted order, with the leaf level of the index containing the pointer to the page and the row number in the data page. In non-clustered index:

(a) The physical order of the rows is not the same as the index order.

(b) Typically created on column used in JOIN, WHERE, and ORDER BY clauses.

(c) Good for tables whose values may be modified frequently.

Microsoft SQL Server creates non-clustered indices by default when CREATE INDEX command is given. There can be more than one non-clustered index on a database table. There can be as many as 249 nonclustered indexes per table. It also creates a clustered index on a primary key by default.

Clutered

At a time, only one clustered index can be created on a given database level as it changes the data block resulting in the row data being stored in order. Clustered indices can greatly increase overall speed of retrieval, but usually only where the data is accessed sequentially in the same or reverse order of the clustered index, or when a range of items is selected.

Some databases separate the data and index blocks into separate files, others put two completely different data blocks within the same physical file(s). Since the physical records are in this sort order on disk, the next row item in the sequence is immediately before or after the last one, and so fewer data block reads are required. The primary feature of a clustered index is therefore the ordering of the physical data rows in accordance with the index blocks that point to them. Create an object where the physical order of rows is same as the index order of the rows and the bottom(leaf) level of clustered index contains the actual data rows. They are known as "index organized tables" under Oracle database.

The order in which columns are listed in the index definition is important. It is possible to retrieve a set of row identifiers using only the first indexed column. However, it is not possible or efficient (on most databases) to retrieve the set of row identifiers using only the second or greater indexed column.

For example, imagine a telephone directory that is organized by city first, then by last name, and then by first name. If you are given the city, you can easily extract the list of all phone numbers for that city. However, in this phone book it would be very tedious to find all the phone numbers for a given last name. You would have to look within each city's section for the entries with that last name. Some databases can do this, others just won't use the index.

Applications and Limitations

Indices are useful for many applications but comes up with few limitations. Consider the following SQL statement: SELECT first_name FROM people WHERE last_name = 'Smith';. To process this statement without an index the database software must look at the last_name column on every row in the table (this is known as a full table scan). With an index the database simply follows the B-tree data structure until the Smith entry has been found; this is much less computationally expensive than a full table scan.

Consider this SQL statement: SELECT email_address FROM customers WHERE email_address LIKE '%@yahoo.com';. This query would yield an email address for every customer whose email address ends with "@yahoo.com", but even if the email_address column has been indexed the database still must perform a full table scan. This is because the index is built with the assumption that words go from left to right.

With a wildcard at the beginning of the search-term, the database software is unable to use the underlying b-tree data structure (in other words, the WHERE-clause is not sargable). This problem can be solved through the addition of another index created on reverse(email_address) and a SQL query like this: SELECT email_address FROM customers WHERE reverse(email_address) LIKE reverse('%@yahoo.com');. This puts the wild-card at the right-most part of the query (now moc.oohay@%) which the index on reverse(email_address) can satisfy.

Types

Dense Index

It is a file with pairs of keys and pointers for every record in the data file. Every key in this file is associated with a particular pointer to a record in the sorted data file. In clustered indices with duplicate keys, the dense index points to the first record with that key.

Sparse Index

In database sparse index is a file with pairs of keys and pointers for every block in the data file. Every key in this file is associated with a particular pointer to the block in the sorted data file. In clustered indices with duplicate keys, the sparse index points to the lowest search key in each block. primary key is a sparse index.

Bitmap Index

It's special type of index that carry the bulk of its data as bit arrays bitmaps and answers most queries by performing bitwise logical operations on these bitmaps. The most commonly used index, such as B+trees, are most efficient if the values it indexes do not repeat or repeat a smaller number of times.

In contrast, the bitmap index is designed for cases where the values of a variable repeat very frequently. For example, the gender field in a customer database usually contains two distinct values: male or female. For such variables, the bitmap index can have a significant performance advantage over the commonly used trees.

Reverse Index

It reverses the key value before entering it in the index. like of value of 1743 becomes 3471 in the index. This index is useful for indexing data such as sequence numbers, where new key values monotonically increase.

Index Implementations

Indices can be implemented using a variety of data structures. Popular indices include balanced trees, B+ trees, Fractal Tree™ indexes and hashes. In Microsoft SQL Server, the leaf node of the clustered index corresponds to the actual data, not simply a pointer to data that resides elsewhere, as is the case with a non-clustered index. Each relation can have a single clustered index and many unclustered indices.

Index Concurrency Control

An index is typically being accessed concurrently by several transactions and processes, and thus needs concurrency control. While in principle indexes can utilize the common database concurrency control methods, specialized concurrency control methods for indexes exist, which are applied in conjunction with the common methods for a substantial performance gain.

Covering Index

A covering index can dramatically speed up data retrieval but may itself be large due to the additional keys, which slow down data insertion & update. To reduce such index size, some systems allow non-key fields to be included in the index. Non-key fields are not themselves part of the index ordering but only included at the leaf level, allowing for a covering index with less overall index size.

In cases an index is used to locate to the data records. from which the required data is read. In other words, the index is only used to locate data records in the table and not to return data.

A covering index is a special case where the index itself contains the required data field(s) and can return the data.

Consider the following table (other fields omitted):

ID	Name	Other Fields
12	Plug	...
13	Lamp	...
14	Fuse	...

To find the Name for ID 13, an index on (ID) will be useful, but the record must still be read to get the Name. However, an index on (ID, Name) contains the required data field and eliminates the need to look up the record.

Standardization

There is no standard about creating indexes because the ISO SQL Standard does not cover physical aspects, and indexes are one of the physical part of databse conception among others like storage (tablespace or filegroups). However RDBMS vendors all give a CREATE INDEX syntax with some specific options which depends on functionalities they provide to customers.

Buzzy has a great story to tell in his book – be sure to check it out. But what was really exciting was that he said creating a website and then a Fan Page were really 2 turning points in his experience as an author. First the website gave him instant credibility. He had self published his book but was also shopping it around to major publishing houses as well. After creating his website and meeting some key people he did indeed get picked up by Penguin books. The really cool story is that he didn't even know how to use a computer! Someone told him to start a Facebook account and his wife showed him how – it was all very new to him. Shortly after, he connected to someone who knew someone and... Now his book is being made into a major motion picture! All because of a connection through his Facebook Fan Page.

If you have a book, or are thinking of writing one or co-authoring one, establishing an online presence is critical! I know it has helped me when marketing my two books, Direct Selling Power and Incredible Business.

Here are the various things I would recommend:

1. Static website that includes a "store" page where visitors can purchase the book through a shopping cart system such as Paypal "add to cart" buttons, or 1shoppingcart. It isadvisald tocreate website through through WordPress, as it is almost free (just pay for domain and hosting) and highly indexed by the search engines.
2. Blog where you can give away some of your writing for free – post articles, excerpts, samples from your book. Or use it to share about things not in your book – about your life, your travels, your hobbies. A blog will boost your website's search engine rankings while also giving readers a chance to "try before they buy" – including potential publishers, magazines, or event planners. I would recommend a WordPress blog associated with a WordPress website, but if you have a regular HTML website, still install WordPress in a /blog/ folder so it is attached to your main domain.
3. People love showing off what they like and are involved in, and they love the interaction they can have with an

author through a Fan Page. Customize your Fan Page so you can send people to your site for more information on your book – or better yet, customize a shopping page right within your Fan Page.

4. On your website and/or blog, and on your Facebook Fan page, have some way to capture people's email addresses. They want to hear from you – let them know once a month or so what you've been up to. Share an article related to your topic. Announce events or book signings or classes you'll be conducting.
5. Again, similar to Facebook, people want to be in touch with you. Be sure you have a Twitter account set up. Feed the Fan Page to the Twitter account, and check regularly for replies. Twitter is another doorway to your website and therefore your book!
6. Other Social Media Profiles. Be sure you are listing your position as Author on other social media platforms such as LinkedIn, BizNik, Yelp, and others. Post across the internet when you are doing anything around your book marketing.
7. Free Teleclass. With my 2nd book, Incredible Business, the co-authors and I are conducting a Virtual Book Launch in the month of October (sign up here!) and this is a great way to showcase your expertise and give people a taste of what they can find in your book. You could simply schedule a teleclass through free conferencecall. com and invite all your contacts to attend.
8. Offer an ebook version of your book, or even a chapter of it, that people can buy or download with purchase. More and more today people are preferring this format and it satisfies their need for instant gratification!

Website Using Microsoft Publisher

This is the fast moving age where people have little or no time to talk with you. In this tight situation, a website can solve your problem by sending your ideas to other visitors. Microsoft Publisher comes with a variety of tools to help create a website that meets most people's needs.

Open the Microsoft Publisher program. The "New Publication" wizard will open. If it doesn't, click "File, New" from the menu at the top of the screen.

Select "Web Sites and Email" in the New Publication dialog box. Click on "Web Sites" in the drop-down menu.

Choose one of four options: Easy Web Site Builder, 3-Page Web Site, Product Sales, or Professional Services. On the right side of the screen, a preview panel will show how each choice looks. You can also use the scroll bar on the right to slowly look at each available option.

Create a website quickly with the Easy Site Builder. Simply check boxes in the Easy Site Builder pop-up dialog box. You are asked about the objectives of your site and the necessary web elements will be added to the site to help meet those individualized needs.

Fill in your personal information on the next pop-up dialog box, such as name, address, and phone number. The information you add depends on the purpose of your website.

Choose website options from the left-side window. You can decide the font type, color scheme, the layout of text and buttons, and even change the overall design scheme using the available selections.

Close all dialog boxes and start editing your web page. Add text and graphics to showcase your purpose. Add additional pages by clicking "Insert-Page" on the top menu bar and your selected design elements will already be in place.

Preview your website from the File menu. The Publish button is also located in the File menu. You must have a website host to publish to the Internet. Otherwise publish it to a folder on your computer. There are seven ways to boost your e Bay Sales :

In many respects eBay is like any other sales channel and success requires marketing and attention to detail. Understand the most basic reasons for poor eBay sales and learn the cost effective ways in which you can increase your eBay sales.

Why Low eBay sales : The Problem

It is known fact that "You can sell anything on eBay" which leads to the impression that making money on eBay is easy. Unfortunately nothing in life is ever straight forward and building sales on eBay takes planning, time and a certain amount of trial and error.

Suggestions

Many sellers do not get the basics of eBay selling right, putting them at an immediate disadvantage. Here, are suggestions for improving your eBay presence in the following 5 areas:

- Present yourself as a reputable seller. By creating a strong brand you can stand out from the crowd and reassure buyers that you are a safe bet.
- Improve product presentation. Listings which do not give full information about the product or the terms and conditions of purchase put off buyers.
- Remove barriers to sales. Making it easy for potential customers to make a purchase.
- Take advantage of free marketing for your eBay business. Marketing is expensive and so it is important to make best use of the all the free ways of promoting your products.
- Use Listing software. This will speed the process of listing on eBay.

BUILDING BRANDS VIA EBAY BUSINESS

Present yourself as a reputable seller —In the online as in the offline world people are attracted to brands that they can trust.

If you can build a brand around your eBay business you increase the chance of return traffic, repeat business and referrals. Choose a sensible username. Take care over choosing your username. Customers are more likely to remember Floorheatingltd than xxxtigger.

Develop a brand and logo. If you are going to be considered as a professional seller on eBay it is important to have a strong corporate identity. This brand should be implemented throughout the eBay platform.

Build a website. Most businesses have a website and your business should be no exception. A website will reassure buyers that they are dealing with an established business and it is worth spending the money necessary to get a professional website built.

Open an eBay shop—An eBay shop is a seller s footprint on eBay. Each shop has its own URL and displays all the items which that user has for sale. The shop can also be customized to your branding and can be used to increase sales in the following ways:

- List your entire inventory. Items can be listed for a fraction of the price of auction listings giving your business a way of vastly expanding the number of items available for sale.
- Up selling to customers. Place selected items in the auction listings and use these to drive traffic to your store where they can make additional purchases.

eBay shop owners sell up to 25% more items than other

Customize your product presentation—On eBay buyers cannot see or touch the items which are for sale. It is therefore vital to create a comprehensive listing showing all aspects of a product and providing all the information, such as P&P, required to make a purchase. The more reassured a browser is, the more likely they are to make a purchase. We have all seen listings of products where the description is short and the picture out of focus. The product could be great but there is no way of knowing it.

A good listing should include the following information

- Multiple, high quality pictures of each item. Needless to say these should be in focus and should show each items from several angles. Any damage should be recorded.
- Comprehensive description.
- Full description of the item including all features, dimensions and any damage. Postage costs. These should cover international postage if possible.
- Return policy.
- Payments accepted.

Presentation is everything in sales and so a well designed HTML template for your product will make you look like a professional, trustworthy seller.

Market your eBay business for free—As an eBay seller it is important to make use of all the opportunities available to drive traffic to your products and eBay shop.

- Link to your eBay shop. All you listings, about me page, email and eBay shop custom pages should link back to your eBay shop and encourage buyers to take a look at your other listings.
- Cross promote with other eBay users. Within eBay there is the facility to make arrangements with other eBay sellers to cross promote each others products. Make arrangements with seller who sell complimentary products to yours.
- Auctiva shopping window. Auctiva (www.auctiva.com) produce a free eBay scrolling product bar. This goes at the bottom of each listing and displays scrolling pictures of the other products which the user has for sale. Use this to promote your other products to browsers. According to Vendio such galleries increase sales by 18%.

- Optimize your eBay Shop for search engines. Within the eBay shop set up it is possible to input keywords for which you would like your shop optimized, and also to make a feed file available for shopping comparison sites.
- Use Froogle. Froogle is Google s shopping comparison site. It accepts fixed price products and unlike all the other comparison sites it is free. Create a feed file (basically a spreadsheet with product descriptions, product URLS and image URLs) of your eBay shop items and submit this is Froogle.
- Online shop malls. There are several eBay shop listing sites which can be used to list your shop, the most popular being www.listmystore.com.
- Use the right category. When selling items make an effort to use the most appropriate category and fill in item specifics. Buyers will use these features to browse items.
- About Me page. Each eBay user is entitled to an About Me page. This is an opportunity to tell buyers a bit more about your company and reassure them that they are dealing with a reputable seller. The About Me page is a free advert for your business on eBay. Amazingly less than 6% of users make use of it and so it will make your business stand out.
- Choose your keywords carefully. To find items, buyers search on the keywords in the title. Avoid using words like LooK or fantastic as these are rarely searched upon.

Use enhanced listing features.—If you believe eBay the listing enhancement options have a noticeable effect on selling price:

- First photo (Free!) - increases chances of selling by 15%
- Gallery - Typically sell for 12% more
- Subtitle - Typically sell for 10% more

Remove old barriess to sales—In general the more information on items and the more delivery and payment options you give buyers, the more likely they are to make a purchase. Sell internationally.

Selling internationally can be a bit of a headache but items listed internationally, on average, sell for 16% more. Accept multiple payment methods. Offering a number of payment options reassures buyers. It is also becoming increasingly important to offer PayPal as a payment option. Although expensive (2-3.4% of transaction value) it is extremely convenient and over 90% of eBay listings offer it as a method of payment.

Use listing software—Using listing and auction management software can speed up the process of listing items and managing auctions. Ebay provides free tools such as turbo lister and seller manager. However, as your business grows it will be necessary to use more sophisticated tools such as Marketworks or Channeladvisor.

At Auction Partner we recommend our client to use the free tools before investing in the more complex (but more powerful) software solutions.

Next Steps

Some of the suggestions in this document are easy to implement whilst some will require planning and a considerable investment of time. Employing a consultancy like Auction Partner, will speed the process of optimizing your business but will cost more than an in-house solution.

If you have limited resources it is recommended that you take a staged approach, concentrating on the quick fixes to initially, and reassessing as your business grows.

How to Increase Book Sales Profits

Over the years, authors have found that it is increasingly more difficult to secure book signing events in bookstores. Authors not only clamor to get space for their books on the bookshelf, but jockey for space on the bookstore's floor for book signings. The more well known the author, the greater chance for securing a bookstore book signing event.

Don't despair! If you use your imagination and apply a little "smarts" to match venue with your book topic, you can attract success with book signing events. Here is a five-step process to increase book sale profits by appearing in unusual places:

Sales is the combined effect of topic, audience and opportunity. Take care of the title of the book and target reades. Suppose, if you write a book about computer troubleshooting, what better place to set up a signing than in a computer store on a busy weekend afternoon? Have you written a book for kids with puppies or kittens in the story? Target pet food and supply stores as potential partners for hosting a book signing. If you're a romance novelist, "Victoria's Secret" comes to mind. And your autographed book of poetry will make a great Mother's Day gift… from a Hallmark store event.

Whether you publish your book or one published by publishing house, you know that everything about tha book promotion or majority for your book falls squarely on your shoulders. In the "old days" the traditional bookstore book signing event was paramount to every author's marketing plan. What you gain from a book signing is obvious: book sales. Yet, to attract the interest of a potential venue, you need to focus on what that venue will gain from your book signing. For example, the store will receive free publicity from any of your marketing efforts, including media, and, of course, a percentage of the sales made that day. The longer your list is of benefits to the store, the greater your chances of striking a book signing agreement. You may have great success with small and independent stores and businesses simply because you will likely be dealing directly with the owner or manager and can avoid the "red tape" associated with franchises and corporations. Yet, don't dismiss approaching large businesses and stores. Many have the authority to approve a handful of events each year to provide community support, eliminating the need to get corporate approval.

Step Three: Get books into the Store

Corporate and franchise businesses have a much more complicated approval process for adding your book to inventory. However, you may be able to work out a simple, temporary consignment arrangement. The store buys a certain amount of books to cover the book signing and can return the rest for a full refund.

Be sure to suggest the store keeps a small inventory of signed books for people who may miss the actual book signing schedule but come to the store looking for the book. If consignment sales go well, your book may automatically be added to inventory.

Marketing of Book Signing

Marketing your book signing is not expensive or difficult—it simply takes some preplanning. Print up inexpensive flyers or bookmarks for the venue to use as bag stuffers a few weeks prior to the book signing. Be sure to discuss this idea with the venue ahead of time to make sure there is agreement to use them. Invite the venue to send out an announcement about the book signing to its customer mailing or emailing list and put a notice on its (and your) website about the upcoming event. You can also hand out bookmarks during the event to buyers and non-buyers alike—make sure the venue's name and your website are both included on the bookmark.

Media can give wide coverage to the popularity of your book. Local media are happy to promote local authors and your unusual location for the book signing will be of specific interest (another benefit to mention to the venue). Contact media well in advance of the event and on the day of the event.

Once the event is over, be sure to express your appreciation to the store for hosting your book signing. Follow up with a handwritten thank-you note. The impression you leave with the venue will be remembered when you're ready to promote your next book!

OpenURL

It designed to enable linking from information resources such as abstracting and indexing databases (sources) to library services (targets), such as academic journals, whether online or in printed or other formats. OpenURL is a standardized format of Uniform Resource Locator (URL) intended to enable Internet users to more easily find a copy of a resource that they are allowed to access. Although OpenURL can be used with any kind of resource on the

Internet, it is most heavily used by libraries to help connect patrons to subscription content.

The linking is mediated by "link resolvers", or "link-servers", which parse the elements of an OpenURL and provide links to appropriate targets available through a library by the use of an OpenURL knowledge base.

The source that generates an OpenURL is typically a bibliographic citation or bibliographic record in a database that indexes the information resources often found in libraries, such as articles, books, patents, etc. Examples of such databases include Ovid, Web of Science, SciFinder, Modern Languages Association Bibliography and Google Scholar. A target is a resource or service that helps satisfy a user's information needs. Examples of targets include full-text repositories, online journals, online library catalogs and other Web resources and services.

The National Information Standards Organization (NISO) has developed OpenURL and its data container (the ContextObject) as American National Standards Institute (ANSI) standard Z39.88. On 22 June 2006, the Online Computer Library Center (OCLC) was named the maintenance agency for the standard. The most common application of OpenURL is to assist in the resolution of a request for a web resource (such as an online article). An OpenURL includes information about the referenced resource itself, and context information — both the context in which the OpenURL occurs (for example, a page of search results from a library catalog) and the context of the request (for example, the particular user making the request). If a different context is expressed in the URL, a different copy ends up resolved to. Changes in context are predictable, and do not require the original creator of the hyperlink (for example, the journal publisher) to handcraft different URLs for different contexts.

For example, changing either the base URL or a parameter in the query string can mean that the OpenURL resolves to a copy of a resource in a different library. So the same OpenURL, contained for instance in an electronic journal, can be adjusted by any library to provide access to their own copy of the resource, without completely overwriting the journal's hyperlink. The journal provider, in turn, is no longer required to provide a different version of the journal, with different hyperlinks, for each subscribing library.

Format

An OpenURL consists of a base URL, which carry the address of the us :r's institutional link-server, followed by a query string, which contains contextual data, typically in the form of key-value pairs. The contextual data is most often bibliographic data, but as of version 1.0 OpenURL can also include information about the requester, the resource containing the hyperlink, the type of service required, and so forth. For example:

OpenURL was created by Herbert Van de Sompel, a librarian at the University of Ghent, in the late 1990s. His link-server software, SFX, was purchased by the library automation company Ex Libris Ltd. which popularized OpenURL in the information industry.

In 2006, a research report found some problems affecting the efficiency of OpenURL linking and recommended the creation of a group to establish best practice solutions. The KBART (Knowledge Bases And Related Tools) working group has been set up to progress the recommendations of the research report.

Applications and Tools

Several companies market link server systems, including OCLC (WorldCat Link Manager), Swets (SwetsWise Linker), Serials Solutions (360 Link, formerly known as Article Linker), Innovative Interfaces, Inc. (WebBridge), EBSCO (LinkSource), Ovid (LinkSolver), SirsiDynix (Resolver), Fretwell-Downing (OL2), TDNet (TOUR), WT Cox Subscriptions (Journal Finder), R.R. Bowker (Ulrichs Resource Linker) and Infor (Vlink). Open-source link resolvers include CUFTS and Umlaut. There are also open-source tools for manipulating OpenURLs and the Code4Lib community maintains a list of these.

OpenURL is normally implemented by information providers by dynamically inserting an appropriate base URL into web pages sent to an authenticated user. OpenURL COinS is a specification that allows free services like Wikipedia to provide OpenURLs by cooperating with client side software agents. Federated search software presents OpenURL links in record fields by employing the library's subscriber links to link servers facilitating access to full-text resources from bibliographic record hyperlinks.

PUBLISHER, AUTHOR AND COPYRIGHT ACT

The process of publication is the production and transformation of literature or of some information—the activity of making information available to the general public. In some cases, authors may be their own publishers, meaning: originators and developers of content also provide media to deliver and display the content. Publishing and communication are similar activities in that they both involve making material available to the public. Under Australian law, they are two separate rights that belong to the copyright owner. Publishing includes the stages of the development, acquisition, copyediting, graphic design, production – printing (and its electronic equivalents), and marketing and distribution of newspapers, magazines, books, literary works, musical works, software and other works dealing with information, including the electronic media. The time and number of people involved in the process is dependent on the size of the publishing company, with larger companies having more degrees of assessment between unsolicited submission and publication. Unsolicited submissions have a very low rate of acceptance, with some sources estimating that publishers ultimately choose about three out of every ten thousand unsolicited manuscripts they receive.

Only unpublished and original work will be acceptable for publication from the publisher's sides. He will check contents of the book and its market potential. You communicate your work to the public when you or another authorised person make it available online or electronically transmit it to the public.

An act of communication to the public can also be an act of publication. If you make your work available online, and it has not previously been made available to the public, you are arguably "publishing" it in terms of the Copyright Act. This is because you are supplying reproductions to the public - the public can download a reproduction to view, save or print.

Digital Information System

Copyright is an indispensable part of a publicationhouse. It is the prime duty of a publisher to protect the copyright of his authros. Publishers and author are depend on each other. If you act as a publisher, you need to respect the rights of your authors while at the same time ensuring the viability of your publication. Traditionally, the term refers to the distribution of printed works such as books (the "book trade") and newspapers. With the advent of digital information systems and the Internet, the scope of publishing has expanded to include electronic resources, such as the electronic versions of books and periodicals, as well as micropublishing, websites, blogs, video games and the like.

As a legal concept publication is very importance given below:

1. As the process of giving formal notice to the world of a significant intention, for example, to marry or enter bankruptcy;
2. As the essential precondition of being able to claim defamation; that is, the alleged libel must have been published, and
3. For copyright purposes, where there is a difference in the protection of published and unpublished works.

A freelance journalist work for newspapers on a content basis. Large-scale newspapers employ full-fledged journalist for writing, re-writing, and editing news. At a small press, it is possible to survive by relying entirely on commissioned material. But as activity increases, the need for works may outstrip the publisher's established circle of writers. For works written independently of the publisher, writers often first submit a query letter or proposal directly to a literary agent or to a publisher. Submissions sent directly to a publisher are referred to as unsolicited submissions, and the majority come from previously unpublished authors. If the publisher accepts unsolicited manuscripts, then the manuscript is placed in the slush pile, which publisher's readers sift through to identify manuscripts of sufficient quality or revenue potential to be referred to acquisitions editors for review. The acquisitions editors send their choices to the editorial staff.

Some publishers follow strict rules for accepting a book for publication. Some gives royaly to the authors, while others give complementary copies against royality. At these companies, unsolicited manuscripts are thrown out, or sometimes returned, if the author has provided pre-paid postage. Established authors are often represented by a literary agent to market their work to publishers and negotiate contracts. Literary agents take a percentage of author earnings (varying between 10 - 15 per cent) to pay for their services.

Some writers follow a non-standard route to publication. For example, this may include bloggers who have attracted large readerships producing a book based on their websites, books based on Internet memes, instant "celebrities" such as Joe the Plumber, retiring sports figures and in general anyone whom a publisher feels could produce a marketable book. Such books often employ the services of a ghostwriter.

For a submission to reach publication, it must be championed by an editor or publisher who must work to convince other staff of the need to publish a particular title. An editor who discovers or champions a book that subsequently becomes a best-seller may find their own reputation enhanced as a result of their success.

ACCEPTANCE AND NEGOTIATION

Once a work is accepted, commissioning editors negotiate the purchase of intellectual property rights and agree on royalty rates.

The authors of traditional printed materials typically sell exclusive territorial intellectual property rights that match the list of countries in which distribution is proposed (i.e. the rights match the legal systems under which copyright protections can be enforced). In the case of books, the publisher and writer must also agree on the intended formats of publication — mass-market paperback, "trade" paperback and hardback are the most common options.

The situation is slightly more complex, if electronic formatting is to be used. Where distribution is to be by CD-ROM or other physical media, there is no reason to treat this form differently from a paper format, and a national copyright is an acceptable approach. But the possibility of Internet download without the ability to restrict physical distribution within national boundaries presents legal problems that are usually solved by selling language or translation rights rather than national rights. Thus, Internet access across the European Union is relatively open because of the laws forbidding discrimination based on nationality, but the fact of publication in, say, France, limits the target market to those who read French. Having agreed on the scope of the publication and the formats, the parties in a book agreement must then agree on royalty rates, the percentage of the gross retail price that will be paid to the author, and the advance payment. This is difficult because the publisher must estimate the potential sales in each market and balance projected revenue against production costs.

Royalty

Royalties usually range between 10-12% of recommended retail price. An advance is usually one-third of first print run total royalties. For example, if a book has a print run of 5000 copies and will be sold at $14.95 and the author receives 10% royalties, the total sum payable to the author, if all copies are sold is $7475 (10% x $14.95 x 5000). The advance in this instance would roughly be $2490. Advances vary greatly between books, with established authors commanding large advances.

Pre-production Stages

Although listed as distinct stages, parts of these occur concurrently. As editing of text progresses, front cover design and initial layout takes place and sales and marketing of the book begins.

Editorial Stage

Editing may also involve structural changes and requests for more information. Some publishers employ fact checkers, particularly regarding non-fiction works. A decision is taken to publish a book or improve the quality of a work through rewriting and smaller changes and than later staff will edit the work. Publishers may maintain a house style, and staff will copy edit to ensure that the work matches the style and grammatical requirements of each market. Editors often choose or refine titles and headlines.

Design Stage

The design stage may include artwork, desiging or making layout for the work. In publishing, the word "art" also indicates photographs. This process prepares the work for printing through processes such as typesetting, dust jacket composition, specification of paper quality, binding method and casing, and proofreading.

The quality of book determines its production cost and it's response in the market. More picutres in the books means more production cost. For standard fiction titles, design is usually restricted to typography and cover design. For books containing illustrations or images, design takes on a much larger role in laying out how the page looks, how chapters begin and end, colours, typography, cover design and ancillary materials such as posters, catalogue images and other sales materials. Non-fiction illustrated titles are the most design intensive books, requiring extensive use of images and illustrations, captions, typography and a deep involvement and consideration of the reader experience.

Nowadays, everything is computerized like of typesetting, page layout, the production of negatives, plates from the negatives and, for hardbacks, the preparation of brasses for the spine legend and imprint are now all computerized. Prepress computerization evolved mainly in about the last twenty years of the 20th century. If the work is to be distributed electronically, the final files are saved as formats appropriate to the target operating systems of the hardware used for reading. These may include PDF files.

Sales and Marketing Stage

Sales and marketing are related to each other. Sales peoples make their plan to meet potential customers and promote books in best possible way. Publishing companies often produce advanced information sheets that may be sent to customers or overseas publishers to gauge possible sales. As early interest is measured, this information feeds back through the editorial process and may affect the formatting of the book and the strategy employed to sell it. For example, if interest from foreign publishers is high, co-publishing deals may be established whereby publishers share printing costs in producing large print runs thereby lowering the per-unit cost of the books. Conversely, if initial feedback is not strong, the print-run of the book may be reduced, the marketing budget cut or, in some cases, the book is dropped from publication altogether.

Phase of Printing

Pagination, proof reading, editing and design work are initial stages of the book production. After all these activities the printing phase of book begins. The initial step is the creation of a pre-press proof, which is sent for final checking and sign-off by the publisher. This proof shows the book precisely as it will appear once printed and is the final opportunity for the publisher to find and correct any errors. Some printing companies use electronic proofs rather than printed proofs. Once the proofs have been approved by the publisher, printing—the physical production of the published work—begins.

A new printing process is printing on demand. The book is written, edited, and designed as usual, but it is not printed until the publisher receives an order for the book from a customer. This procedure ensures low costs for storage, and reduces the likelihood of printing more books than will be sold.

Selling of Books

Books are most commonly sold through booksellers and other retailers. Newspapers and magazines are typically sold directly by the publisher to subscribers, and then distributed either through the postal system or by newspaper carriers. Periodicals are also frequently sold through newsagents and vending machines. The final stage in publication is making the work available the public and it ready for sale. In previous centuries, an author was frequently also his own editor, printer, and bookseller, but these functions are usually separated now. Once a book, newspaper, or other publication is printed, the publisher may use a variety of channels to distribute it. Within the book industry, some copies of the finished book are often flown to publishers as sample copies to aid sales or to be sent for pre-release reviews. The remaining books often travel from the printing facility via sea freight. As such, the delay between the approval of the pre-press proof and the arrival of books in warehouse, much less in a retail store, can be some months. For books that are tied into movie release dates (particularly children's films), publishers will arrange books to arrive in store up to two months prior to the movie release to build interest in the movie.

Derided in the 1911 Encyclopedia Britannica as "a purely commercial affair" that cared more about profits than about literary quality,publishing is fundamentally a business, with a need for the expenses of creating, producing, and distributing a book or other publication not to exceed the income derived from its sale.

Advertising and Marketing Tasks

The publisher usually controls the advertising and other marketing tasks, but may subcontract various aspects of the process to specialist publisher marketing agencies. In many companies, editing, proofreading, layout, design and other aspects of the production process are done by freelancers. Dedicated in-house salespeople are sometimes replaced by companies who specialize in sales to bookshops, wholesalers and chain stores for a fee. This trend is accelerating as retail book chains and supermarkets have centralized their buying.

If the entire process up to the stage of printing is handled by an outside company or individuals, and then sold to the publishing company, it is known as book packaging. This is a common strategy between smaller publishers in different territorial markets where the company that first buys the intellectual property rights then sells a package to other publishers and gains an immediate return on capital invested. Indeed, the first publisher will often print sufficient copies for all markets and thereby get the maximum quantity efficiency on the print run for all. Some businesses maximize their profit margins through vertical integration; book publishing is not one of them. Although newspaper and magazine companies still often own printing presses and binderies, book publishers rarely do. Similarly, the trade usually sells the finished products through a distributor who stores and distributes the publisher's wares for a percentage fee or sells on a sale or return basis.

The advent of the Internet has therefore posed an interesting question that challenges publishers, distributors and retailers. In 2005, Amazon.com announced its purchase of Booksurge and selfsanepublishing, a major print on demand operation. This is probably intended as a preliminary move towards establishing an Amazon imprint. One of the largest bookseller chains, Barnes & Noble, already runs its own successful imprint with both new titles and classics — hardback editions of out-of-print former best sellers. Similarly, Ingram Industries, parent company of Ingram Book Group (a leading US book wholesaler), now includes its own print-on-demand division called Lightning Source. Among publishers, Simon & Schuster recently announced that it will start selling its backlist titles directly to consumers through its website.

Book clubs are almost entirely direct-to-retail, and niche publishers pursue a mixed strategy to sell through all available outlets — their output is insignificant to the major booksellers, so lost revenue poses no threat to the traditional symbiotic relationships between the four activities of printing, publishing, distribution and retail.

INDUSTRY SUB-DIVISIONS

Newspaper Publishing

While, travelling on Bahadur Shah Jafar Marg (Near ITO) in New Delhi, one can see big sign-boards of Times of India, Indian

Express, Pioneer and Business Standards newspapers. We can read news on newspapers. Most newspapers are primarily sold to subscribers or are distributed as advertising-supported free newspapers. In India, newspaper owners get ahigh respect in society.

Periodical Publishing

Nominally, periodical publishing involves publications that appear in a new edition on a regular schedule. Newspapers and magazines are both periodicals, but within the industry, the periodical publishing is frequently considered a separate branch that includes magazines and even academic journals, but not newspapers. About one-third of publishers in the United States publish periodicals (not including newspapers).

Book Publishing

Daryaganj is the hub of Indian Publishers, and they publish books from kids level to postgraduate level. SOme publishers are established,while few one have recently started publishing books with E-books available on Internet, Publications of Books has become a risky affair. Most books are published by a small number of very large book publishers, but thousands of smaller book publishers exist. Many small- and medium-sized book publishers specialize in a specific area. Additionally, thousands of authors have created their own publishing companies, and self-published their own works.

Within the book publishing industry, the "publisher of record" for a book is the entity in whose name the book's ISBN is registered. The publisher of record may or may not be the actual publisher.

Directory Publishing

Directory publishing is a specialized genre within the publishing industry. These publishers produce mailing lists, telephone books, and other types of directories. With the advent of the Internet, many of these directories are now online.

Academic Publishing

Publishing books on academic subjects of higher studies is the main purpose of academic publication. Academic publishing does not publish general books like novels, fiction,sports etc. Some, like university presses, are owned by scholarly institutions. Others are commercial businesses that focus on academic subjects.

With the arrival of Information Technology, now we have acess to foriegn books and research and development work by professors and scientists. But this improvement in the efficiency of communication created a challenge for libraries, which have had to accommodate the weight and volume of literature.

The main functions that academic publishers provide is to manage the process of peer review. Their role is to facilitate the impartial assessment of research and this vital role is not one that has yet been usurped, even with the advent of social networking and online document sharing.

Today, publishing academic journals and textbooks is a large part of an international industry. Critics claim that standardised accounting and profit-oriented policies have displaced the publishing ideal of providing access to all. In contrast to the commercial model, there is non-profit publishing, where the publishing organization is either organised specifically for the purpose of publishing, such as a university press, or is one of the functions of an organisation such as a medical charity, founded to achieve specific practical goals. An alternative approach to the corporate model is open access, the online distribution of individual articles and academic journals without charge to readers and libraries. The pioneers of Open Access journals are BioMed Central and the Public Library of Science (PLoS). Many commercial publishers are experimenting with hybrid models where older articles or government funded articles are made free, and newer articles are available as part of a subscription or individual article purchase.

Tie-in Publishing

Technology not only makes our life comfort, but also entertain us in many ways. Like home-theatre, music system, amusement parks and the list is very long. Some publications have tie-up agreement for promotions on entertainment channels.

The BBC has its own publishing division that does very well with long-running series such as Doctor Who. Some of the major publishers have entire divisions devoted to a single franchise, e.g. Ballantine Del Rey Lucasbooks has the exclusive rights to Star Wars in the United States; Random House UK (Bertelsmann)/Century LucasBooks holds the same rights in the United Kingdom. The game industry self-publishes through BL Publishing/Black Library (Warhammer) and Wizards of the Coast (Dragonlance, Forgotten Realms, etc.). These multimedia works are cross-marketed aggressively and sales frequently outperform the average stand-alone published work, making them a focus of corporate interest.

INDEPENDENT PUBLISHING ALTERNATIVES

Writers in a specialized field or with a narrower appeal have found smaller alternatives to the mass market in the form of small presses and self-publishing. More recently, these options include print on demand and ebook format. These publishing alternatives provide an avenue for authors who believe that mainstream publishing will not meet their needs or who are in a position to make more money from direct sales than they could from bookstore sales, such as popular speakers who sell books after speeches. Authors are more readily published by this means due to the much lower costs involved.

Latest Developments

The 21st century has brought a number of new technological changes to the publishing industry. These changes include e-books, print on demand and accessible publishing. E-books have been quickly growing in availability since 2005. Google, Amazon.com and Sony have been leaders in working with publishers and libraries to digitize books. As of early 2011 Amazon's Kindle reading device is a significant force in the market, along with the Apple iPad and the Nook.

The ability to quickly and cost effectively Print on Demand has meant that publishers no longer have to store books at warehouses, if the book is in low or unknown demand. This is a huge advantage to small publishers who can now operate without large overheads and large publishers who can now cost effectively sell their backlisted items.

Accessible publishing uses the digitization of books to mark up books into XML and then produces multiple formats from this to sell to consumers, often targeting those with difficulty in reading. Formats include a variety larger print sizes, specialized print formats for dyslexia, eye tracking problems and macular degeneration, as well as Braille, DAISY, Audiobooks and e-books.

Green publishing means adapting the publishing process to minimise environmental impact. One example of this is the concept of on demand printing, using digital or print-on-demand technology. This cuts down the need to ship books since they are manufactured close to the customer on a just-in-time basis.

A further development is the growth of on-line publishing where no physical books are produced. The ebook is created by the author and uploaded to a website from where it can be downloaded and read by anyone.

Standardization

Refer to the ISO divisions of ICS 01.140.40 and 35.240.30 for further information.

Legal Issues

Publication is the distribution or transformation of news to the public. The Berne Convention requires that this only be done with the consent of the copyright holder, which is initially always the author. In the Universal Copyright Convention, "publication" is defined in article VI as "the reproduction in tangible form and the general distribution to the public of copies of a work from which it can be read or otherwise visually perceived." In providing a work to the general public, the publisher takes responsibility for the publication in a way that a mere printer or a shopkeeper does not. For example, publishers may face charges of defamation, if they produce and distribute libelous material to the public, even if the libel was written by another person.

Privishing

It's an industry term and used in industry for publishing a book in such small amount of rupees of marketing, advertising, or sales support from the publisher, that the book effectively does not reach the public. The book, whilst nominally published, is almost impossible to obtain through normal channels such as bookshops, often cannot be special-ordered and will have a notable lack of support from its publisher, including refusals to reprint the title. A book that is privished may be referred to as "killed". Depending on the motivation, privishing may constitute breach of contract, censorship, or good business practice (e.g., not printing more books than the publisher believes will sell in a reasonable length of time).

References

1. Using Clustered Indices, MSDN, retrieved 2010-08-27
2. Database Systems: The Complete Book. Hector Garcia-Molina, Jeffrey D. Ullman, Jennifer D. Widom
3. Gavin Powell (2005-12). "Chapter 12: Building Fast-Performing Data Models". Beginning Database Design ISBN 978-0-7645-7490-0. Wrox Publishing. http://searchsecurity.techtarget.com/generic/0, 295582, sid87_gci1184450,00.html.
4. "Clustered Index Structures". SQL Server 2005 Books Online (September 2007). http://msdn2.microsoft.com/en-us/library/ms177443.aspx.
5. Daren Bieniek, Randy Dess, Mike Hotek, Javier Loria, Adam Machanic, Antonio Soto, Adolfo Wiernik (2006-01). "Chapter 4: Creating Indices". SQL Server 2005 Implementation and Management. Microsoft Press. http://www.microsoft.com/mspress/books/9364.aspx.

6. http://www.powerhomebiz.com/062006/ebay.htm
7. http://www.writerprofits.com

Epstein, Jason. Book Business: Publishing Past, Present, and Future.

1. Schiffrin, André (2000). The Business of Books: How the International Conglomerates Took Over Publishing and Changed the Way We Read.
2. Ugrešiæ, Dubravka (2003). Thank You for Not Reading.
3. Abelson et al. (2005). Open Networks and Open Society: The Relationship between Freedom, Law, and Technology

Chapter–4

Managing Electronic Materials

Terrorists are also computer-savvy, and other than weapons they know how to atttack on the security-related websites of the targeted country. After 9/11 attacks American Government is very conscious for the safety of their security data. Automated Trusted Information Exchange is a technology term used in computing and it's a computer database containing homeland security and terrorist threat information, which is part of the U.S. government's Regional Information Sharing Systems (RISS) program.

The Homeland Security Information Network (HSIN) is a web-based platform, run by the Department of Homeland Security, which is designed to allow local, state, tribal, and federal government agencies to share "Sensitive but Unclassified (SBU)" information with each other over a secure channel. The Department of Homeland Security has publicly announced that the network has so far been hacked at least twice in 2009—once in March and once in April.

The Joint Regional Information Exchange System (JRIES) began in December 2002 as an all-source intelligence / information sharing system, designed initially as a grassroots pilot system to connect the California Anti-Terrorism Information Center, the New York Police Department, and the Defense Intelligence Agency (DIA). These groups designed JRIES, which was first deployed in

February 2003, to facilitate the exchange of suspicious activity reports, register events potentially related to terrorist activity, and foster real-time intelligence and law enforcement collaboration in a secure environment across federal, state, and local jurisdictions. JRIES used a commercial, off-the-shelf software collaboration tool application to enable multiple groups to share the information securely.

A JRIES executive board, composed of representatives from the participating groups, provided guidance and structure to help manage the system. JRIES proved useful during the northeast blackout in 2003 when information posted on the system allowed users across the country to quickly learn that the event was not related to terrorism. The system provided a very simple and efficient way for the law enforcement community to obtain situational awareness concurrently, without the need for hundreds of phone calls. Although DIA originally operated and maintained JRIES, DIA transferred program management of the system to the U.S. Department of Homeland Security (DHS) in September 2003, due to funding constraints. DIA was concerned that managing JRIES to support domestic intelligence activities conflicted with its military intelligence role. As of February 2004, approximately 100 organizations–with more than 1,000 law enforcement and intelligence analysts from federal, state, and local government agencies–were using JRIES. After acquiring JRIES, DHS recognized that the system's utility could be expanded beyond its existing counter-terrorism intelligence and threat awareness mission because JRIES met DHS' requirements for senior executive communications, crisis planning and management, and coordination and communications with first responder, emergency management, and military organizations. As such, in February 2004, DHS announced the expansion of JRIES as its primary communication, collaboration, situational awareness, and information-sharing system. The DHS Secretary renamed JRIES as the Homeland Security Information Network (HSIN) in order to reflect the system's broader scope.

By December 2004, DHS had deployed HSIN to all 50 states, 53 major urban areas, five U.S. territories, the District of Columbia, and several international partners. DHS extended HSIN access beyond the law enforcement community to include state homeland security advisors, governors' offices, emergency managers, first responders, the National Guard, and an international component. DHS equipped each location with two laptops installed with the commercial, off-the-shelf software collaboration tool application.

In March 2005 because of the lack of scalability to accomadate a large increase in users, DHS decided to move HSIN away from the current software collaboration tool and to develop a series of web-based portals as replacements. Nonetheless, DHS continues to operate both the commercial software collaboration tool application and a portal to support the law enforcement community.

DHS has expanded the role of HSIN through a state and local initiative. The goals of this initiative are to identify and address requirements of state and local communities of interest, as well as to provide robust training to promote effective use of the network. As of January 2006, eight states had deployed HSIN throughout their respective departments and agencies. Declaring HSIN the primary system for operational information sharing and collaboration, the DHS Secretary asked that the department's senior managers as well as headquarters and field personnel support the ongoing growth and utilization of HSIN.

Prior to DHS' implementation and expansion of HSIN, reports by various nonprofit, industry, audit, and congressional organizations documented problems with homeland security information sharing and the need for a single, effective collaboration system.

The Multistate Anti-Terrorism Information Exchange Program, also known by the acronym MATRIX, was a federally funded data mining system originally developed for the Florida Department of Law Enforcement described as a tool to identify terrorist subjects. The system was reported to analyze government and commercial databases to find associations between suspects or to discover locations of or completely new "suspects". The database and technologies used in the system were housed by Seisint, a Florida-based company since acquired by Lexis Nexis.

The Matrix program was shut down in June 2005 after federal funding was cut in the wake of public concerns over privacy and state surveillance.

Regional Information Sharing Systems (RISS) is an information-sharing program funded by the U.S. Federal government whose purpose is to connect databases from local and regional law enforcement so that they can use each other's data for criminal investigations. In 1997, RISS created RISSNET, a network to interconnect many local, state, regional, and tribal law enforcement databases. In 2002, RISSNET was connected with the FBI's Law Enforcement Online system. The National Criminal Intelligence Sharing Plan (NCISP) is an intelligence-sharing initiative that links the computer databases of local, state, regional, tribal law enforcement agencies with those of the U.S. federal government. In 2003, the National Criminal Intelligence Sharing Plan (NCISP) declared that RISSNET would be the official "backbone" for all unclassified, but sensitive criminal intelligence data traffic.. Later that year, members were also given access to the Automated Trusted Information Exchange (ATIX) database, which contains information on homeland security and terrorist threats.

Main Features

- recursive and multithreaded checking
- output in colored or normal text, HTML, SQL, CSV, XML or a sitemap graph in different formats
- HTTP/1.1, HTTPS, FTP, mailto:, news:, nntp:, Telnet and local file links support
- restriction of link checking with regular expression filters for URLs
- proxy support
- username/password authorization for HTTP and FTP and Telnet
- honors robots.txt exclusion protocol
- Cookie support

- HTML and CSS syntax check
- Antivirus check
- Different interfaces: command line, GUI and web interface
- ... and a lot more check options documented in the manual page.

Screenshots

Basic Usage

To check a URL like http://www.example.org/myhomepage/ it is enough to enter http://www.example.org/myhomepage/ in the GUI client or web interface, or execute linkchecker http://www.example.org/myhomepage/ on the command line.

This check will validate recursively all pages starting with http://www.example.org/myhomepage/. Additionally, all external links pointing outside of www.example.org will be checked but not recursed into.

Other Linkcheckers

If this software does not fit your requirements, you can check out other linkcheckers.

Books Development

Our great epics like Ramayana and Mahabharta were written Tam Patra,as that time no one has heard of paper. In some cultures, writing was chiseled on stone or clay.

The invention of paper in Han Dynasty China around 105 A.D. allowed writing to become portable. The Chinese developed a thin yet strong paper for writing and arranged the paper in accordion folded books, handscrolls, or sewn bindings. As paper and bookmaking moved east to Japan, south through India, and west to the Middle East with the trade routes, new forms and structures emerged according to cultural and religious needs.

PRESERVATION OF BOOKS

Although, the damage of a books is natural but careful handling of a book can delay the decaying process. The repeated incorrect handling and storage of a book can quickly transform a new book into a worn or even an unusable one. The right handling and storage in a stable, cool, clean, non-humid environment, can prolong its life. The environment around the book, is a major concern because unacceptable levels of temperature and humidity will accelerate deterioration. For example, the high humidity in an attic or basement can promote mold growth, cockle pages, and attract insects. Extremely low humidity, and hot radiators, can dry out leather bindings.

Direct sun-light, with a large ultraviolet (UV) component, will fade leather and cloth. Blue leather fades to dull green and red leather to brown, especially along the spine of the book.

Dust, dirt and grime from handling can adversely effect books as well. Many people shelve their books in closed glass cases away from brightly lit windows or damp exterior walls to minimize the amount of dust and grime that will accumulate.

How we handle and use a book contributes to its longevity. If a book will not lay flat, do not use force to open further. The covers should always be supported when the book is open.

Many books are damaged by the habit of pulling the books off the shelf with the head cap or the top of the spine. It is a much better practice to push the two adjoining books inward and remove the book by grasping the spine. Place similar sized books, next to each other on the shelf vertically, packing them neither too loosely or tightly. This will help to prevent warping of a tall book next to a short book.

The use of paper clips and marking pens to make notations should be discouraged since clips will rust or crimp the pages and pens often bleed through the pages, obscuring text. The folding down of page corners is also damaging as it will often cause the page corner to break off over time. The practice of using rubber bands or string to tie-up a book should be avoided because both will cut into brittle pages and damage fragile covers. A flat, soft ribbon (such as cotton twill tape), can be used to tie up the books as an immediate and temporary solution. An excellent way to protect fragile books is with a box that is custom made to the dimensions of the book. Books with dry flaking leather covers can be wrapped in paper or polyester jackets to keep the fragments and dirt from transferring to hands, adjoining books and the rest of the pages. In the past, leather books were treated with a leather dressing; however the application of an oil or leather dressing can have an adverse effect and is, therefore, not recommended.

Codex, or Multi-section Book

The first example of the codex, or a book made of sheets gathered together like a modern book, was in the 1st century A.D. During this period in northern Africa, books were made of sheets of parchment or papyrus, and "bound" together with rings. Later books were given covers and actually sewn together. Throughout Europe, parchment was considered a superior material for writing, and monasteries produced beautiful vellum or parchment books and illustrations for religious texts. Paper wasn't made in Europe until the 12th century, eleven hundred years after its invention in China, when the first paper mills began operation in Spain and Italy.

Eventually, paper gained acceptance with scribes and bookbinders and its popularity soared by the development of movable type printing in the late 15th century. These early European papers were far superior to the papers of today, because they were made from cotton rags or linen, which are pure sources of cellulose. With the advent of machine made paper in the early 19th century, and the use of ground wood pulp instead of cotton and linen by the 1850's, paper quality declined radically.

But, ground wood pulp as a papermaking material did allow paper to be made cheaply and quickly. By the mid-19th century, common people could own books, read newspapers and serialized novels and stories. Unfortunately, these "advances" in technology led to a decline in paper quality. Ground wood pulp contains a complex acid called lignin, which is essentially self-destructive, causing paper to become brown and brittle with time. It is safe to say that almost any book printed after the 1850's is made of a ground wood pulp paper, unless it was from a fine press or it specifies the paper as acid-free.

The First Step: Triage

Just like we care our cored ones. We also have to preserve books for our future. Some books are more valuable than others, and "value" can be a very subjective term. In the book world, there are rare books, a designation that refers to books that are old or financially valuable, to books which are finely printed and bound, or to books which have been owned by famous people. Librarians, curators, and collectors develop categories for rare books, or special collections.

In your home, you might have books which are "special", and books which are "ordinary". In the special category there might be an oversized art book, a favorite novel or book of poems, a family Bible, or a scrapbook of mementos or photographs. In addition, you might also have old yearbooks, textbooks from school or college, books of literature, books about a profession or trade. These are groups of books which are not looked at very often, but remain important reference tools. Books like paperbacks would constitute the "ordinary" category, books which might have once been enjoyed, but are easily replaced.

The first thing you need to do to take proper care of your book collection is to ask a series of questions: how many books do you have? which books are most valuable? do you need to keep all the books in your collection? are there any books which could be given to schools or libraries?

Once you prioritize the items in your collection, the job of preservation is simplified. The enemies of books—insects, mold, and damage from light—do not discriminate between expensive books and cheap paperbacks. This article will outline suggested steps for preventive preservation, explaining specific ways to create a better environment for your collection.

Temperature and Humidity : Enemies of Books

Books are made of organic materials, paper and board made from pulp, cloth made from natural fibers, leathers from tanned animal skins. All organic materials begin to deteriorate in reaction to the environment. Fluctuations in temperature and humidity cause these materials to expand and contract, which in turn can cause books to warp and buckle, crack and fall apart. While temperature and humidity affect paper, cloth, and leather differently, fluctuations in temperature and humidity do even more damage on books because they are composite objects. All the parts are joined together to make an operating, three dimensional object, with folds and hinges.

Books are hygroscopic, meaning that they readily absorb and release moisture. The amount of moisture in the air can be measured as relative humidity (referring to the water vapor in the air relative to the greatest amount of water vapor the air could hold at the same temperature). Relative humidity is expressed in percentages, and in Hawai's humid environment, the relative humidity averages between 60% and 75%. High humidity causes mold growth, and increased insect activity. Moreover, daily and seasonal fluctuations in humidity are extremely damaging to books.

Temperature is also an important consideration. The higher the temperature, the faster the book will deteriorate, as the rate of chemical reactions is doubled with each increase in temperature of 18 degrees F. Hawai's temperature averages from 60 to 90 degrees Fahrenheit. As a result, books and paper objects are self-destructing in the high heat, which, combined with high humidity, leaves books extremely vulnerable.

Recommendations

The good news is that there is something you can do to slow down the deterioration. You can lower the temperature, or at least attempt to stabilize the fluctuations through air conditioning, and lower the relative humidity by using a dehumidifier. Stability is the key ingredient: libraries and museums recommend the ideal temperature of 70 degrees F and a relative humidity of 50-55% for the storage of valuable collections. These ideal conditions can be difficult to maintain throughout the house, so think micro-environments.

Some people live in single room which they seal off from air condition and humidity. In this room, they store all of their books, photographs, leather, and other materials that are sensitive to high humidity. You can also make airtight storage containers out of large Tupperware locking tubs, or another inert material (not wood, for reasons which will be explained under the Storage section), and line the container with silica desicant. Place the silica packets or loose silica gel in the bottom of the airtight container, then build a ragboard "shelf" to separate the items from the desicant. When the desicant has absorbed a significant amount of moisture it will change color. Then you can dry it out in your oven and reuse it. Obviously, this will not work for an entire collection of books, but will be better than nothing for your most valuable treasures. Photographs, slides, and other photographic materials are extremely sensitive to high humidity, and also respond well to controlled micro-environments.

Pest and Mold : Enemies of Books

There are few things worse than the heartbreak caused by pulling a favorite book off the shelf and finding evidence of insects or mold. Unfortunately, humid climate makes India a paradise for mold and insects. This 18th century family Bible was in a Kaneohe home, untended on a shelf for years. When the owners recently renovated their home and moved their books, they discovered page after page destroyed by insects. Insects are an inevitable part of living in the tropics.

Opulent homes and beach shacks have one thing in common: a never-ending war against pests! India has a large rat and cockroach population, and most homes also have ants and other insects. Be aware that insects need food, and books are a gourmet meal with sugary glues and paper sizing. Common sense tells you not to leave food out in your kitchen, but many people do not realize that wood, leather, paper, tapa, and other materials in books are all "food" to insects.

Mold is another enemy of books. Mold spores, which thrive in relative humidity above 60-70%, have an easy time growing and living in our environment. The best way to reduce the incidence of mold growth is to follow the recommendations in the Temperature and Humidity section and attempt to stabilize the environment. Mold thrives in dark humid places, so air circulation is crucial. Periodically, check areas where books are stored and examine for insect and mold activity. To prevent insect infestations, follow the same guidelines you would to protect your house from termites and other pests: fix broken screens, reduce the ways that insects enter the house, line cracks and crevices (away from children and pets) with boric acid, and be aware of the items you bring into the house. Bringing cardboard boxes, cuttings from the garden, and items which have been stored outside into the house also allow insects to invade.

Common sense and good housekeeping can often prevent problems that affect art and book collections.

Light : Another enemy of Books

Light accelerates the deterioration of paper. Light embrittles and weakens the fibers in paper, made of cellulose. Exposure to light can cause paper to bleach, yellow or darken, and inks, pigments and dyes can fade or change color. Exposure to light is always damaging, and the damage is irreversible. The most damaging sources of light are the sun and artificial flourescent lighting — due to high concentrations of ultraviolet (UV) waves.

Recommendations

Light levels can be lowered through the use of drapes or blinds, (which also helps to lower the temperature in the home or office). UV-filtering plastic films or UV-filtering Plexiglas can be used on windows, and UV-filtering sleeves can be used on flourescent tubes. This reduces ultra-violet waves, but does not filter them out completely.

Humans : Main Enemy of Books

Poor handlings of books by careless fellow ruins the life of the books. People smash books down on xerox machines and break the spines, drop them and tear the paper, spill drinks on them and stain the pages, inflicting damage of every sort. Taking the time to care for books as objects is an important step for their preservation.

Books should not be pulled off their shelves by their spines, as this will break the spine or covers. Take care in photocopying; try to find a machine that has the platen on the side, so that the book can be placed face down on one page at a time, with the book kept at a 45 degree angle. Books need to be stored upright on shelves, unless they are oversized, when flat storage is best. Books should not lean from side to side on the shelf, or be stored on their foredge, as this breaks the covers away from the pages, or textblock. Paper and cloth bindings should not be shelved next to leather, as acidity and oils can migrate from book to book.

Storage : Friends of Books

Proper storage is a main step in preservation of books. How and where you store your books is important.

Recommendations: Shelving

Wood should be avoided as a material for shelving valuable books. Wooden shelves and furniture contain acids which accelerate the deterioration of books and paper.

In addition, wood is treated with chemicals like formaldehyde leaving fumes and gasses that are absorbed by books. If you have to use wood, there are safeguards you can take to protect your collection. Seal the wood, preferably with a water-based polyurethane. This will not provide a complete barrier from acids and off-gassing destructive elements, but it helps tremendously. Ideally you should allow the sealant to air for three weeks after drying. Then, to provide complete protection, shelves should be lined with aluminum foil, glass, plexiglas, or a combination of these with 100% ragboard.

AIR CIRCULATION

The use of only ragboard alone will not provide a barrier against the acids and gasses in wood.

It is crucial for book storage, especially in India humid climate. Many people have closed cabinets where they store their books. High humidity due to lack of air circulation, plus dark, closed cabinets provide a fertile ground for mold growth. Shelving against exterior walls should be avoided as well, as this put books in contact with excess moisture and humidity. Allow at least three inches between the wall and the book shelves to assure circulation.

Regular Check-ups

The regular ckeck-ups are vital for preservation of books. Books should be removed from shelves periodically. At this time, inspect the books for dust or evidence of pests. If books are dusty, dust with a dry, clean brush in a ventilated area or outdoors. Shelves should be dusted with a magnetic wiping cloth so the dust is absorbed and not simply rearranged on the shelves. Use products like Dust Bunny, Dust Magnet, One Wipe, Endust. If you use your vacuum cleaner, vacuum with the soft brush attachment and change the bag at regular intervals.

Custom Book Boxes

Placing books inside custom book boxes is one defense against the destructive forces of nature. Valuable or damaged books can be stored in archival quality boxes for their protection. Archival quality enclosures protect vulnerable books from light and excessive handling. Archival quality refers to materials that are pH neutral, either through the use of high quality raw materials or paper pulp which has been treated with an alkaline reserve. The term permanent, or permanent durable is being used increasingly to replace the term acid-free among conservators. After Hurricane Iniki, many libraries lost roofs and suffered excessive water damage, leaving wet and moldy books. The damage was irrepairable. But libraries which had boxed their valuable books found that the boxes were damaged, but the books inside escaped unharmed.

Boxes can be fancy or plain, custom made or in standard sizes. They can be made of acid-free paper or binder's board covered in cloth or leather. A number of companies offer a range of boxes and acid-free storage supplies at competitive prices. The following companies offer only acid-free, archival quality storage materials, and conservators endorse their products. You can call the 800 number and request a free catalog, then browse for the appropriate solution to your storage problems.

SYMBOLIC LINK

In computing, a symbolic link is a special file that consists a reference to another filr or directory in the form of an absolute or relative path and that affects pathname resolution.Symbolic links were already present by 1978 in mini-computer operating systems from DEC and Data General's RDOS. Today they are supported by the POSIX operating-system standard, most Unix-like operating systems such as Linux and Mac OS X, and also Windows operating systems such as Windows Vista, Windows 7 and to some degree in Windows 2000 and Windows XP.

Symbolic links operate transparently for most operations: programs which read or write to files named by a symbolic link will behave as if operating directly on the target file. However, programs that need to handle symbolic links specially (e.g., backup utilities) may identify and manipulate them directly. A symbolic link merely contains a text string that is interpreted and followed by the operating system as a path to another file or directory. It is a file on its own and can exist independently of its target. If a symbolic link is deleted, its target remains unaffected. If the target is moved, renamed or deleted, any symbolic link that used to point to it continues to exist but now points to a non-existing file. Symbolic links pointing to non-existing files are sometimes called broken, orphaned, dead or dangling. In computing, a hard link is a directory entry that associates a name with a file on a file system. A directory is itself a special kind of file that contains a list of such entries. The term is particular to file systems which allow multiple hard links to be created for the same file. This has the effect of creating multiple names for the same file, causing an aliasing effect: if the file is opened by one of its names, and changes are made to its content, then these changes will also be visible when the file is opened by an alternative name. By contrast, a soft link on such filesystems is not a link to a file itself, but to a file name; this also creates aliasing, but in a different way.

Directories are files, so multiple hard links to directories are possible; however, their unrestricted creation is usually avoided, because of the cyclic structures this may create. Hard links—that is, multiple hard links to the same file—are supported by POSIX-compliant and partially POSIX-compliant operating systems, such as Linux, Android, Apple's Mac OS X, Windows NT4 and later Windows NT operating systems. Support also depends on the type of file system being used. For instance, the NTFS file system supports it, while FAT does not.

Are Symbolic links are different from hard links. THe answer is "Yes". Hard links are not normally main point to directories, and they cannot link paths on different volumes or file systems. Symbolic links may point to any file or directory irrespective of the volumes on which the source and destination reside. Whereas hard links always refer to an existing file, symbolic links may contain arbitrary text that doesn't point to anything.

Some Unix as well as Linux distributions use symbolic links extensively in an effort to reorder the file system hierarchy. This is accomplished with several mechanisms, such as variant and context-dependent symbolic links. This offers the opportunity to create a more intuitive or application-specific directory tree and to reorganize the system without having to redesign the core set of system functions and utilities.

Storage of Symbolic Links

Early implementations of symbolic links stored the symbolic link information as data in regular files. The file contained the textual reference to the link's target, and an indicator denoting it as a symbolic link.

This method was slow and an inefficient use of disk-space on small systems. An improvement, called fast symlinks, allowed storage of the target path within the data structures used for storing file information on disk (inodes). This space normally stores a list of disk block addresses allocated to a file. Thus, symlinks with short target paths are accessed quickly. Systems with fast symlinks often fall back to using the original method if the target path exceeds the available inode space. The original style is retroactively termed a slow symlink. It is also used for disk compatibility with other or older versions of operating systems.

Although storing the link value inside the inode saves a disk block and a disk read, the operating system still needs to parse the path name in the link, which always requires reading additional inodes and generally requires reading other, and potentially many, directories, processing both the list of files and the inodes of each of them until it finds a match with the link's path components. Only when a link points to a file in the same directory do "fast symlinks" provide significantly better performance than other symlinks. The vast majority of POSIX-compliant implementations use symlink inodes. However, the POSIX standard does not require the entire set of file status information common to regular files to be implemented for symlinks. This allows implementations to use other solutions, such as storing symlink data in directory entries.

The file system permissions of a symbolic link usually have relevance only to rename or removal operations of the link itself, not to the access modes of the target file which are controlled by the target file's own permissions. The reported size of a symlink is the number of characters in the path it points to.

Mac OS aliases

In Mac OS and some Linux distributions, applications or users can also employ aliases, which have the added feature of following the target, even if it is moved to another location on the same volume.

Microsoft Windows

Windows 7 & Vista symbolic link

Windows 7 and Windows Vista support symbolic links for both files and directories with the command line utility mklink. Unlike junction points, a symbolic link can also point to a file or remote Server Message Block (SMB) network path. Additionally, the NTFS symbolic link implementation provides full support for cross-filesystem links. However, the functionality enabling cross-host symbolic links requires that the remote system also support them, which effectively limits their support to Windows Vista and later Windows operating systems.

Symbolic links are designed to aid in migration and application compatibility with POSIX operating systems. Microsoft aimed for Vista's symbolic links to "function just like UNIX links".However, the implementation varies from Unix symbolic links in several ways. For example, Vista users must manually indicate when creating a symbolic link whether it is a file or a directory. Vista has a limit of 31 symbolic links in a single path. Only users with the new Create Symbolic Link privilege, which only administrators have by default, can create symbolic links. If this is not the desired behavior, it must be changed in the Local Security Policy management console.

NTFS Junction Points

The Windows 2000 version ofNTFS introduced reparse points, which enabled, among other things, the use of Volume Mount Points and junction points. Junction points are for directories only, and moreover, local directories only; junction points to remote shares are unsupported. The Windows 2000 and XP Resource Kits include a program called linkd to create junction points; a more powerful one named Junction was distributed by Sysinternals' Mark Russinovich.

How Shortcuts are treated?

Shortcuts are treated like ordinary files by the file system and by software programs that are not aware of them. Only software programs that understand shortcuts (such as the Windows shell and file browsers) treat them as references to other files.

Shortcuts, which are supported by the graphical file browsers of some operating systems, may resemble symbolic links but differ in a number of important ways. One difference is what type of software is able to follow them:

Symbolic links are automatically resolved by the file system. Any software program, upon accessing a symbolic link, will see the target instead, whether the program is aware of symbolic links or not.

Another difference are the capabilities of the mechanism:

Microsoft Windows shortcuts normally refer to a destination by an absolute path (starting from the root directory), whereas POSIX symbolic links can refer to destinations via either an absolute or a relative path. The latter is useful if both the location and destination of the symbolic link share a common path prefix, but that prefix is not yet known when the symbolic link is created (e.g., in an archive file that can be unpacked anywhere).

Microsoft Windows application shortcuts contain additional metadata that can be associated with the destination, whereas POSIX symbolic links are just strings that will be interpreted as absolute or relative pathnames.

Windows shortcuts maintain their connection even when the target is moved, unlike symbolic links. Windows XP will search for a broken link's target before offering to delete it.

Cygwin simulates POSIX-compliant symbolic links in the Microsoft Windows file system. It uses identical programming and user utility interfaces as Unix (see above), but creates Windows shortcuts (.lnk files) with additional information used by Cygwin at the time of symlink resolution. Cygwin symlinks are compliant with both Windows and POSIX standards.

Some differences exist, however. Cygwin has no way to specify shortcut-related information - such as working directory or icon - as there is no place for such parameters in ln -s command. To create standard Microsoft .lnk files Cygwin provides the mkshortcut and readshortcut utilities

Command for Symbolic Links

The command creating symbolic links is makelink, which is also used for hard links. Internally the dos.library returns an error code indicating that a target is a soft link if you try to perform actions on it that are only legal for a file, and applications that wish to follow the symbolic link then needs to explicitly make a call to follow the link and retry the operation. The AmigaDOS shell will follow links automatically.

Variable Symbolic Links

A variable symbolic link is a symbolic link that has a variable name embedded in it. This allows some flexibility in filesystem order that is not possible with a standard symbolic link. Variables embedded in a symbolic links may include user and or environment specific information.

Symbolic links may be implemented in a context-dependent or variable fashion, such that the link points to varying targets depending on a configuration parameter, run-time parameter, or other instantaneous condition. In the OS/2 operating system, symbolic links resemble shadows in the graphical Workplace Shell.

Standardized Format

OpenURL is a standardized format of Uniform Resource Locator (URL) intended to enable Internet users to more easily find a copy of a resource that they are allowed to access. Although OpenURL can be used with any kind of resource on the Internet, it is most heavily used by libraries to help connect patrons to subscription content.

The OpenURL standard is designed to enable linking from information resources such as abstracting and indexing databases (sources) to library services (targets), such as academic journals, whether online or in printed or other formats. The linking is mediated by "link resolvers", or "link-servers", which parse the elements of an OpenURL and provide links to appropriate targets available through a library by the use of an OpenURL knowledge base.

A target is a resource or service that helps satisfy a user's information needs. Examples of targets include full-text repositories, online journals, online library catalogs and other Web resources and services.

The National Information Standards Organization (NISO) has developed OpenURL and its data container (the ContextObject) as American National Standards Institute (ANSI) standard Z39.88. On 22 June 2006, the Online Computer Library Center (OCLC) was named the maintenance agency for the standard.

Link Resolver: A link resolver is a service that produces menus in response to OpenURL queries. In short, it provides links between source (origination) and target (destination) databases. The initial OpenURL link is generated by a target database but the menus are determined by the resolver, which incorporates a knowledgebase of customized services. Therefore, the menu suggests only databases and catalogs available to a specific population of users.

At USU, we use the Serials Solutions product, ArticleLinker, to generate these links. Source databases generate an OpenURL and display the ArticleLinker icon. Clicking the icon causes the URL to query our resolver; the resolver then produces a service menu (customized for USU faculty, students, and staff) with options for obtaining more information (generally the full text of bibliographic citations).

Abstracting and indexing databases are good examples of source databases. Target databases are a bit more complex, but generally, include fulltext databases, e-journal packages, aggregators, library catalogs, etc. It is also possible to set a link resolver to query a search engine, populate an interlibrary loan request form, query a citation search database, and many other innovative services. The only restriction is that both the source and the target databases must be "OpenURL compliant."

What does an OpenURL look like?

An OpenURL appears below. In the first segment (red) you can see the server address of our link resolver where the URL will obtain information pertinent to USU users (e.g. what databases and services might be able to provide information about this citation) and in the second segment you can see the encoded information about the citation (e.g. that Academic Search Premier generated the citation, that this is a journal article; that the journal title is New Literary History, etc.).

The source that generates an OpenURL is typically a bibliographic citation or bibliographic record in a database that indexes the information resources often found in libraries, such as articles, books, patents, etc. Examples of such databases include Ovid, Web of Science, SciFinder, Modern Languages Association Bibliography and Google Scholar.

There are many reasons why a catalog search might fail. The most frequent problem occurs when the citation refers to a book or a book chapter. Often there are multiple editions of books and if you search by ISBN, the edition that we own might be different from the one referenced in the bibliographic citation. Therefore, it is always best to try both the ISBN and the title search. Problems also occur when metadata has been incorrectly encoded and the online catalog is told to search by the wrong type of title (i.e. the metadata reflects "article title" in the "journal title" field). It is always good to double-check a failed ArticleLinker search in the catalog.

Some full text providers are not set-up to link all the way to the article level. In such cases, ArticleLinker takes you to the journal level and you must navigate down. Other providers give you the option of linking to both the journal level and the article level.

Lots of things can cause a problem with ArticleLinker including typographical errors in the metadata or citation, incorrectly reported holdings in the knowledgebase, and incorrectly formatted metadata. The good news is that as the standard has matured, problems have become less frequent; however, any OpenURL resolver will still occasionally, misfire. ArticleLinker now provides a form to refine the citation search when it returns no results. It is best to check the data that has populated this form to see if the search has been correctly executed

Common Application

The most common application of OpenURL is to assist in the resolution of a request for a web resource (such as an online article). An OpenURL includes information about the referenced resource itself, and context information — both the context in which the OpenURL occurs (for example, a page of search results from a library catalog) and the context of the request (for example, the particular user making the request). If a different context is expressed in the URL, a different copy ends up resolved to. Changes in context are predictable, and do not require the original creator of the hyperlink (for example, the journal publisher) to handcraft different URLs for different contexts.

For example, changing either the base URL or a parameter in the query string can mean that the OpenURL resolves to a copy of a resource in a different library. So the same OpenURL, contained for instance in an electronic journal, can be adjusted by any library to provide access to their own copy of the resource, without completely overwriting the journal's hyperlink. The journal provider, in turn, is no longer required to provide a different version of the journal, with different hyperlinks, for each subscribing library..

Format

An OpenURL consists of a base URL, which contains the address of the user's institutional link-server, followed by a query string, which contains contextual data, typically in the form of key-value pairs. The contextual data is most often bibliographic data, but as of version 1.0 OpenURL can also include information about the requester, the resource containing the hyperlink, the type of service required, and so forth. For example:

A breakdown of the query string above shows that the following values are set:

1. The URL version url_ver = Z39.88-2004
2. Custom metadata rft_val_fmt = info:ofi/fmt:kev:mtx:book
3. And an object named "rft" is set which could be represented as rft = { isbn:"0836218310", btitle:"The Far Side Gallery 3" }

OpenURL was created by Herbert Van de Sompel, a librarian at the University of Ghent, in the late 1990s. His link-server software, SFX, was purchased by the library automation company Ex Libris Ltd. which popularized OpenURL in the information industry.

In 2006 a research report found some problems affecting the efficiency of OpenURL linking and recommended the creation of a group to establish best practice solutions. The KBART (Knowledge Bases And Related Tools) working group has been set up to progress the recommendations of the research report.

Applications and tools

Several companies market link server systems, including OCLC (WorldCat Link Manager), Swets (SwetsWise Linker), Serials Solutions (360 Link, formerly known as Article Linker), Innovative Interfaces, Inc. (WebBridge), EBSCO (LinkSource), Ovid (LinkSolver), SirsiDynix (Resolver), Fretwell-Downing (OL2), TDNet (TOUR), WT Cox Subscriptions (Journal Finder), R.R. Bowker (Ulrichs Resource Linker) and Infor (Vlink). Open-source link resolvers include CUFTS and Umlaut. There are also open-source tools for manipulating OpenURLs and the Code4Lib community maintains a list of these.

OpenURL is usually implemented by information providers by dynamically inserting an appropriate base URL into web pages sent to an authenticated user. OpenURL COinS is a specification that allows free services like Wikipedia to provide OpenURLs by cooperating with client side software agents. Federated search software presents OpenURL links in record fields by employing the library's subscriber links to link servers facilitating access to full-text resources from bibliographic record hyperlinks.

A link resolver enables linking within a library that can interpret incoming OpenURLs, take the local holdings and access privileges of that library into account, and display links to the appropriate resources. A link resolver lets a library provide a range of library-configured links and services, including links to full text versions, a local catalogue to check print holdings, document delivery or ILL services, databases, search engines, and so on.

Why libraries need local link resolvers

DOIs point to the authoritative version of content on the publisher's web site and to publisher-designated resources. However, for the user working in a library context, it is often useful to be directed to other resources. For example, the library may not subscribe to a particular electronic journal, it but may have access to the desired article through an aggregated database or print holdings. In addition, a library may want to provide a range of linking options beyond what is available at the publisher's web site.

How the process works?

Localized linking via DOI redirection occurs in this sequence, as shown in the following illustration:

1. Library installs a local linking server.
2. User in the library context clicks a DOI link.
3. A cookie on the user's machine alerts the DOI proxy server to redirect this DOI to the local linking server.
4. The local linking server receives the metadata needed for local resolution either from the source of the link or from CrossRef via OpenURL.

PACKAGE MANAGEMENT SYSTEM

In software, it's a collection of software tools to automatic the process of installing, upgrading, configuring, and removing software packages for a computer's operating system in a consistent manner. It typically maintains a database of software dependencies and version information to prevent software mismatches and missing prerequisites.

Packages are distributions of software, applications and data. Packages also contain metadata, such as the software's name, description of its purpose, version number, vendor, checksum, and a list of dependencies necessary for the software to run properly. Upon installation, metadata is stored in a local package database. Operating systems based on Linux and other Unix-like systems typically consist of hundreds or even thousands of distinct software packages; in the former case, a package management system is a convenience, in the latter case it becomes essential.

Ian Murdock has commented that package management is "the single biggest advancement Linux has brought to the industry", that it blurs the boundaries between operating system and applications, and that it makes it "easier to push new innovations [...] into the marketplace and [...] evolve the OS".

A package management system is often called an "install manager". This can lead to confusion between a package management system and an installer. The differences include:

Package Management System	Installer
Typically part of the operating system.	Each product comes bundled with its own installer.
Uses a single installation database.	Performs its own installation, sometimes recording information about that installation in a registry.

Can verify and manage all packages on the system.	Only works with its bundled product.
Single package management system vendor.	Multiple installe vendors.
Single package format.	Multiple installation formats.

A package, for package managers, denotes a specific set of files bundled with the appropriate metadata for use by a package manager. This can be confusing, as some programming languages often use the word "package" as a specific form of software library. Furthermore, that software library can be distributed in a package of files bundled for a package manager.

Main Functions

Package management systems are charged with the task of organizing all of the packages installed on a system. Main function of Package management system given below :

- Verifying file checksums to ensure correct and complete packages.
- Verifying digital signatures to authenticate the origin of packages.
- Applying file archivers to manage encapsulated files.
- Upgrading software with latest versions, typically from a software repository.
- Grouping of packages by function to help eliminate user confusion.
- Managing dependencies to ensure a package is installed with all packages it requires.

Some additional challenges are met by only a some package management systems.

Challenges with shared libraries

Computer systems which rely on dynamic library linking, instead of static library linking, share executable libraries of machine instructions across packages and applications. In these systems, complex relationships between different packages requiring different versions of libraries results in a challenge colloquially known as "dependency hell". On Microsoft Windows systems, this is also called "DLL hell" when working with dynamically linked libraries. Good package management systems become vital on these systems.

Front-ends for Locally Compiled Packages

System administrators may install and maintain software using tools other than package management software. For example, a local administrator may download unpackaged source code, compile it, and install it. This may effect the state of the local system to fall out of synchronization with the state of the package manager's database. The local administrator will be required to take additional measures, such as manually managing some dependencies or integrating the changes into the package manager.

There are tools available to ensure that locally compiled packages are integrated with the package management. For distributions based on .deb and .rpm files as well as Slackware Linux, there is CheckInstall, and for recipe-based systems such as Gentoo Linux and hybrid systems such as Arch Linux, it is possible to write a recipe first, which then ensures that the package fits into the local package database.

Maintenance of Configuration

Particularly troublesome with software upgrades of configuration files. Since package management systems, at least on Unix systems, originated as extensions of file archiving utilities, they can usually only either overwrite or retain configuration files, rather than applying rules to them. There are exceptions to this that usually apply to kernel configuration (which, if broken, will render the computer unusable after a restart). Problems can be caused if the format of configuration files changes.

For instance, if the old configuration file does not explicitly disable new options that should be disabled. Some package management systems, such as Debian's dpkg, allow configuration during installation. In other situations, it is desirable to install packages with the default configuration and then overwrite this configuration, for instance, in headless installations to a large number of computers. (This kind of pre-configured installation is also supported by dpkg.)

Repositories

In order to give users more control over the types of software that they are allowing to be installed on their system (and sometimes due to legal or convenience reasons on the distributors' side), software is often downloaded from a number of software repositories.

Upgrade Suppression

When a user interacts with the package management software to bring about an upgrade, it is customary to present the user with the list of things to be done (usually the list of packages to be upgraded, and possibly giving the old and new version numbers), and allow the user to either accept the upgrade in bulk, or select individual packages for upgrades. Many package management systems can be configured to never upgrade certain packages, or to upgrade them only when critical vulnerabilities or instabilities are found in the previous version, as defined by the packager of the software. This process is sometimes called version pinning.

For instance:

1. yum supports this with the syntax exclude=open office*, pacman with IgnorePkg = openoffice (to suppress upgrading openoffice in both cases)
2. dpkg and dselect support this partially through the hold flag in package selections
3. APT extends the hold flag through the complex "pinning" mechanism

Users can also blacklist a package

1. aptitude has "hold" and "forbid" flags

2. portage supports this through the package.mask configuration file

Cascading Package Removal

Some of the more advanced package management features offer "cascading package removal", in which all packages that depend on the target package and all packages that only the target package depends on, are also removed.

Common Package Management Systems and Formats

Package Formats

Every package manage relies the format and matadata of the packages, it can manage. That is, package managers need groups of files to be bundled for the specific package manager along with appropriate metadata, such as dependencies. Often, a core set of utilities manages the basic installation from these packages and multiple package managers use these utilities to provide additional functionality.

For example, yum relies on rpm as a backend. Yum extends the functionality of the backend by adding features such as simple configuration for maintaining a network of systems. As another example, the Synaptic Package Manager provides a graphical user interface by using the Advanced Packaging Tool (apt) library, which, in turn, relies on dpkg for core functionality. Alien is a program that converts between different Linux package formats. It supports conversion between Linux Standard Base conform RPM, deb, Stampede (.slp) and Slackware (tgz) packages.

Free and Open Source Software Systems

By the name free and open software packages under similar and compatible licenses are available for use number of systems. These packages can be combined and distributed using configurable and internally complex packaging systems to handle many permutations of software and manage version-specific dependencies and conflicts. Some packaging systems of free and open source software are also themselves released as free and open source software.

One typical difference between package management in proprietary operating systems, such as Mac OS X and Windows, and those in free and open source software, such as Linux, is that free and open source software systems permit third-party packages to also be installed and upgraded through the same mechanism, whereas the PMS of Mac OS X and Windows will only upgrade software provided by Apple and Microsoft, respectively (with the exception of some third party drivers in Windows). The ability to continuously upgrade third party software is typically added by adding the URL of the corresponding repository to the package management's configuration file.

Application-level Package Managers

Besides the systems-level application managers, there are some add-on package managers for operating systems with limited capabilities and for programming languages where developers need the latest libraries.

In contrast to systems-level application managers, application-level package managers focus on a small part of the software system. They typically reside within a directory tree that is not maintained by the systems-level package manager (like c:\cygwin or /usr/local/fink). However, this is not the case for the package managers that deal with programming libraries. This leads to a conflict as both package managers claim to "own" a file and might break upgrades.

References

1. "How package management changed everything". ianmurdock.com. http://ianmurdock.com/2007/07/21/how-package-management-changed-everything/. Retrieved 2008-03-01.
2. Chris, Tucker (2007–03–15). Optimal Package Install/Uninstall Manager. UC San Diego. p. 1. http://

hcseweb.ucsd.edu/~rjhala/papers/opium.pdf. Retrieved 2010–08–03.

3. "Linux repository classification schemes". braintickle.blogspot.com. http://braintickle.blogspot. com/ 2006/01/linux-repository-classification.html. Retrieved 2008-03-01.
4. "CentOS yum pinning rpms". centos.org. Archived from the original on 2007-11-02. http://web.archive.org/web/ 20071102203232/http://lists.centos.org/pipermail/centos/ 2005-May/046320.html. Retrieved 2008-03-01.
5. "pacman(8) Manual Page". archlinux.org. http:// www.archlinux.org/pacman/pacman.8.html. Retrieved 2008-03-01.
6. "How to keep specific versions of packages installed (complex)". debian.org. http://www.debian.org/doc/ manuals/apt-howto/ch-apt-get.en.html#s-pin. Retrieved 2008-03-01.
7. "Apt pinning to blacklist a package". http:// linux.derkeiler.com/Mailing-Lists/Debian/2009-07/ msg00476.html. Retrieved 2010-08-19.
8. "Regional Information Sharing Systems" (in English). RISS (Official Site). http://www.riss.net/. Retrieved 17 December 2009.

1. "Regional Information Sharing Systems (RISS)" (in English). Institute for Intergovernmental Research. http:/ /www.iir.com/RISS/. Retrieved 17 December 2009.
2. "RISS Overview" (in English). RISS (Official site). http:/ /www.riss.net/overview.aspx. Retrieved 17 December 2009.
3. "Automated Trusted Information Exchange (ATIX)". ATIX (official site). http://www.riss.net/atix.aspx. Retrieved 17 December 2009.
4. Harris, William. "Homeland Security Information Network: Moving Past the Missteps Toward Better

Information Sharing". Testimony to U.S. House of Representatives. http://homeland.house.gov/SiteDocuments/20070510132121-04354.pdf. Retrieved 18 December 2009.

5. "Homeland Security Information Network". Department of Homeland Security (official site). http://www.dhs.gov/files/programs/gc_1156888108137.shtm. Retrieved 18 December 2009.
6. "Homeland Security Information Network". FEMA (official site). http://www.fema.gov/emergency/nrf/HSIN.htm. Retrieved 18 December 2009.
7. "GAO-07-822T Information Technology: Homeland Security Information Network". US Government Accountability Office (GAO). http://www.gao.gov/new.items/d07822t.pdf. Retrieved 18 December 2009.
8. Bain, Ben (May 13, 2009). "Information-sharing platform hacked". Federal Computer Week. http://www.fcw.com/Articles/2009/05/13/Web-DHS-HSIN-intrusion-hack.aspx. Retrieved 18 December 2009.
9. Symbolic Links, MSDN Library, Win32 and COM Development, 2008-01-18
10. CreateSymbolicLink Function, MSDN Library, Win32 and COM Development
11. Symbolic Link Programming Considerations, MSDN
12. Mark Russinovich: Inside the Windows Vista Kernel: Part 1 – File-based symbolic links, Microsoft Technet, February 2007.
13. Sysinternals Junction documentation
14. Microsoft .lnk files in Cygwin
15. Cygwin User's Guide, Cygwin.

CHAPTER–5

E-LEARNING AND COMMUNICATION TECHNOLOGIES

DISTRIBUTED SEARCH AND MATERIALS MANAGEMENT

As far as the medical information on Internet is concerned, there are numerous websites dedicated to healthcare tips and information. The UK National electronic Library for Health (NeLH) is addressing this issue by providing a single-entry portal to evidence-based medical information on the Internet enhanced with a quality tag assigned by professional experts.

In order to fully utilize the potential of an Internet-based library, the NeLH is distributed and consists of a number of Virtual Branch Libraries (VBLs), each dedicated to a particular disease or a medical area. VBLs are dynamically updated and their design reflects the needs of each particular user base. However, users accessing a single VBL may want to search the entire NeLH or should have the option of being able to search the entire NeLH. Therefore, support for a distributed search according to an adopted topology of VBL servers is essential.

Distributed web crawling is a distributed computing technique whereby Internet search engines employ many computers to index the Internet via web crawling. The idea is to spread out the required resources of computation and bandwidth to many computers and networks. Cho and Garcia-Molina (Cho and Garcia-Molina, 2002) studied two types of policies:

Dynamic Policy

With this type of policy, a central server assigns new URLs to different crawlers dynamically. This allows the central server to, for instance, dynamically balance the load of each crawler.

With dynamic assignment, typically the systems can also add or remove downloader processes. The central server may become the bottleneck, so most of the workload must be transferred to the distributed crawling processes for large crawls.

There are two configurations of crawling architectures with dynamic assignments that have been described by Shkapenyuk and Suel (Shkapenyuk and Suel, 2002):

(a) A small crawler configuration, in which there is a central DNS resolver and central queues per Web site, and distributed downloaders.

(b) A large crawler configuration, in which the DNS resolver and the queues are also distributed.

Static Policy

For static assignment, a hashing function can be used to transform URLs (or, even better, complete website names) into a number that corresponds to the index of the corresponding crawling process. With this type of policy, there is a fixed rule stated from the beginning of the crawl that defines how to assign new URLs to the crawlers.

As there are external links that will go from a Web site assigned to one crawling process to a website assigned to a different crawling process, some exchange of URLs must occur.

To reduce the overhead due to the exchange of URLs between crawling processes, the exchange should be done in batch, several URLs at a time, and the most cited URLs in the collection should be known by all crawling processes before the crawl (e.g.: using data from a previous crawl) (Cho and Garcia-Molina, 2002).

An effective assignment function must have three main properties: each crawling process should get approximately the same number of hosts (balancing property), if the number of crawling processes grows, the number of hosts assigned to each process must shrink (contra-variance property), and the assignment must be able to add and remove crawling processes dynamically. Boldi *et al.* (Boldi *et al.*, 2004) propose to use consistent hashing, which replicates the buckets, so adding or removing a bucket does not require re-hashing of the whole table to achieve all of the desired properties.,

Most modern commercial search engines use this technique. Google and Yahoo use thousands of individual computers to crawl the Web.Newer projects are attempting to use a less structured, more ad-hoc form of collaboration by enlisting volunteers to join the effort using, in many cases, their home or personal computers. LookSmart is the largest search engine to use this technique, which powers its Grub distributed web-crawling project.

This solution uses computers that are connected to the Internet to crawl Internet addresses in the background. Upon downloading crawled web pages, they are compressed and sent back together with a status flag (e.g. changed, new, down, redirected) to the powerful central servers. The servers, which manage a large database, send out new URLs to clients for testing.

According to the FAQ about Nutch, an open-source search engine website, the savings in bandwidth by distributed web crawling are not significant, since "A successful search engine requires more bandwidth to upload query result pages than its crawler needs to download pages..."

Patrons of the library can search library catalog online to locate various resources - books, periodicals, audio and visual materials, or other items under control of the library. Patrons may reserve or renew item, provide feedback, and manage their account.

With a good vision, we have planned to cross some milestones towards making an ideal library, by developing a digital library and establishing networking with other libraries to bridge the gap in information availability.

A library catalog is a register of all bibliographic terms found in a library or group of libraries, such as a network of libraries at several locations. A bibliographic item can be any information entity (e.g., books, computer files, graphics, realia, cartographic materials, etc.) that is considered library material (e.g., a single novel in an anthology), or a group of library materials (e.g., a trilogy), or linked from the catalog (e.g., a webpage) as far as it is relevant to the catalog and to the users (patrons) of the library.

The card catalog was a familiar sight to library users for generations, but it has been effectively replaced by the online public access catalog (OPAC). Some still refer to the online catalog as a "card catalog". Some libraries with OPAC access still have card catalogs on site, but these are now strictly a secondary resource and are seldom updated. Many of the libraries that have retained their physical card catalog post a sign advising the last year that the card catalog was updated. Some libraries have eliminated their card catalog in favour of the OPAC for the purpose of saving space for other use, such as additional shelving.

An Online Public Access Catalog (OPAC or Library Catalog) is an online database of materials held by a library or group of libraries. Users search a library catalog principally to locate books and other material physically located at a library. Although a handful of experimental systems existed as early as the 1960s, the first large-scale online catalogs were developed at Ohio State University in 1975 and the Dallas Public Library in 1978. These and other early online catalog systems tended to closely reflect the card catalogs that they were intended to replace. Using a dedicated terminal or telnet client, users could search a handful of pre-coordinate indexes and browse the resulting display in much the same way they had previously navigated the card catalog.

Virtual Classroom

A virtual classroom duplicates the capabilities found in a real classroom. A virtual classroom provides:

- A place to meet: Students and teachers use their computers to go to a virtual meeting place instead of a classroom.
- Take attendance: A list of students is recorded.
- Teaching Options: Teachers can choose from a variety of synchronous technologies including:
    - Slide presentation
    - Audio and video conferencing
    - Application sharing
    - Shared whiteboard
- Instant Messaging : Students can indicate when they want to speak by virtually raising their hand. Teachers can let students speak through audio and video conferencing. Teachers and students can use instant messaging and chat.
- Questionaire : Teachers can put questions to students.
- Breakout Sessions: Students can work together in groups.

Most companies that sell virtual classroom software provide all of these capabilities in a single package.

AUDIO AND VIDEO CONFERENCING

Audio conferencing can be implemented in dual ways. Firstly, Computers connected to the Internet. Common names for this kind of implementation are IP Audio Conferencing or Voice-over-IP. Secondly, Phone conferences. People dial the same number to participate in an audio conference.

Video conferencing can also be implemented in two ways:

- Computers connected to the Internet. The computers need digital cameras.
- Special video conferencing devices that connect over the Internet or over phone lines.

Chat

It allows several stranges to communicate with each other. Each participant uses a computer to type their comments. The other participants can see the name of the person and their comments.

Shared Whiteboard

A shared whiteboard lets a group of people communicate by typing comments, drawing, highlighting and pointing. A shared whiteboard is a common feature within virtual classroom software packages.

Application Sharing

One can demonstrate how to use software applications to remote learners with application sharing. A teacher can also let the learner take control of the application to practice performing tasks.

Instant Messaging

It's also similar to chat. One person communicates to another via typing the text. Instant messaging also provides some additional features. With instant messaging, you can keep a list of list of people that you might like to chat with. The list will indicate if they are online, offline, available for chat or busy. These features make instant messaging an excellent tool for learning from peers.

Search Mechanisms

Throughout the 1980s, the number and sophistication of online catalogs grew. The first commercial systems appeared, and would by the end of the decade largely replace systems built by libraries themselves. Library catalogs began providing improved search mechanisms, including Boolean and keyword searching, as well as ancillary functions, such as the ability to place holds on items that had been checked-out.

At the same time, libraries began to develop applications to automate the purchase, cataloging, and circulation of books and other library materials. These applications, collectively known as an integrated library system (ILS) or library management system, included an online catalog as the public interface to the system's inventory. Most library catalogs, then, are closely tied to their underlying ILS system.

E-LEARNING

E-learning consists of all forms of electronically supported learning and teaching. The information and communication systems, whether networked or not, serve as specific media to implement the learning process.The term will still most likely be utilized to reference out-of-classroom and in-classroom educational experiences via technology, even as advances continue in regard to devices and curriculum.

You know that people learn in many different ways and at different times. To support these different learning needs, you will need different e-learning delivery methods. You also will need a way to develop and manage e-learning.

E-learning is essentially the computer and network-enabled transfer of skills and knowledge. E-learning applications and processes include Web-based learning, computer-based learning, virtual classroom opportunities and digital collaboration. Content is delivered via the Internet, intranet/extranet, audio or video tape, satellite TV, and CD-ROM. It can be self-paced or instructor-led and includes media in the form of text, image, animation, streaming video and audio.

Abbreviations like CBT (Computer-Based Training), IBT (Internet-Based Training) or WBT (Web-Based Training) have been used as synonyms to e-learning. Today one can still find these terms being used, along with variations of e-learning such as elearning, Elearning, and eLearning. The worldwide e-learning industry is estimated to be worth over $48 billion according to conservative estimates.Developments in internet and multimedia technologies are the basic enabler of e-learning, with consulting, content, technologies, services and support being identified as the five key sectors of the e-learning industry.

Higher Education

In a study, Allen and Seamen claim that almost a quarter of all students in post-secondary education were taking fully online courses in 2008, and a report by Ambient Insight Research says that in 2009, 44 per cent of post-secondary students in the USA were taking some or all of their courses online, and projected that this figure would rise to 81 percent by 2014. This is the age of online learning where teachers and students do notmeet face-to-face, but they interact via Internet. Many Indian teachers are giving classes to their American students who are weak in English Grammar including science subjects. Nearly, five year's back By 2006, 3.5 million students were participating in on-line learning at institutions of higher education in the United States.According to the Sloan Foundation reports, there has been an increase of around 12–14 percent per year on average in enrollments for fully online learning over the five years 2004–2009 in the US post-secondary system, compared with an average of approximately 2 per cent increase per year in enrollments overall. Thus it can be seen that e-learning is moving rapidly from the margins to being a predominant form of post-secondary education, at least in the USA. Many higher education, for-profit institutions, now offer on-line classes. By contrast, only about half of private, non-profit schools offer them.

The Sloan report, based on a poll of academic leaders, indicated that students generally appear to be at least as satisfied with their online classes as they are with traditional ones. Private institutions may become more involved with on-line presentations as the cost of instituting such a system decreases. Properly trained staff must also be hired to work with students online. These staff members need to understand the content area, and also be highly trained in the use of the computer and Internet. Online education is rapidly increasing, and online doctoral programs have even developed at top research universities.

K-12 Learning

In America, K-12 schools are the greatest craze among parents who want to educate their children in these schools. Some E-Learning environments take place in a traditional classroom, others allow students to attend classes from home or other locations.

Four decades back, Stanford University psychology professors Patrick Suppes and Richard C. Atkinson experimented with using computers to teach math and reading to young children in elementary schools in East Palo Alto, California. Stanford's Education Program for Gifted Youth is descended from those early experiments. Early e-learning systems, based on Computer-Based Learning/Training often attempted to replicate autocratic teaching styles whereby the role of the e-learning system was assumed to be for transferring knowledge, as opposed to systems developed later based on Computer Supported Collaborative Learning (CSCL), which encouraged the shared development of knowledge.

As early as 1993, William D. Graziadei described an online computer-delivered lecture, tutorial and assessment project using electronic mail. In 1997 he published an article which described developing an overall strategy for technology-based course development and management for an educational system. He said that products had to be easy to use and maintain, portable, replicable, scalable, and immediately affordable, and they had to have a high probability of success with long-term cost-effectiveness.

William D. Graziadei, Sharon Gallagher,Ronald N. Brown,Joseph Sasiadek Building Asynchronous and Synchronous Teaching-Learning Environments: Exploring a Course/Classroom Management System Solution. In 1997 Graziadei, W.D., et al., published an article entitled "Building Asynchronous and Synchronous Teaching-Learning Environments: Exploring a Course/ Classroom Management System Solution". They described a process at the State University of New York (SUNY) of evaluating products and developing an overall strategy for technology-based course development and management in teaching-learning. The product(s) had to be easy to use and maintain, portable, replicable, scalable, and immediately affordable, and they had to have a high probability of success with long-term cost-effectiveness. Today many technologies can be, and are, used in e-learning, from blogs to collaborative software, ePortfolios, and virtual classrooms. Most eLearning situations use combinations of these techniques.

E-Learning 2.0

This is a neologism for CSCL systems that came about during the emergence of Web 2.0 From an E-Learning 2.0 perspective, conventional e-learning systems were based on instructional packets, which were delivered to students using assignments. Assignments were evaluated by the teacher. In contrast, the new e-learning places increased emphasis on social learning and use of social software such as blogs, wikis, podcasts and virtual worlds such as Second Life. This phenomenon has also been referred to as Long Tail Learning See also (Seely Brown & Adler 2008). E-Learning 2.0, by contrast to e-learning systems not based on CSCL, assumes that knowledge (as meaning and understanding) is socially constructed. Learning takes place through conversations about content and grounded interaction about problems and actions.

However, it should be noted that many early online courses, such as those developed by Murray Turoff and Starr Roxanne Hiltz in the 1970s and 80s at the New Jersey Institute of Technology, courses at the University of Guelph in Canada, the British Open University, and the online distance courses at the University of British Columbia (where Web CT, now incorporated into Blackboard Inc. was first developed), have always made heavy use of online discussion between students. Also, from the start, practitioners such as Harasim (1995) have put heavy emphasis on the use of learning networks for knowledge construction, long before the term e-learning, let alone e-learning 2.0, was even considered.

There is also an increased use of virtual classrooms (online presentations delivered live) as an online learning platform and classroom for a diverse set of education providers such as Minnesota State Colleges and Universities and Sachem School District.

It is not exaggerated to say that social networks have become an easy available mode of E-learning 2.0. Social networks have been used to foster online learning communities around subjects as diverse as test preparation and language education. Mobile Assisted Language Learning is a term used to describe using handheld computers or cell phones to assist in language learning. Some feel, however, that schools have not caught up with the social networking trends. Few traditional educators promote social networking in a healthy and promotional way. Advocates of social learning claim that one of the best ways to learn something is to teach it to others.

Approaches to E-learning Services

Computer along with Internet have revolutionized the process of E-learning. Now, we are using the word E-books virtual learning frequently. The Sloan Commission reports on the status of e-learning,which refer to web enhanced, web supplemented and web dependent to reflect increasing intensity of technology use.

Bates and Poole (2003) and the OECD (2005)suggest that different forms of e-learning can be considered as a continuum, from no e-learning, i.e. no use of computers and/or the Internet for teaching and learning, through classroom aids, such as making classroom lecture Powerpoint slides available to students through a course web site or learning management system, to laptop programs, where students are required to bring laptops to class and use them as part of a face-to-face class, to hybrid learning, where classroom time is reduced but not eliminated, with more time devoted to online learning, through to fully online learning, which is a form of distance education. In the Bates and Poole continuum, 'blended learning' can cover classroom aids, laptops and hybrid learning, while 'distributed learning' can incorporate either hybrid or fully online learning.

It can be seen that e-learning can describe range of applications by no means clear even in peer reviewed research publications which form of e-learning is being discussed.However, Bates and Poole argue that when instructors say they are using e-learning, this most often refers to the use of technology as classroom aids, although over time, there has been a gradual increase in fully online learning.

Computer-based Learning and Training

Computer-based learning, sometimes abbreviated to CBL, refers to the use of computers as a key component of the educational environment. While this can refer to the use of computers in a classroom, the term more broadly refers to a structured environment in which computers are used for teaching purposes.

Cassandra B. Whyte researched about the ever increasing role that computers would play in higher education. This evolution, to include computer-supported collaborative learning, in addition to data management, has been realized. The type of computers have changed over the years from cumbersome, slow devices taking up much space in the classroom, home, and office to laptops and handheld devices that are more portable in form and size and this minimalization of technology devices will continue.

Computer-Based Trainings (CBTs) are elf-paced activities accessible via a computer or CBTs typically present content in a linear fashion, much like reading an online book or manual. For this reason they are often used to teach static processes, such as using software or completing mathematical equations. The term

Computer-Based Training is often used interchangeably with Web-based training (WBT) with the primary difference being the delivery method. Where CBTs are typically delivered via CD-ROM, WBTs are delivered via the Internet using a web browser.

Assessing learning in a CBT usually comes in the form of multiple choice questions, or other assessments that can be easily scored by a computer such as drag-and-drop, radial button, simulation or other interactive means. Assessments are easily scored and recorded via online software, providing immediate end-user feedback and completion status. Users are often able to print completion records in the form of certificates. CBTs provide learning stimulus beyond traditional learning methodology from textbook, manual, or classroom-based instruction. For example, CBTs offer user-friendly solutions for satisfying continuing education requirements. Instead of limiting students to attending courses or reading printed manuals, students are able to acquire knowledge and skills through methods that are much more conducive to individual learning preferences. For example, CBTs offer visual learning benefits through animation or video, not typically offered by any other means.

CBTs can be a good alternative to printed learning materials since rich media, including videos or animations, can easily be embedded to enhance the learning. Another advantage to CBTs are that they can be easily distributed to a wide audience at a relatively low cost once the initial development is completed.

However, CBTs pose some learning challenges as well. Typically the creation of effective CBTs requires enormous resources. The software for developing CBTs (such as Flash or Adobe Director) is often more complex than a subject matter expert or teacher is able to use. In addition, the lack of human interaction can limit both the type of content that can be presented as well as the type of assessment that can be performed. Many learning organizations are beginning to use smaller CBT/WBT activities as part of a broader online learning program which may include online discussion or other interactive elements.

Computer-supported Collaborative Learning (CSCL)

Computer-supported collaborative learning (CSCL) is one of the most promising innovations to improve teaching and learning with the help of modern information and communication technology. Most recent developments in CSCL have been called E-Learning 2.0, but the concept of collaborative or group learning whereby instructional methods are designed to encourage or require students to work together on learning tasks has existed much longer. It is widely agreed to distinguish collaborative learning from the traditional 'direct transfer' model in which the instructor is assumed to be the distributor of knowledge and skills, which is often given the neologism E-Learning 1.0, even though this direct transfer method most accurately reflects Computer-Based Learning systems (CBL).

In Datacloud: Toward a New Theory of Online Work, Johndan Johnson-Eilola describes a specific computer-supported collaboration space: The Smart Board. According to Johnson-Eilola, a "Smart Board system provides a 72-inch, rear projection, touchscreen, intelligent whiteboard surface for work" (79). In Datacloud, Johnson-Eilola asserts that "[w]e are attempting to understand how users move within information spaces, how users can exist within information spaces rather than merely gaze at them, and how information spaces must be shared with others rather than being private, lived within rather than simply visited" (82).

He explains how the Smart Board system offers an information space that allows his students to engage in active collaboration. He makes three distinct claims regarding the functionality of the technology: 1) The Smart Board allows users to work with large amounts of information, 2) It offers an information space that invites active collaboration, 3) The work produced is often "dynamic and contingent" (82).

Johnson-Eilola further explains that with the Smart Board "...information work becom[es] a odied experience" (81). Users have the opportunity to engage with—inhabit—the technology by direct manipulation. Moreover, this space allows for more than one user; essentially, it invites multiple users. When using smart boards information is able to be introduced to students in a new, fun, and engaging way. Teachers and/or students are able to draw on the board using different colors. This can help focus ones attention on particular areas of the screen. The marks made on the smart board are able to be erased. This makes it easy to show the information in its original form. When using smart boards teaching and learning become a more active experience for both the student and the teacher.

Locus of Control remains an important consideration in successful engagement of E-learners whether using the Smart Board or another E-learning modality. According to the work of Cassandra B. Whyte, the continuing attention to aspects of motivation and success in regard to E-learning should be kept in context and concert with other educational efforts. Information about motivational tendencies can help educators, psychologists, and technologists develop insights to help students perform better academically.

Technology-enhanced Learning (TEL)

Technology enhanced learning (TEL) has the goal to provide socio-technical innovations (also improving efficiency and cost effectiveness) for e-learning practices, regarding individuals and organizations, independent of time, place and pace. The field of TEL therefore applies to the support of any learning activity through technology.

Technology Issues

Along with the terms learning technology, instructional technology, and Educational Technology, the term is generally used to refer to the use of technology in learning in a much broader sense than the computer-based training or Computer Aided Instruction of the 1980s. It is also broader than the terms Online Learning or Online Education which generally refer to purely web-based learning. In cases where mobile technologies are used, the term M-learning has become more common. E-learning, however, also has implications beyond just the technology and refers to the actual learning that takes place using these systems.

E-learning is naturally suited to distance learning and flexible learning, but can also be used in conjunction with face-to-face teaching, in which case the term Blended learning is commonly used. E-Learning pioneer Bernard Luskin argues that the "E" must be understood to have broad meaning if e-Learning is to be effective. Luskin says that the "e" should be interpreted to mean exciting, energetic, enthusiastic, emotional, extended, excellent, and educational in addition to "electronic" that is a traditional national interpretation. This broader interpretation allows for 21st century applications and brings learning and media psychology into the equation. In higher education especially, the increasing tendency is to create a Virtual Learning Environment (VLE) (which is sometimes combined with a Management Information System (MIS) to create a Managed Learning Environment) in which all aspects of a course are handled through a consistent user interface standard throughout the institution. A growing number of physical universities, as well as newer online-only colleges, have begun to offer a select set of academic degree and certificate programs via the Internet at a wide range of levels and in a wide range of disciplines.

While some programs require students to attend some campus classes or orientations, many are delivered completely online. In addition, several universities offer online student support services, such as online advising and registration, e-counseling, online textbook purchase, student governments and student newspapers.

E-Learning can also refer to educational web sites such as those offering learning scenarios, worksheets and interactive exercises for children. The term is also used extensively in the business sector where it generally refers to cost-effective online training.

The recent trend in the E-Learning sector is screencasting. There are many screencasting tools available but the latest buzz is all about the web based screencasting tools which allow the users to create screencasts directly from their browser and make the video available online so that the viewers can stream the video directly.

The advantage of such tools is that it gives the presenter the ability to show his ideas and flow of thoughts rather than simply explain them, which may be more confusing when delivered via simple text instructions. With the combination of video and audio, the expert can mimic the one on one experience of the classroom and deliver clear, complete instructions. From the learner's point of view this provides the ability to pause and rewind and gives the learner the advantage of moving at their own pace, something a classroom cannot always offer.

COMMUNICATION TECHNOLOGIES USED IN E-LEARNING

It generally categorized as asynchronous or synchronous. Asynchronous activities use technologies such as blogs, wikis, and discussion boards. The idea here is that participants may engage in the exchange of ideas or information without the dependency of other participants involvement at the same time. Electronic mail (Email) is also asynchronous in that mail can be sent or received without having both the participants' involvement at the same time. Asynchronous learning also gives students the ability to work at their own pace. This is particularly beneficial for students who have health problems. They have the opportunity to complete their work in a low stress environment. Synchronous activities involve the exchange of ideas and information with one or more participants during the same period of time. A face to face discussion is an example of synchronous communications. Synchronous activities occur with all participants joining in at once, as with an online chat session or a virtual classroom or meeting.

Virtual classrooms and meetings can often use a mix of communication technologies. Participants in a virtual classroom use icons called emoticons to communicate feelings and responses to questions or statements. Other communication technologies available in a virtual classroom include text notes, microphone rights, and breakout sessions. Breakout sessions allow the participants to work collaboratively in a small group setting to accomplish a task.

In asynchronous online courses, students proceed at their own pace. If they need to listen to a lecture a second time, or think about a question for awhile, they may do so without fearing that they will hold back the rest of the class. Through online courses, students can earn their diplomas more quickly, or repeat failed courses without the embarrassment of being in a class with younger students. Students also have access to an incredible variety of enrichment courses in online learning, and can participate in internships, sports, or work and still graduate with their class.

In many models, the writing community and the communication channels relate with the E-learning and the M-learning communities. Both the communities provide a general overview of the basic learning models and the activities required for the participants to join the learning sessions across the virtual classroom or even across standard classrooms enabled by technology. Many activities, essential for the learners in these environments, require frequent chat sessions in the form of virtual classrooms and/or blog meetings.

Learning Management System (LMS) and Learning Content Management System (LCMS)

A learning management system (LMS) is software used for delivering, tracking and managing training/education. LMSs range from systems for managing training/educational records to software for distributing courses over the Internet and offering features for online collaboration. A learning content management system (LCMS) is software for authoring, editing and indexing e-learning content (courses, reusable content objects). An LCMS may be solely dedicated to producing and publishing content that is hosted on an LMS, or it can host the content itself. The Aviation Industry Computer-Based Training Committee (AICC) specification provides support for content that is hosted separately from the LMS.

A LMS allows for teachers and administrators to track attendance, time on task, and student progress. LMS also allows for not only teachers and administrators to track these variables but parents and students as well. Parents can log on to the LMS to track grades. Students log on to the LMS to submit homework and to access the course syllabus and lessons.

Computer-aided Assessment

Computer-aided Assessment (also but less commonly referred to as E-assessment), ranging from automated multiple-choice tests to more sophisticated systems is becoming increasingly common. With some systems, feedback can be geared towards a student's specific mistakes or the computer can navigate the student through a series of questions adapting to what the student appears to have learned or not learned. The best examples follow a Formative Assessment structure and are called "Online Formative Assessment". This involves making an initial formative assessment by sifting out the incorrect answers. The author/teacher will then explain what the pupil should have done with each question. It will then give the pupil at least one practice at each slight variation of sifted out questions. This is the formative learning stage. The next stage is to make a Summative Assessment by a new set of questions only covering the topics previously taught. Some will take this even further and repeat the cycle such as BOFA which is aimed at the Eleven plus exam set in the UK.

The word learning design has sometimes come to refer to the type of activity enabled by software such as the open-source system LAMS which supports sequences of activities that can be both adaptive and collaborative. The IMS Learning Design specification is intended as a standard format for learning designs, and IMS LD Level A is supported in LAMS V2.elearning has been replacing the traditional settings due to its cost effectiveness.

Electronic Performance Support Systems (EPSS)

Electronic performance support systems (EPSS) is a "computer-based system that improves worker productivity by providing on-the-job access to integrated information, advice, and learning experiences". 1991, Barry Raybould

Content Issues

Content is a core component of E-learning and includes issues such as pedagogy and learning object re-use.

Pedagogical Elements

Pedagogical elements are an attempt to define structures or units of educational material. For example, this could be a lesson, an assignment, a multiple choice question, a quiz, a discussion group or a case study. These units should be format independent, so although it may be in any of the following methods, pedagogical structures would not include a textbook, a web page, a video conference or Podcast.

When beginning to create E-Learning content, the pedagogical approaches need to be evaluated. Simple pedagogical approaches make it easy to create content, but lack flexibility, richness and downstream functionality. On the other hand, complex pedagogical approaches can be difficult to set up and slow to develop, though they have the potential to provide more engaging learning experiences for students. Somewhere between these extremes is an ideal pedagogy that allows a particular educator to effectively create educational materials while simultaneously providing the most engaging educational experiences for students.

Pedagogical Approaches or Perspectives

It is possible to use various pedagogical approaches for eLearning which include:

- instructional design – the traditional pedagogy of instruction which is curriculum focused, and is developed by a centralized educating group or a single teacher.
- social-constructivist – this pedagogy is particularly well afforded by the use of discussion forums, blogs, wiki and on-line collaborative activities. It is a collaborative approach that opens educational content creation to a wider group including the students themselves. The One Laptop Per Child Foundation attempted to use a constructivist approach in its project

- Laurillard's Conversational Model is also particularly relevant to eLearning, and Gilly Salmon's Five-Stage Model is a pedagogical approach to the use of discussion boards.
- Cognitive perspective focuses on the cognitive processes involved in learning as well as how the brain works.
- Emotional perspective focuses on the emotional aspects of learning, like motivation, engagement, fun, etc.
- Behavioural perspective focuses on the skills and behavioural outcomes of the learning process. Role-playing and application to on-the-job settings.
- Contextual perspective focuses on the environmental and social aspects which can stimulate learning. Interaction with other people, collaborative discovery and the importance of peer support as well as pressure.
- Mode Neutral Convergence or promotion of 'transmodal' learning where online and classroom learners can coexist within one learning environment thus encouraging interconnectivity and the harnessing of collective intelligence.

Reusability, Standards and Learning Objects

Much effort has been put into the technical reuse of electronically-based teaching materials and in particular creating or re-using Learning Objects. These are self contained units that are properly tagged with keywords, or other metadata, and often stored in an XML file format. Creating a course requires putting together a sequence of learning objects. There are both proprietary and open, non-commercial and commercial, peer-reviewed repositories of learning objects such as the Merlot repository. A common standard format for e-learning content is SCORM whilst other specifications allow for the transporting of "learning objects" (Schools Framework) or categorizing metadata (LOM).

These standards themselves are early in the maturity process with the oldest being 8 years old. They are also relatively vertical specific: SIF is primarily pK-12, LOM is primarily Corp, Military and Higher Ed, and SCORM is primarily Military and Corp with some Higher Ed. PESC- the Post-Secondary Education Standards Council- is also making headway in developing standards and learning objects for the Higher Ed space, while SIF is beginning to seriously turn towards Instructional and Curriculum learning objects.

In the US pK12 space there are a host of content standards that are critical as well- the NCES data standards are a prime example. Each state government's content standards and achievement benchmarks are critical metadata for linking e-learning objects in that space.

An excellent example of e-learning that relates to knowledge management and reusability is Navy E-Learning, which is available to Active Duty, Retired, or Disable Military members. This on-line tool provides certificate courses to enrich the user in various subjects related to military training and civilian skill sets. The e-learning system not only provides learning objectives, but also evaluates the progress of the student and credit can be earned toward higher learning institutions. This reuse is an excellent example of knowledge retention and the cyclical process of knowledge transfer and use of data and records.

The network structure is defined within the GSM standards. Additionally each interface between the different elements of the GSM network is also defined. This facilitates the information interchanges can take place. It also enables to a large degree that network elements from different manufacturers can be used. However as many of these interfaces were not fully defined until after many networks had been deployed, the level of standardisation may not be quite as high as many people might like.

- Um interface The "air" or radio interface standard that is used for exchanges between a mobile (ME) and a base station (BTS / BSC). For signalling, a modified version of the ISDN LAPD, known as LAPDm is used.
- Abis interface This is a BSS internal interface linking the BSC and a BTS, and it has not been totally

standardised. The Abis interface allows control of the radio equipment and radio frequency allocation in the BTS.

- A interface The A interface is used to provide communication between the BSS and the MSC. The interface carries information to enable the channels, timeslots and the like to be allocated to the mobile equipments being serviced by the BSSs. The messaging required within the network to enable handover etc to be undertaken is carried over the interface.
- B interface The B interface exists between the MSC and the VLR . It uses a protocol known as the MAP/B protocol. As most VLRs are collocated with an MSC, this makes the interface purely an "internal" interface. The interface is used whenever the MSC needs access to data regarding a MS located in its area.
- C interface The C interface is located between the HLR and a GMSC or a SMS-G. When a call originates from outside the network, i.e. from the PSTN or another mobile network it ahs to pass through the gateway so that routing information required to complete the call may be gained. The protocol used for communication is MAP/C, the letter "C" indicating that the protocol is used for the "C" interface. In addition to this, the MSC may optionally forward billing information to the HLR after the call is completed and cleared down.
- D interface The D interface is situated between the VLR and HLR. It uses the MAP/D protocol to exchange the data related to the location of the ME and to the management of the subscriber.
- E interface The E interface provides communication between two MSCs. The E interface exchanges data related to handover between the anchor and relay MSCs using the MAP/E protocol.

- F interface The F interface is used between an MSC and EIR. It uses the MAP/F protocol. The communications along this interface are used to confirm the status of the IMEI of the ME gaining access to the network.
- G interface The G interface interconnects two VLRs of different MSCs and uses the MAP/G protocol to transfer subscriber information, during e.g. a location update procedure.
- H interface The H interface exists between the MSC the SMS-G. It transfers short messages and uses the MAP/H protocol.
- I interface The I interface can be found between the MSC and the ME. Messages exchanged over the I interface are relayed transparently through the BSS.

Although the interfaces for the GSM cellular system may not be as rigorouly defined as many might like, they do at least provide a large element of the definition required, enabling the functionality of GSM network entities to be defined sufficiently.

COMMAND-LINE INTERFACE

A command-line interface (CLI) is a mechanism for interacting with a computer operating system or software by typing commands to perform specific tasks. This text-only interface contrasts with the use of a mouse pointer with a graphical user interface (GUI) to click on options, or menus on a text user interface (TUI) to select options. This method of instructing a computer to perform a given task is referred to as "entering" a command: the system waits for the user to conclude the submitting of the text command by pressing the "Enter" key (a descendant of the "carriage return" key of a typewriter keyboard). A command-line interpreter then receives, parses, and executes the requested user command. The command-line interpreter may be run in a text terminal or in a terminal emulator window as a remote shell client such as PuTTY. Upon completion, the command usually returns output to the user in the form of text lines on the CLI. This output may be an answer if the command was a question, or otherwise a summary of the operation.

The concept of command line interface orginated when teletype writer were connected to computers in the 1950s, and offered results on demand, compared to batch oriented mechanical punched card input technology. Dedicated text-based CRT terminals followed, with faster interaction and more information visible at one time, then graphical terminals enriched the visual display of information. Currently personal computers encapsulate all three functions (batch processing, CLI, GUI) in software.

The CLI continues to co-evolve with GUIs like those provided by Microsoft Windows, Mac OS and the X Window System. In some applications, such as MATLAB and AutoCAD, a CLI is integrated with the GUI, with some benefits of both. A CLI is used whenever a large vocabulary of commands or queries, coupled with a wide (or arbitrary) range of options, can be entered more rapidly as text than with a pure GUI. This is typically the case with operating system command shells. CLIs are used by systems with insufficient resources to support a graphical user interface. Some computer language systems (such as Python, Forth, LISP and many dialects of BASIC) provide an interactive command-line mode to allow for experimentation.

CLIs are often used by programmers and system administrators, in engineering and scientific environments, and by technically advanced personal computer users. CLIs are also popular among people with visual disability, since the commands and feedbacks can be displayed using Refreshable Braille displays.

A program that implements such a text interface is often called a command-line interpreter or shell. Examples include the various Unix shells (sh, ksh, csh, tcsh, bash, etc.), the historical CP/M CCP, and MS-DOS/IBM-DOS's COMMAND.COM, the latter two based heavily on DEC's RSX and RSTS CLIs.

In November 2006, Microsoft released version 1.0 of Windows PowerShell (formerly codenamed Monad), which combined features of traditional Unix shells with their object-oriented .NET Framework. MinGW and Cygwin are open-source packages for Windows that offer a Unix-like CLI. Microsoft provides MKS Inc.'s ksh implementation MKS Korn shell for Windows through their Services for UNIX add-on.

The latest versions of the Macintosh operating system are based on a variation of Unix called Darwin. On these computers, users can access a Unix-like command-line interface called Terminal found in the Applications Utilities folder. (This terminal uses bash by default.) Some applications provide both a CLI and a GUI. The engineering/scientific numerical computation package MATLAB provides no GUI for some calculations, but the CLI can handle any calculation. The three-dimensional-modelling program Rhinoceros 3D provides a CLI as well as a distinct scripting language. In some computing environments, such as the Oberon or Smalltalk user interface, most of the text which appears on the screen may be used for giving commands.

Anatomy of a Shell CLI

A CLI can generally be considered as consisting of syntax and semantics. The syntax is the grammar that all commands must follow. In the case of operating systems (OS), MS-DOS and Unix each define their own set of rules that all commands must follow. In the case of embedded systems, each vendor, such as Nortel, Juniper Networks or Cisco Systems, defines their own proprietary set of rules that all commands within their CLI conform to. These rules also dictate how a user navigates through the system of commands. The semantics define what sort of operations are possible, on what sort of data these operations can be performed, and how the grammar represents these operations and data—the symbolic meaning in the syntax.

Two different CLIs may agree on either syntax or semantics, but it is only when they agree on both that they can be considered sufficiently similar to allow users to use both CLIs without needing to learn anything, as well as to enable re-use of scripts. A simple CLI will display a prompt, accept a "command line" typed by the user terminated by the Enter key, then execute the specified command and provide textual display of results or error messages. Advanced CLIs will validate, interpret and parameter-expand the command line before executing the specified command, and optionally capture or redirect its output.

Unlike a button or menu item in a GUI, a command line is typically self-documenting, stating exactly what the user wants done. In addition, command lines usually include many defaults that can be changed to customize the results. Useful command lines can be saved by assigning a character string or alias to represent the full command, or several commands can be grouped to perform a more complex sequence — for instance, compile the program, install it, and run it — creating a single entity, called a command procedure or script which itself can be treated as a command. These advantages mean that a user must figure out a complex command or series of commands only once, because they can be saved, to be used again.

The commands given to a CLI shell are often in one of the following forms are give below :

- [doSomething] [how] [toFiles]
- [doSomething] [how] [sourceFile] [destinationFile]
- [doSomething] [how] < [inputFile] > [outputFile]
- [doSomething] [how] | [doSomething] [how] | [do Something] [how] > [outputFile]

doSomething is, in effect, a verb, how an adverb (for example, should the command be executed "verbosely" or "quietly") and toFiles an object or objects (typically one or more files) on which the command should act. The '>' in the third example is a redirection operator, telling the command-line interpreter to send the output of the command not to the screen but to the file named on the right of the '>'. This will overwrite the file. Using '>>' will redirect the output and append it to the file. Another redirection operator is the pipe ('|'), which tells the CLI to use the output of one command as the input to the next command; this "operator-stream" mechanism can be very powerful.

CLI and Resource Protection

In some CLIs, the commands issued are not coupled to any conceptual place within a command hierarchy. A user can specify relative or absolute paths to any command or data. Examples of this include MS-DOS, Windows, and UNIX, which provide forms of a change directory command which allows access to any directory in the system. In some systems, protection of resources is provided by a system of resource ownership by privileged groups, and password-protected user accounts which are members of specific groups.

MS-DOS provides no such resource protection, nor do versions of Windows prior to the Windows NT family. (Both of these were designed as single-user systems, where it was assumed that the owner would simply not allow people that she/he did not fully trust to have physical access to the computer at all. UNIX, by contrast, originated as a time-sharing system in corporate and university environments.) Other CLIs (such as those in network routers) limit the set of commands that a user can perform to a subset, determined by location within a command hierarchy, grouped by association with security, system, interface, etc. The location within this hierarchy and the options available are often referred to as a mode. In these systems the user might traverse through a series of sub-hierarchies, each with their own subset of commands. For example, if the CLI had two modes called interface and system, the user would enter the word 'interface' at the command prompt and then enter an interface mode, where a certain subset of commands and data are available. At this point system commands are not accessible and would not be accessible until the user explicitly exits the interface mode and enters the system mode.

Command Prompt

A command prompt (or just prompt) is a sequence of (one or more) characters used in a command-line interface to indicate readiness to accept commands. Its intent is to literally prompt the user to take action. A prompt usually ends with one of the characters $, %, #, :, > and often includes other information, such as the path of the current working directory.

On many Unix system and derivative systems, it is common for the prompt to end in a $ or % character if the user is a normal user, but in a # character if the user is a superuser ("root" in Unix terminology). It is common for prompts to be modifiable by the user. Depending on the environment, they may include colors, special characters, and other elements like the current time, in order, for instance, to make the prompt more informative or visually pleasing, to distinguish sessions on various machines, or to indicate the current level of nesting of commands.

In DOS's COMMAND.COM and in the Windows NT's command-line interpreter cmd.exe the prompt is modifiable by issuing a prompt command or by changing the value of the %PROMPT% environment variable. The default of most modern systems, the C:\> style is obtained, for instance, with "prompt PG". The default of older DOS systems, C> is obtained by just "prompt", although on some systems this produces the newer C:\> style; on those systems "prompt NG" can be used to switch to the older style.

On many Unix systems, the $PS1 variable can be used, although other variables also may have an impact on the prompt (depending on what shell is being used). In the bash shell, a prompt of the form

[time] user@host: work_dir $

could be set by issuing the command

export PS1='[\t] \u@\H: \W $'

In zsh the $RPROMPT variable controls an optional "prompt" on the right hand side of the display. It is not a real prompt in that the location of text entry does not change. It is used to display information on the same line as the prompt, but right justified.

In RISC OS, the command prompt is a '*' symbol, and thus (OS)CLI commands are often referred to as "star commands".It is also possible to access the same commands from other command lines (such as the BBC BASIC command line), by preceding the command with a '*'.

Arguments

A command-line argument or parameter is an argument sent to a program being called. In principle a program can take many command-line arguments, the meaning and importance of which depend entirely upon the program.

When a command processor is active a program is typically invoked by typing its name followed by command-line arguments (if any). For example, in Unix and Unix-like environments, an example of a command-line argument is:

rm file.s

"file.s" is a command-line argument which tells the program rm to remove the file "file.s".

Programming languages such as C, C++ and Java allow a program to interpret the command-line arguments by handling them as string parameters in the main function.

Command-line option

A command line option or simply option (also known as a command line parameter, or sometimes flag or switch) modifies the operation of a computer program; the effect is determined by the programmer, and can be anything desired. Parameters follow the program pathname on the command line, separated by spaces. A space before the first parameter is not always required.

For example, in the OpenVMS operating system, the command directory is used to list the files inside a directory. By default—that is, when the user simply types directory—it will list only the names of the files. By appending the option /owner (to form the command directory/owner), the user can instruct the directory command to also display the ownership of the files.

The format of switches varies widely between operating systems. In most cases the syntax is by convention rather than an operating system requirement; the entire command line is simply a string passed to a program, which can process it in any way the programmer wants; a few characters such as, typically, the pipe or vertical bar character "|", have reserved meanings and are prohibited. For example, most operating systems could in principle handle

NonStandardProgram +83 Multi word terminated by numeric 12 :x -a

Sometimes different programs use different syntax in the same operating system. For example:

- Switches may be indicated by -, /, or either.
- Parameters may or may not be case-sensitive
- Sometimes switches and related arguments are run together, sometimes separated by whitespace, and sometimes by a character, typically : or =. Thus "Prog -fFilename", "Prog -f Filename", "Prog -f:Filename", "Prog -f=Filename".
- Some programs allow single-character switches to be combined; others do not. -fA may be the same as -f -A, may be incorrect, or may even be a valid but different parameter.

Given this variability it is impossible to know a priori what arguments a program can recognise, and what syntax to use without consulting program documentation. It is usual for a program to display a brief summary of its parameters when invoked with a command-line which is typically one of: no parameters; ?; -?; -h; / ?; /h; -help; or —help. Entering a program name without parameters in the hope that it will display parameters can be hazardous, as some programs and scripts execute without further ado.

The Space character

In many areas of computing, particularly in the command line, the space character can cause problems as it has two distinct and incompatible functions: as part of a command or parameter, or as a parameter or name separator. Ambiguity can be prevented either by prohibiting embedded spaces, or by enclosing a name with embedded spaces between quote characters. For example

Long path/Long program name Parameter one Parameter two...

is ambiguous (is "program name" part of the program name, or two parameters?);

Long_path/Long_program_name Parameter_one Parameter_two ...,

LongPath/LongProgramName ParameterOne ParameterTwo...

and

"Long path/Long program name" "Parameter one" "Parameter two" ...

are not. Unix-based operating systems tend not to use embedded spaces; Microsoft Windows tends to use quotes.

A command-line interpreter also called a command line shell, command language interpreter, or abbreviated as CLI is a computer program that reads lines of text entered by a user and interprets them in the context of a given operating system or programming language.

Command-line interpreters allow users to issue various commands in a very efficient (and often terse) way. This requires the user to know the names of the commands and their parameters, and the syntax of the language that is interpreted.

History

From the 1960s onwards, user interaction with computers was primarily by means of command-line interfaces, initially on machines like the ASR-33 Teletype, but then on early CRT-based computer terminals such as the VT52. All of these devices were purely text based, with no ability to display graphic or pictures.For business application programs, text-based menus were used, but for more general interaction the command line was the interface.

From the early 1970s the Unix operating system on minicomputers pioneered the concept of a powerful command-line environment, which Unix called the "shell", with the ability to "pipe" the output of one command in as input to another, and to save and re-run strings of commands as "shell scripts" which acted like custom commands.

The command-line was also the main interface for the early home computers such as the Commodore PET, Apple II and BBC Micro - almost always in the form of a BASIC interpreter. When more powerful business orientated microcomputers arrived with CP/M and later MSDOS computers such as the IBM PC, the command-line began to borrow some of the syntax and features of the Unix shells such as globbing and piping of output. The command-line was first seriously challenged by the new GUI approach in 1984 with the Apple Macintosh 128K, but it took until 1990 and Windows 3.0 before most users converted. While most computer users now use a GUI almost exclusively, more advanced users have access to powerful command-line environments:

- MS Windows users have the classic cmd.exe "DOS"-like environment, but also the new PowerShell interfaces
- Appleand Linux users have the classic Unix bash shell
- Routers from CiscoJuniper Networks and many others are commonly configured from the command-line.

Scripting

Most command-line interpreters support scripting, to various extents. (They are, after all, interpreters of an interpreted programming language, albeit that in many cases the language is unique to the particular command-line interpreter.) They will interpret scripts (variously termed shell scripts or batch files) written in the language that they interpret. Some command-line interpreters also incorporate the interpreter engines of other languages, such as REXX, in addition to their own, allowing the executing of scripts, in those languages, directly within the command-line interpreter itself.

Conversely, scripting programming languages, in particular those with an eval function (such as REXX, Perl, Python, Ruby or Jython), can be used to implement command-line interpreters. For a few operating systems, most notably DOS, such a command interpreter provides a more flexible command line interface than the one supplied. In other cases, such a command interpreter can present a highly customised user interface employing the user interface and input/output facilities of the language.

References

1. Borgman C (1996). "Why are Online Catalogs Still Hard to Use?". Journal of the American Society for Information Science 47 (7): 499.
2. Husain R & Alam Ansari M (2006). "From Card Catalog to Web OPACs". DESIDOC Bulletin of Information Technology 26 (2): 41–7.
3. Borgman C (1996), 493-503.
4. Antelman K, Lynema E, Pace AK (2006). "Toward a Twenty-First Century Library Catalog". Information Technology & Libraries 25 (3): 128–139.
5. Breeding M (2008). "Open Source Library Automation". Library Technology Reports 44 (8): 5–10.
6. "WorldCat facts and statistics". Online Computer Library Center. 2009. http://www.oclc.org/ca/en/worldcat/statistics/default.htm. Retrieved November 4, 2009.

1. RISC OS 3 User Guide, Part 3: Outside the desktop (page 125) Published by Acorn Computers Limited, ISBN1 85250 124 2, Edition 2 Part number 0496,075 Issue 1 March 1992
2. With the exception of ASCII art
3. via Finder, Applications, Utilities, Terminal.app
4. "The Cisco IOS command-line interface (CLI) is the primary user interface..."

5. "...the software that you use whenever you access the router..."
6. Tavangarian D., Leypold M., Nölting K., Röser M.,(2004). Is e-learning the Solution for Individual Learning? Journal of e-learning, 2004.
7. EC (2000). Communication from the Commission: E-Learning – Designing "Tejas at Niit" tomorrow's education. Brussels: European Commission
8. Nagy, A. (2005). The Impact of E-Learning, in: Bruck, P.A.; Buchholz, A.; Karssen, Z.; Zerfass, A. (Eds). E-Content: Technologies and Perspectives for the European Market. Berlin: Springer-Verlag, pp. 79–96
9. "Sloan Consortium"
10. Allen, I. E. and Seaman, J. (2008) Staying the Course: Online Education in the United States, 2008 Needham MA: Sloan Consortium
11. Allen, I.E. and Seaman, J. (2003) Sizing the Opportunity: The Quality and Extent of Online Education in the United States, 2002 and 2003 Wellesley, MA: The Sloan Consortium
12. Ambient Insight Research (2009) US Self-paced e-Learning Market Monroe WA: Ambient Insight Research
13. Hebert, D. G. (2007). "Five Challenges and Solutions in Online Music Teacher Education". Research and Issues in Music Education.
14. Graziadei, W. D., et al., 1997. Building Asynchronous and Synchronous Teaching-Learning Environments: Exploring a Course/Classroom Management System Solution
15. Karrer, T (2006) What is eLearning 2.0? Elearningtech.blogspot.com
16. Karrer, T (2007) Understanding eLearning 2.0. Learning circuit

17. Downes, S (2005) E-Learning 2.0. Downes.ca
18. Redecker, Christine (2009). "Review of Learning 2.0 Practices: Study on the Impact of Web 2.0 Innovations on Education and Training in Europe". JRC Scientific and technical report. (EUR 23664 EN – 2009).
19. Karrer, T (2008) Corporate Long Tail Learning and Attention Crisis Elearningtech.blogspot.com
20. Seely Brown, John; Adler, Richard P. (2008). "Minds on Fire:Open Education, the Long Tail, and Learning 2.0". Educause review (January/February 2008): 16–32. http://net.educause.edu/ir/library/pdf/ERM0811.pdf.
21. Hiltz, S. (1990) 'Evaluating the Virtual Classroom', in Harasim, L. (ed.) Online Education: Perspectives on a New Environment New York: Praeger, pp. 133–169
22. Mason. R. and Kaye, A. (1989) Mindweave: Communication, Computers and Distance Education Oxford, UK: Pergamon Press
23. Bates, A. (2005) Technology, e-Learning and Distance Education London: Routledge
24. Harasim, L., Hiltz, S., Teles, L. and Turoff, M. (1995) Learning Networks: A Field Guide to Teaching and Learning Online Cambridge, MA: MIT Press.
25. WebEx Education Platform
26. Dunlap, J. C., & Lowenthal, P. R. (2009). Horton hears a tweet. EDUCAUSE Quarterly, 32(4). Retrieved from http://www.educause.edu/EDUCAUSE+Quarterly/EDUCAUSEQuarterlyMagazineVolum/HortonHearsaTweet/192955
27. Crane, Beverley E. "Using Web 2.0 Tools in the k-12 Classroom" Neal-Shuman Publishers Inc., 2009, p.3

Chapter–6

Role of Search Interfaces with Applications

Pronounced see-dee-rom. Short for Compact Disc-Read-Only Memory, a type of optical disk capable of storing large amounts of data — up to 1GB, although the most common size is 650MB (megabytes). A single CD-ROM has the storage capacity of 700 floppy disks, enough memory to store about 300,000 text pages.

CD-ROMs are stamped by the vendor, and once stamped, they cannot be erased and filled with new data. To read a CD, you need a CD-ROM player. All CD-ROMs conform to a standard size and format, so you can load any type of CD-ROM into any CD-ROM player. In addition, CD-ROM players are capable of playing audio CDs, which share the same technology.

CD-ROMs are particularly well-suited to information that requires large storage capacity. This includes large software applications that support color. graphics, sound, and especially video.

A CD-ROM is a pre-pressed compact disc that contains data accessible to, but not writable by, a computer for data storage and music playback. The 1985 "Yellow Book" standard developed by Sony and Philips adapted the format to hold any form of binary data. CD-ROMs are popularly used to distribute computer software, including video games and multimedia applications, though any data can be stored (up to the capacity limit of a disc). Some CDs hold both computer data and audio with the latter capable of being played on a CD player, while data (such as software or digital video) is only usable on a computer (such as ISO 9660 format PC CD-ROMs). These are called enhanced CDs.

Although many people use lowercase letters in this acronym, proper presentation is in all capital letters with a hyphen between CD and ROM. At the time of the technology's introduction it had more capacity than computer hard drives common at the time. The reverse is now true, with hard drives far exceeding CDs, DVDs and Blu-ray, though some experimental descendants of it such as HVDs may have more space and faster data rates than today's biggest hard drive.

A Compact Disc (also known as a CD) is an optical disc used to store digital data. It was originally developed to store and playback sound recordings exclusively, but later expanded to encompass data storage CD-ROM, write-once audio and data storage CD-R, rewritable media CD-RW, Video Compact Discs (VCD), Super Video Compact Discs (SVCD), PhotoCD, PictureCD, CD-i, and Enhanced CD. Audio CDs and audio CD players have been commercially available since October 1982.

Standard CDs have a diameter of 120 millimetres (4.7 in) and can hold up to 80 minutes of uncompressed audio (700 MB of data). The Mini CD has various diameters ranging from 60 to 80 millimetres (2.4 to 3.1 in); they are sometimes used for CD singles, storing up to 24 minutes of audio or delivering device drivers. CD-ROMs and CD-Rs remain widely used technologies in the computer industry. The CD and its extensions are successful: in 2004, worldwide sales of CD audio, CD-ROM, and CD-R reached about 30 billion discs. By 2007, 200 billion CDs had been sold worldwide.Compact Discs are increasingly being replaced or supplemented by other forms of digital distribution and storage, such as downloading and flash drives, with audio CD sales dropping nearly 50% from their peak in 2000.

The Compact Disc is a spin-off of Laserdisc technology. Sony first publicly demonstrated an optical digital audio disc in September

1976. In September 1978 they demonstrated an optical digital audio disc with a 150 minute playing time, and with specifications of 44,056 Hz sampling rate, 16-bit linear resolution, cross-interleaved error correction code, that were similar to those of the Compact Disc introduced in 1982. Technical details of Sony's digital audio disc were presented during the 62nd AES Convention, held on March 13–16, 1979, in Brussels.

On March 8, 1979 Philips publicly demonstrated a prototype of an optical digital audio disc at a press conference called "Philips Introduce Compact Disc"in Eindhoven, Netherlands. On March 6, 2009, Philips received an IEEE Milestone with the following citation: "On 8 March 1979, N.V. Philips' Gloeilampenfabrieken demonstrated for the international press a Compact Disc Audio Player. The demonstration showed that it is possible by using digital optical recording and playback to reproduce audio signals with superb stereo quality. This research at Philips established the technical standard for digital optical recording systems."

Later in 1979, Sony and Philips Consumer Electronics (Philips) set up a joint task force of engineers to design a new digital audio disc. Led by Kees Schouhamer Immink and Toshitada Doi, the research pushed forward laser and optical disc technology that began independently by Philips and Sony in 1977 and 1975, respectively.

After a year of experimentation and discussion, the taskforce produced the Red Book, the Compact Disc standard. Philips contributed the general manufacturing process, based on video Laserdisc technology. Philips also contributed eight-to-fourteen modulation (EFM), which offers both a long playing time and a high resilience against disc defects such as scratches and fingerprints, while Sony contributed the error-correction method, CIRC.

The Compact Disc Story, told by a former member of the taskforce, gives background information on the many technical decisions made, including the choice of the sampling frequency, playing time, and disc diameter. The taskforce consisted of around four to eight persons, though according to Philips, the Compact Disc was thus "invented collectively by a large group of people working as a team." The first test CD was pressed in Langenhagen near Hannover, Germany, by the Polydor Pressing Operations plant. The disc contained a recording of Richard Strauss's Eine Alpensinfonie (in English, An Alpine Symphony), played by the Berlin Philharmonic and conducted by Herbert von Karajan. The first public demonstration was on the BBC television program Tomorrow's World when The Bee Gees' album Living Eyes (1981) was played. In August 1982 the real pressing was ready to begin in the new factory, not far from the place where Emil Berliner had produced his first gramophone record 93 years earlier. By now, Deutsche Grammophon, Berliner's company and the publisher of the Strauss recording, had become a part of PolyGram. The first CD to be manufactured at the new factory was The Visitors (1981) by ABBA. The first album to be released on CD was Billy Joel's 52nd Street, that reached the market alongside Sony's CD player CDP-101 on October 1, 1982 in Japan.

DIGITAL AUDIO REVOLUTION

In the united states and other markets, early years on March 2, 1983 CD players and discs (16 titles from CBS Records) were released in the United States and other markets. This event is often seen as the "Big Bang" of the digital audio revolution. The new audio disc was enthusiastically received, especially in the early-adopting classical music and audiophile communities and its handling quality received particular praise. As the price of players gradually came down, the CD began to gain popularity in the larger popular and rock music markets. The first artist to sell a million copies on CD was Dire Straits, with its 1985 album Brothers in Arms. The first major artist to have his entire catalogue converted to CD was David Bowie, whose 15 studio albums were made available by RCA Records in February 1985, along with four Greatest Hits albums. In 1988, 400 million CDs were manufactured by 50 pressing plants around the world.

The CD was planned to be the successor of the gramophone record for playing music, rather than primarily as a data storage medium. From its origins as a musical format, CDs have grown to encompass other applications. In June 1985, the computer readable CD-ROM (read-only memory) and, in 1990, CD-Recordable were introduced, also developed by both Sony and Philips. The CD's compact format has largely replaced the audio cassette player in new automobile applications, and recordable CDs are an alternative to tape for recording music and copying music albums without defects introduced in compression used in other digital recording methods. Other newer video formats such as DVD and Blu-ray have used the same form factor as CDs, and video players can usually play audio CDs as well. With the advent of the MP3 in the 2000s, the sales of CDs has dropped in seven out of the last eight years. In 2008, large label CD sales dropped 20%, although independent and DIY music sales may be tracking better according to figures released March 30, 2009.

Physical Details

A. A polycarbonate disc layer has the data encoded by using bumps.

B. A shiny layer reflects the laser.

C. A layer of lacquer protects the shiny layer.

D. Artwork is screen printed on the top of the disc.

E. A laser beam reads the CD and is reflected back to a sensor, which converts it into electronic data

A CD is made from 1.2 millimetres (0.047 in) thick, polycarbonate plastic and weighs 15–20 grams. From the center outward, components are: the center spindle hole (15 mm), the first-transition area (clamping ring), the clamping area (stacking ring), the second-transition area (mirror band), the program (data) area, and the rim. The inner program area occupies a radius from 25 to 58 mm. A thin layer of aluminium or, more rarely, gold is applied to the surface making it reflective. The metal is protected by a film of lacquer normally spin coated directly on the reflective layer. The label is printed on the lacquer layer, usually by screen printing or offset printing.

CD one stored as a series of tiny indentations known as "pits", encoded in a spiral track moulded into the top of the polycarbonate layer. The areas between pits are known as "lands". Each pit is approximately 100 nm deep by 500 nm wide, and varies from 850 nm to 3.5 μm in length. The distance between the tracks, the pitch, is 1.6 μm.

Scanning velocity is 1.2–1.4 m/s (constant linear velocity) – equivalent to approximately 500 rpm at the inside of the disc, and approximately 200 rpm at the outside edge. (A disc played from beginning to end slows down during playback.) The program area is 86.05 cm^2 and the length of the recordable spiral is (86.05 cm^2 / 1.6 μm) = 5.38 km. With a scanning speed of 1.2 m/s, the playing time is 74 minutes, or 650 MB of data on a CD-ROM. A disc with data packed slightly more densely is tolerated by most players (though some old ones fail). Using a linear velocity of 1.2 m/s and a track pitch of 1.5 μm yields a playing time of 80 minutes, or a data capacity of 700 MB. Even higher capacities on non-standard discs (up to 99 minutes) are available at least as recordables, but generally the tighter the tracks are squeezed, the worse the compatibility.

A CD is read by focusing a 780 nm wavelength (near infrared) semiconductor laser through the bottom of the polycarbonate layer. The change in height between pits and lands results in a difference in the way the light is reflected. By measuring the intensity change with a photodiode, the data can be read from the disc.

The pits and lands themselves do not directly represent the zeros and ones of binary data. Instead, non-return-to-zero, inverted encoding is used: a change from pit to land or land to pit indicates a one, while no change indicates a series of zeros. There must be at least two and no more than ten zeros between each one, which is defined by the length of the pit. This in turn is decoded by reversing the eight-to-fourteen modulation used in mastering the disc, and then reversing the Cross-Interleaved Reed-Solomon Coding, finally revealing the raw data stored on the disc.

CDs are susceptible to damage from both normal use and environmental exposure. Pits are much closer to the label side of a disc, enabling defects and contaminants on the clear side to be out of focus during playback. Consequently, CDs are more likely to suffer damage on the label side of the disk. Scratches on the clear side can be repaired by refilling them with similar refractive plastic, or by careful polishing.

DISC SHAPES AND DIAMETERS

The digital data on a CD begins at the center of the disc and proceeds toward the edge, which allows adaptation to the different size formats available. Standard CDs are available in two sizes. By far, the most common is 120 millimetres (4.7 in) in diameter, with a 74- or 80-minute audio capacity and a 650 or 700 MB data capacity. This diameter has been adopted by subsequent formats, including Super Audio CD, DVD, HD DVD, and Blu-ray Disc. 80 mm discs ("Mini CDs") were originally designed for CD singles and can hold up to 24 minutes of music or 210 MB of data but never became popular. Today, nearly every single is released on a 120 mm CD, called a Maxi single.

Logical Formats

Audio CD

The logical format of an audio CD (officially Compact Disc Digital Audio or CD-DA) is described in a document produced by the format's joint creators, Sony and Philips in 1980. The document is known colloquially as the "Red Book" after the color of its cover. The format is a two-channel 16-bit PCM encoding at a 44.1 kHz sampling rate per channel. Four-channel sound is an allowable option within the Red Book format, but has never been implemented. Monaural audio has no existing standard on a Red Book CD; mono-source material is usually presented as two identical channels on a 'stereo' track.

44.1 kHz Sample Rate

The selection of the sample rate was based primarily on the need to reproduce the audible frequency range of 20 Hz – 20 kHz. The Nyquist–Shannon sampling theorem states that a sampling rate of more than twice the maximum frequency of the signal to be recorded is needed, resulting in a required rate of at least 40 kHz.

The exact sampling rate of 44.1 kHz was inherited from a method of converting digital audio into an analog video signal for storage on U-matic video tape, which was the most affordable way to transfer data from the recording studio to the CD manufacturer at the time the CD specification was being developed. The device that converts an analog audio signal into PCM audio, which in turn is changed into an analog video signal is called a PCM adaptor.

This technology could store six samples (three samples per stereo channel) in a single horizontal line. A standard NTSC video signal has 245 usable lines per field, and 59.94 fields/s, which works out to be 44,056 samples/s/stereo channel. Similarly, PAL has 294 lines and 50 fields, which gives 44,100 samples/s/stereo channel. This system could store 14-bit samples with some error correction, or 16-bit samples with almost no error correction. There was a long debate over the use of 14-bit (Philips) or 16-bit (Sony) quantization, and 44,056 or 44,100 samples/s (Sony) or approximately 44,000 samples/s (Philips). When the Sony/Philips task force designed the Compact Disc, Philips had already developed a 14-bit D/A converter, but Sony insisted on 16-bit. In the end, 16 bits and 44.1 kilosamples per second prevailed. Philips found a way to produce 16-bit quality using its 14-bit DAC by using four times oversampling.

Storage Capacity and Playing Time

The partners aimed at a playing time of 60 minutes with a disc diameter of 100 mm (Sony) or 115 mm (Philips). Sony vice-president Norio Ôga suggested extending the capacity to 74 minutes to accommodate Wilhelm Furtwängler's recording of Ludwig van Beethoven's Symphony Number Nine from the 1951 Bayreuth Festival.

The additional 14-minute playing time subsequently required changing to a 120 mm disc. Kees Immink, Philips' chief engineer, however, denies this, claiming that the increase was motivated by technical considerations, and that even after the increase in size, the Furtwängler recording would not have fit on one of the earliest CDs. According to a Sunday Tribune interview, the story is slightly more involved. In 1979, Philips owned PolyGram, one of the world's largest distributors of music.

PolyGram had set up a large experimental CD plant in Hannover, Germany, which could produce huge numbers of CDs having, of course, a diameter of 115 mm. Sony did not yet have such a facility. If Sony had agreed on the 115-mm disc, Philips would have had a significant competitive edge in the market. Sony decided that something had to be done. The long playing time of Beethoven's Ninth Symphony imposed by Ôga was used to push Philips to accept 120 mm, so that Philips' PolyGram lost its edge on disc fabrication. The 74-minute playing time of a CD, which was longer than the 20 minutes per side typical of long-playing (LP) vinyl albums, was often used to the CD's advantage during the early years when CDs and LPs vied for commercial sales. CDs would often be released with one or more bonus tracks, enticing consumers to buy the CD for the extra material. However, attempts to combine double LPs onto one CD occasionally resulted in the opposite situation in which the CD would actually offer fewer tracks than the equivalent LP. Playing times beyond 74 minutes are achieved by decreasing track pitch beyond the original red book standard. Most players can accommodate the more closely spaced data. Christian Thielemann's live Deutsche Grammophon recording of Bruckner's Fifth with the Munich Philharmonic in 2004 clocks at 82:34.

The Kirov Orchestra recording of Pyotr Ilyich Tchaikovsky's The Nutcracker conducted by Valery Gergiev and released by Philips/PolyGram Records (catalogue number 462 114) on October

20, 1998, clocks at 81:14.Disc two of Gold (Deutche Grammophon/ Universal Classics 477 743) by Herbert von Karajan clocks in at 81:21. The Mission of Burma compilation album Mission of Burma, released in 1988 by Rykodisc, previously held the record at 80:08.

Data Structure

The smallest entity in a CD is called a frame, which consists of 33 bytes and contains six complete 16-bit stereo samples (two bytes × two channels × six samples = 24 bytes). The other nine bytes consist of eight CIRC error-correction bytes and one subcode byte, used for control and display.

Each byte is translated into a 14-bit word using eight-to-fourteen modulation, which alternates with three-bit merging words. In total there are 33 × (14 + 3) = 561 bits. A 27-bit unique synchronization word is added, so that the number of bits in a frame totals 588 (of which only 192 bits are music).

These 588-bit frames are in turn grouped into sectors. Each sector contains 98 frames, totaling 98 × 24 = 2352 bytes of music. The CD is played at a speed of 75 sectors per second, which results in 176,400 bytes per second. Divided by two channels and two bytes per sample, this results in a sample rate of 44,100 samples per second.

For CD-Rom data disc the physical frame and sector sizes are the same. Since error concealment cannot be applied to non-audio data in case the CIRC error correction fails to recover the user data, a third layer of error correction is defined, reducing the payload to 2048 bytes per sector for the Mode-1 CD-ROM format.

To increase the data-rate for Video CD, Mode-2 CD-ROM, the third layer has been omitted, increasing the payload to 2336 user-available bytes per sector, only 16 bytes (for synchronization and header data) less than available in Red-Book audio.

Frame

For the Red Book stereo audio CD, the time format is commonly measured in minutes, seconds and frames (mm:ss:ff), where one frame corresponds to one sector, or 1/75th of a second of stereo sound. In this context, the term frame is erroneously applied in editing applications and does not denote the physical frame described above. In editing and extracting, the frame is the smallest addressable time interval for an audio CD, meaning that track start and end positions can only be defined in 1/75 second steps.

Logical Structure

The largest entity on a CD is called a track. A CD can contain up to 99 tracks (including a data track for combined mode discs). Each track can in turn have up to 100 indexes, though players which handle this feature are rarely found outside of pro audio, particularly radio broadcasting. The vast majority of songs are recorded under index 1, with the pre-gap being index 0.

Sometimes hidden tracks are placed at the end of the last track of the disc, often using index 2 or 3. This is also the case with some discs offering "101 sound effects", with 100 and 101 being indexed as two and three on track 99.

The index, if used, is occasionally put on the track listing as a decimal part of the track number, such as 99.2 or 99.3. (Information Society's Hack was one of very few CD releases to do this, following a release with an equally obscure CD+G feature.) The track and index structure of the CD carried forward to the DVD as title and chapter, respectively.

Manufacturing Tolerances

Current manufacturing processes allow an audio CD to contain up to 80 minutes (variable from one replication plant to another) without requiring the content creator to sign a waiver releasing the plant owner from responsibility if the CD produced is marginally or entirely unreadable by some playback equipment. Thus, in current practice, maximum CD playing time has crept higher by reducing minimum engineering tolerances; by and large, this has not unacceptably reduced reliability.

CD-Text

CD-Text is an extension of the Red Book specification for audio CD that allows for storage of additional text information (e.g., album name, song name, artist) on a standards-compliant audio CD. The information is stored either in the lead-in area of the CD, where there is roughly five kilobytes of space available, or in the subcode channels R to W on the disc, which can store about 31 megabytes.

CD + Graphics

Compact Disc + Graphics (CD+G) is a special audio Compact Disc that contains graphics data in addition to the audio data on the disc. The disc can be played on a regular audio CD player, but when played on a special CD+G player, can output a graphics signal (typically, the CD+G player is hooked up to a television set or a computer monitor); these graphics are almost exclusively used to display lyrics on a television set for karaoke performers to sing along with. The CD+G format takes advantage of the channels R through W. These six bits store the graphics information.

CD + Extended Graphics

Compact Disc + Extended Graphics (CD+EG, also known as CD+XG) is an improved variant of the Compact Disc + Graphics (CD+G) format. Like CD+G, CD+EG utilizes basic CD-ROM features to display text and video information in addition to the music being played. This extra data is stored in subcode channels R-W. Very few, if any, CD+EG discs have been published.

Super Audio CD

Super Audio CD (SACD) is a high-resolution read-only optical audio disc format that provides much higher fidelity digital audio reproduction than the Red Book. Introduced in 1999, it was developed by Sony and Philips, the same companies that created the Red Book. SACD was in a format war with DVD-Audio, but neither has replaced audio CDs.

In contrast to DVD-Audio, the SACD format has the feature of being able to produce hybrid discs; these discs contain the SACD audio stream as well as a standard audio CD layer which is playable in standard CD players, thus making them backward compatible.

CD-MIDI

CD-MIDI is a format used to store music-performance data which upon playback is performed by electronic instruments that synthesize the audio. Hence, unlike Red Book, these recordings are not audio.

CD-ROM

The compact disc was a medium used purely of audio in the first few years of its exitsence. However, in 1985 the Yellow Book CD-ROM standard was established by Sony and Philips, which defined a non-volatile optical data computer data storage medium using the same physical format as audio Compact Discs, readable by a computer with a CD-ROM drive.

Video CD (VCD)

Video CD (VCD, View CD, and Compact Disc digital video) is a standard digital format for storing video media on a CD. VCDs are playable in dedicated VCD players, most modern DVD-Video players, personal computers, and some video game consoles.

The VCD standard was created in 1993 by Sony, Philips, Matsushita, and JVC and is referred to as the White Book standard.

Overall picture quality is intended to be comparable to VHS video. Poorly compressed VCD video can sometimes be lower quality than VHS video, but VCD exhibits block artifacts rather than analog noise, and does not deteriorate further with each use, which may be preferable.

352x240 (or SIF) resolution was chosen because it is half the vertical, and half the horizontal resolution of NTSC video. 352x288 is similarly one quarter PAL/SECAM resolution. This approximates the (overall) resolution of an analog VHS tape, which, although it has double the number of (vertical) scan lines, has a much lower horizontal resolution.

Super Video CD

Super Video CD (Super Video Compact Disc or SVCD) is a format used for storing video media on standard Compact Discs. SVCD was intended as a successor to VCD and an alternative to DVD-Video, and falls somewhere between both in terms of technical capability and picture quality.

SVCD has two-thirds the resolution of DVD, and over 2.7 times the resolution of VCD. One CD-R disc can hold up to 60 minutes of standard quality SVCD-format video. While no specific limit on SVCD video length is mandated by the specification, one must lower the video bit rate, and therefore quality, in order to accommodate very long videos. It is usually difficult to fit much more than 100 minutes of video onto one SVCD without incurring significant quality loss, and many hardware players are unable to play video with an instantaneous bit rate lower than 300 to 600 kilobits per second.

Photo CD

Photo CD is a system designed by Kodak for digitizing and storing photos on a CD. Launched in 1992, the discs were designed to hold nearly 100 high quality images, scanned prints and slides using special proprietary encoding. Photo CD discs are defined in the Beige Book and conform to the CD-ROM XA and CD-i Bridge specifications as well.

They are intended to play on CD-i players, Photo CD players and any computer with the suitable software irrespective of the operating system. The images can also be printed out on photographic paper with a special Kodak machine. This format is not to be confused with Kodak Picture CD, which is a consumer product in CD-ROM format.

CD-i

The Philips "Green Book" specifies the standard for interactive multimedia Compact Discs designed for CD-i players. This format is unusual because it hides the initial tracks which contains the software and data files used by CD-i players by omitting the tracks from the disc's TOC (table of contents). This causes audio CD players to skip the CD-i data tracks. This is different from the CD-i Ready format, which puts CD-i software and data into the pregap of track 1.

CDi was the leading format of its time but was supplanted by the politics of competition. Philips Interactive Media lead the way in producing breakthrough titles, including the first interactive coloring book, Sesame Street Disc and children's programs, Groliers and Comptoms encyclopedias and many more pathbreaking programs.

Enhanced CD

Enhanced CD, also known as CD Extra and CD Plus, is a certification mark of the Recording Industry Association of America for various technologies that combine audio and computer data for use in both Compact Disc and CD-ROM players.

The primary data formats for Enhanced Compact Disc's are mixed mode (Yellow Book/Red Book), CD-i, hidden track, and multisession (Blue Book).

VinylDisc

VinylDisc is the hybrid of a standard Audio CD and the vinyl record. The vinyl layer on the disc's label side can hold approximately three minutes of music.

Manufacture

Replicated CDs are mass-produced initially using a hydraulic press. Small granules of heated raw polycarbonate plastic are fed into the press. A screw forces the liquefied plastic into the mold cavity. The mold closes with a metal stamper in contact with the disc surface. The plastic is allowed to cool and harden. Once opened, the disc substrate is removed from the mold by a robotic arm, and a 15 mm diameter center hole (called a stacking ring) is created. The time it takes to "stamp" one CD, is usually 2 to 3 seconds.

This method produces the clear plastic blank part of the disc. After a metallic reflecting layer (usually aluminum, but sometimes gold or other metal) is applied to the clear blank substrate, the disc goes under a UV light for curing and it is ready to go to press. To prepare to press a CD, a glass master is made, using a high-powered laser on a device similar to a CD writer. The glass master is a positive image of the desired CD surface (with the desired microscopic pits and lands). After testing, it is used to make a die by pressing it against a metal disc. The die is a negative image of the glass master: typically, several are made, depending on the number of pressing mills that are to make the CD. The die then goes into a press and the physical image is transferred to the blank CD, leaving a final positive image on the disc.

A small amount of lacquer is applied as a ring around the center of the disc, and rapid spinning spreads it evenly over the surface. Edge protection lacquer is applied before the disc is finished. The disc can then be printed and packed. Manufactured CDs that are sold in stores are sealed via a process called "polywrapping" or shrink wrapping.

Recordable CD

Recordable Compact Discs, CD-Rs, are injection molded with a "blank" data spiral. A photosensitive dye is then applied, after which the discs are metalized and lacquer-coated. The write laser of the CD recorder changes the color of the dye to allow the read laser of a standard CD player to see the data, just as it would with a standard stamped disc. The resulting discs can be read by most CD-ROM drives and played in most audio CD players.

CD-R recordings are designed to be permanent. Over time the dye's physical characteristics may change, however, causing read errors and data loss until the reading device cannot recover with error correction methods. The design life is from 20 to 100 years, depending on the quality of the discs, the quality of the writing drive, and storage conditions. However, testing has demonstrated such degradation of some discs in as little as 18 months under normal storage conditions. This failure is known as CD rot. CD-Rs follow the Orange Book standard.

Recordable Audio CD

The recordable audio CD is designed to be used in a consumer audio CD recorder. These consumer audio CD recorders use SCMS (Serial Copy Management System), an early form of digital rights management (DRM), to conform to the AHRA (Audio Home Recording Act). The Recordable Audio CD is typically somewhat more expensive than CD-R due to (a) lower volume and (b) a 3% AHRA royalty used to compensate the music industry for the making of a copy.

High-capacity Recordable CD

High-capacity Recordable CD are consitsts of :

A higher density recording format that can hold:

- 98.5 minutes of audio on a 12 cm disc (compared to about 80 minutes for Red Book audio).
- 30 minutes of audio on an 8 cm disc (compared to about 24 minutes for Red Book audio).

Rewritable CD

CD-RW is a re-recordable medium that uses a metallic alloy instead of a dye. The write laser in this case is used to heat and alter the properties (amorphous vs. crystalline) of the alloy, and hence change its reflectivity. A CD-RW does not have as great a difference in reflectivity as a pressed CD or a CD-R, and so many earlier CD audio players cannot read CD-RW discs, although most later CD audio players and stand-alone DVD players can. CD-RWs follow the Orange Book standard.

High-speed ReWritable CD

Due to technical limitations, the original ReWritable CD could be written no faster than 4x speed. High Speed ReWritable CD has a different design that permits writing at speeds ranging from 4x to 12x.

Original CD-RW drives can only write to original ReWritable CDs. High Speed CD-RW drives can typically write to both original ReWritable CD discs and High Speed ReWritable CD discs. Both types of CD-RW discs can be read in most CD drives. Higher speed CD-RW discs, Ultra Speed (16x to 24x write speed) and Ultra Speed+ (32x write speed), are now available.

ReWritable Audio CD

The ReWritable Audio CD is designed to be used in a consumer audio CD recorder, which won't (without modification) accept standard CD-RW discs. These consumer audio CD recorders use the Serial Copy Management System (SCMS), an early form of digital rights management (DRM), to conform to the United States' Audio Home Recording Act (AHRA). The ReWritable Audio CD is typically somewhat more expensive than CD-RW due to (a) lower volume and (b) a 3% AHRA royalty used to compensate the music industry for the making of a copy.

Copy Protection

The Red Book audio specification, except for a simple 'anti-copy' bit in the subcode, does not include any copy protection mechanism. Starting in early 2002, attempts were made by record companies to market "copy-protected" non-standard Compact Discs, which cannot be ripped, or copied, to hard drives or easily converted to MP3s. One major drawback to these copy-protected discs is that most will not play on either computer CD-ROM drives, or some standalone CD players that use CD-ROM mechanisms. Philips has stated that such discs are not permitted to bear the trademarked Compact Disc Digital Audio logo because they violate the Red Book specifications. Numerous copy-protection systems have been countered by readily available, often free, software.

Standalone Software

Stand alone software is a software application that does not come bundled within another software application, and does not require another software package to run. Stand alone software is software installed on your computer, vs. online software which runs via your Internet browser.

Examples: Quicken, Microsoft Money and other desktop personal finance software are stand alone software packages requiring nothing more on your computer to run other than an operating system such as Windows.

Standalone software mean:

- Computer software that can work offline, i.e. does not necessarily require network connection to function
- Software that is not a part of some software bundle
- A program that is run as a separate computer process, not an add-on of an existing process, e.g. not a plugin. The term "stand-alone" has been used inconsistently: for instance, on the Apple Macintosh platform, the plugin code has often been referred to as being stand-alone,
- Historically, a standalone program - a program that does not require operating system's services to run
- A portable application, that can be run from a removable storage, without the need for installation procedure.

(Source: http://financialsoft.about.com/od/glossaryindexs/g/StandAlone.htm)

References

1. http://financialsoft.about.com/od/glossaryindexs/g/StandAlone.htm
2. ^"Compact Disc Hits 25th birthday". BBC News. 2007-08-17. http://news.bbc.co.uk/2/hi/technology/6950845.stm. Retrieved 2009-12-01.

3. ^ Plambeck, Joseph (2010-05-30). "As CD Sales Wane, Music Retailers Diversify". The New York Times. http://www.nytimes.com/2010/05/31/business/media/31bestbuy.html.

4. "A Long Play Digital Audio Disc System". AES. http://www.aes.org/e-lib/browse.cfm?elib=2912. Retrieved 2009-02-14.

5. "How the CD Was Developed". BBC News. 2007-08-17. http://news.bbc.co.uk/2/hi/technology/6950933.stm. Retrieved 2007-08-17.

6. "Philips Compact Disc". Philips. http://www.philipsmuseumeindhoven.nl/phe/products/e_cd.htm. Retrieved 2009-02-14.

7. "IEEE CD Milestone". IEEE Global History Network. http://www.ieeeghn.org/wiki/index.php/Milestones:Compact_Disc_Audio_Player,_1979. Retrieved 2010-10-14.

8. Kees A. Schouhamer Immink (1998). "The CD Story". Journal of the AES 46: 458–465. http://www.exp-math.uni-essen.de/~immink/pdf/cdstory.htm. Retrieved 2007-02-09.

9. Kees A. Schouhamer Immink (2007). "Shannon, Beethoven, and the Compact Disc". IEEE Information Theory Newsletter: 42–46. http://www.exp-math.uni-essen.de/~immink/pdf/beethoven.htm. Retrieved 2007-12-12.

10. Knopper, Steve (2009-01-07). Appetite for Self-Destruction: The Rise and Fall of the Record Industry in the Digital Age. Free Press/Simon & Schuster.

11. "The Inventor of the CD". Philips research (from cache). http://web.archive.org/web/20080129201342/www.research.philips.com/newscenter/dossier/optrec/beethoven.html. Retrieved 2009-01-16.

12. Royal Philips Electronics. "Optical Recording". Press release. http://www.research.philips.com/newscenter/dossier/optrec/firstcds.html.
13. Bilyeu, Melinda; Hector Cook, Andrew Môn Hughes (2004). The Bee Gees:tales of the brothers Gibb. Omnibus Press. p. 519. ISBN 9781844490578.
14. "And 25 Years Ago Philips Introduced the CD". GeekZone. http://www.geekzone.co.nz/content. asp?contentid=7304. Retrieved 2008-01-11.
15. "Sony History: A Great Invention 100 Years On". Sony. Archived from the original on 2008-08-02. http://web.archive.org/web/20080802133849/http://www.sony.net/Fun/SH/1 -20/h5.html. Retrieved 2008 11-04.
16. Maxim, 2004
17. The New Schwann Record & Tape Guide Volume 37 No. 2 February 1985
18. MAC Audio News. No. 178, November 1989. pp 19-21 Glenn Baddeley. November 1989 News Update. Melbourne Audio Club Inc.
19. The world's first CD-R was made by the Japanese firm Taiyo Yuden Co., Ltd. in 1988 as part of the joint Philips-Sony development effort.
20. Smith, Ethan (January 2, 2009). "Music Sales Decline for Seventh Time in Eight Years: Digital Downloads Can't Offset 20% Plunge in CD Sales". Wall Street Journal. http://online.wsj.com/article/SB123075988836646491.html?mod=rss_ whats_news_technology&mg=com-wsj. Retrieved 4 March 2009.
21. "CD Baby Payouts Surge « Indie Music Stop". Indiemusicstop.wordpress.com. 2009-03-30. http://indiemusicstop.wordpress.com/2009/04/01/cd-baby-payouts-surge/. Retrieved 2009-12-01.

22. "Q. How Do You Calculate Moment of Inertia?". http://www.cd-testing.com/#i17. Retrieved 2009-08-19. "a typical disc with ... weight of 15 grams ... maximum allowed weight (20g)"

23. Philips. "Beethoven's Ninth Symphony of Greater Importance than Technology". http://www.marantzphilips.nl/The_cd_laser. Retrieved 2007-02-09.

24. AES. "AES Oral History Project: Kees A.Schouhamer Immink". http://www.aes.org/historical/store/oralhistory/?code=OHP-016-DVD. Retrieved 2008-07-29.

25. Cassidy, Fergus (2005-10-23). "Great Lengths" (reprint). Sunday Tribune. http://www.ferguscassidy.ie/ethos-23-Oct-2005.html. Retrieved 2007-12-21.

26. Hoffmann, Frank; Ferstler, Howard (2005). Encyclopedia of Recorded Sound. CRC Press. p. 1289. ISBN 041593835X, 9780415938358.

27. Goldmark, Peter. Maverick inventor; My Turbulent Years at CBS. New York: Saturday Review Press, 1973.

28. Andy McFadden (2010-01-09). "CD-Recordable FAQ". http://www.cdrfaq.org/faq03.html#S3-8. Retrieved 2010-12-30.

1. ISO (1995). "ISO/IEC 10149:1995 – Information technology – Data interchange on read-only 120 mm optical data disks (CD-ROM)". http://www.iso.org/iso/catalogue_detail.htm?csnumber=25869. Retrieved 2010-08-06.

2. EP 689208 "Method for block oriented addressing" – for block layouts see columns 1 and 2

3. Data Interchange on Read-only 120 mm Optical Data Disks (CD-ROM). ECMA. June 1996. http://www.ecma-international.org/publications/standards/Ecma-130.htm. Retrieved 2009-04-26.

4. Note that the CIRC error correction system used in the CD audio format has two interleaved layers.

5. "Optical Media FAQs" (PDF). Archived from the original on 2006-10-22. http://web.archive.org/web/20061022035649/http://memorex.com/downloads/whitepapers/WhitePaper_Reference_ Guide_ Optical_Media_Mar2406.pdf. Retrieved 2007-01-06.
6. Schoen, Seth. "Harry Potter and the Digital Fingerprints", Electronic Frontier Foundation, July 20, 2007. Retrieved October 24, 2007.
29. "BRUCKNER: Symphony No. 5 in B flat major - Munich Philharmonic/Christian Thielemann - DGG". audaud.com. http://www.audaud.com/article.php?ArticleID=410. Retrieved 2011-04-06.
30. "Mission of Burma 1988 Rykodisc compilation information". discogs.com. http://www.discogs.com/Mission-Of-Burma-Mission-Of-Burma/release/1129709. Retrieved 2011-01-18. "This Rykodisc release was the first compact disc to contain 80 minutes of music; 78 minutes had previously been the longest length possible to encode on a CD."
31. "CD-R Unreadable in Less Than Two Years". cdfreaks.com. http://www.cdfreaks.com/news/CD-Recordable-discs-unreadable-in-less-than-two-years.html. Retrieved 2007-02-01.
32. "CD-R ROT". PC-Active.com via archive.org. Archived from the original on 2005-02-04. http://web.archive.org/web/20050204065340/http://www.pc-active.nl/toonArtikel.asp?artikelID=508. Retrieved 2007-02-01.
33. Andy McFadden (2007-08-08). "CD-Recordable FAQ". http://www.cdrfaq.org/. Retrieved 2007-09-20.

CHAPTER–7

MEANING AND SCOPE OF SOFTWARE INTERFACES AND USER INTERFACES

An interface means the point of interaction between components. It can be used in both hardware and software system. This allows a component, whether a piece of hardware such as a graphics card or a piece of software such as an internet browser, to function independently while using interfaces to communicate with other components via an input/output system and an associated protocol.

A computing interface is the medium of communication between the computer and the user by means of peripheral devices such a monitor or a keyboard, an interface with the internet via Internet Protocol, and any other point of communication involving a computer.

The trait of a good user interface is consistency. Good user interface design is about getting a user to have a consistent set of expectations, and then meeting those expectations. Consistency can be bad if not used for a purpose and when it serves no benefit for the end user, though.

An integrated library system (ILS), also known as a library management system (LMS), is an enterprise resource planning system for a library, used to track items owned, orders made, bills paid, and patrons who have borrowed. An ILS usually comprises a relational database, software to interact with that database, and two graphical user interfaces (one for patrons, one for staff). Most ILSes separate software functions into discrete programs called modules, each of them integrated with a unified interface. Examples of modules might include the following given below :

- acquisitions (ordering, receiving, and invoicing materials)
- cataloging (classifying and indexing materials)
- circulation (lending materials to patrons and receiving them back)
- serials (tracking magazine and newspaper holdings)
- the OPAC (public interface for users)

Each patron and item has a unique ID in the database that allows the ILS to track its activity.Larger libraries use an ILS to order and acquire, receive and invoice, catalog, circulate, track and shelve materials. Smaller libraries, such as those in private homes or non-profit organizations (like churches or synagogues, for instance), often forgo the expense and maintenance required to run an ILS, and instead use a library computer system

Innovative Interfaces, Inc. is a provider of integrated library system software that is used by thousands of libraries in over 40 countries. Innovative software is installed in all types of libraries including: academic, public, consortia, school, special libraries, medical libraries and law libraries.

It which is platform-independent and powered by Java. The Millennium is integrated library system can be used to manage all library operations. These include acquisitions of material for the library, cataloging, serials (or periodicals) control, circulation, interlibrary loan (a form of resource sharing), and management of electronic resources.

The public interface most familiar to library users is the library catalog. The computerized form of the library catalog is known as the OPAC (or online public access catalog). Innovative's newest version of their OPAC is called WebPAC Pro. In 2007 the company introduced Encore, a discovery platform that overlays the OPAC and displays search results in a way that reflects the new age of social media. This includes tag clouds and facets to focus searches, tagging, rating and book reviews. Encore Synergy also allows the catalog to search subscribed databases.

The Innovative Users Group was founded in 1991 as an international organization of member libraries who use the Innovative Interfaces, Inc. integrated library system, Millennium. It is an independent organization from Innovative Interfaces, Inc. The Innovative Users Group organizes an annual conference, organizes ballots for user-submitted enhancements, and maintains the IUG Clearinghouse for users to share tutorials, scripts, guides, and other resources created to better use the software.

VIRTUAL USER INTERFACE (VUI)

It is a user interface to a virtual world. It is a terminology that is used to describe the interface to a collection of three dimensional applications, functions and services running in a virtual world. The VUI is the next generation replacement for the current Graphical User Interfaces we find in our traditional desktop environments today.

A VUI client allows multiple users to simultaneously collaborate on and use a single application. You are not required to install or even launch an application in this space just simply move to the last location you were using it. The virtual desktop is far superior to the traditional 2D GUI or menu desktop as the multidimensional capabilities in conjunction with shared back end processing allow a user to run as many applications as they need. Local versions of VUI's will cache server based copies to allow a local client to replicate a hosted VUI environment when working in a non internet connected space. The VUI client is platform independent and will allow access from any device to your back end applications.

SEARCH STRATEGIES

First, the controls for different features should be presented in a consistent manner so that users can find the controls easily.For example, users find it difficult to use software when some commands are available through menus, some through icons, some through right-clicks, some under a separate button at one corner of a screen, some grouped by function, some grouped by "common," some grouped by "advanced." A user looking for a command should have a consistent search strategy for finding it. The more search strategies a user has to use, the more frustrating the search will be. The more consistent the grouping, the easier the search.

Second, the "principle of least astonishment" is crucial. Various features should work in similar ways.For example, some features in Adobe Acrobat are "select tool, then select text to which apply." Others are "select text, then apply action to selection." Commands should work the same way in all contexts.

Third, consistency counsels against user interface changes version-to-version. Change should be minimized, and forward-compatibility should be maintained. For example, the change from the menu bars of Microsoft Office 2003 to the ribbon toolbar of Microsoft Office 2007 caused mixed reactions to the redesign, intended to enhance access to the most used functions.

Consistency is one quality to trade off in user interface design—not the only thing, but one of the most important. In some cases, a violation of consistency principles can provide sufficiently clear advantages that a wise and careful user interface designer may choose to violate consistency to achieve some other important goal. Generally, less mature software has fewer users who are entrenched in the status quo.

Older, more broadly used software must more carefully hew to the status quo to avoid disruptive costs. The most experienced users, and the ones who derive most value from a program, are the users who tend to bear the greatest costs from change. However, of those trade-offs, consistency is one of the most important core principles, and it should be violated least often. Bad user interface design, and poorly implemented changes to an existing user interface, can impose staggering costs on users.

In the industrial design field of human–machine interaction, the user interface is the space where interaction between humans and machines occurs. The goal of interaction between a human and a machine at the user interface is effective operation and control of the machine, and feedback from the machine which aids the operator in making operational decisions. Examples of this broad concept of user interfaces include the interactive aspects of computer operating systems, hand tools, heavy machinery operator controls, and process controls. The design considerations applicable when creating user interfaces are related to or involve such disciplines as ergonomics and psychology.

A user interface is the system by which people (users) interact with a machine. The user interface includes hardware (physical) and software (logical) components. User interfaces exist for various systems, and provide a means of:

- Input, allowing the users to manipulate a system, and/or
- Output, allowing the system to indicate the effects of the users' manipulation.

Generally, the goal of human-machine interaction engineering is to produce a user interface which makes it easy, efficient, and enjoyable to operate a machine in the way which produces the desired result. This generally means that the operator needs to provide minimal input to achieve the desired output, and also that the machine minimizes undesired outputs to the human.

Ever since the increased use of personal computers and the relative decline in societal awareness of heavy machinery, the term user interface has taken on overtones of the (graphical) user interface, while industrial control panel and machinery control design discussions more commonly refer to human-machine interfaces.

Other terms for user interface include "human–computer interface" (HCI) and "man–machine interface" (MMI).

SOFTWARE INTERFACES

It is the range of different kinds of interface at different levels: an operating system may interface with pieces of hardware, applications or programs running on the operating system may need to interact via streams, and in object oriented programs, objects within an application may need to interact via methods.

The use of interfaces allows implementation of a programming style called programming against interfaces. The idea behind this is to base the logic one develops on the sole interface definition of the objects one uses and not to make the code depend on the internal details. This allows the programmer the ability to later change the behavior of the system by simply swapping the object used with another implementing the same interface.

Types of Access

The types of access that interfaces provide between software components can include: constants, data types, types of procedures, exception specifications and method signatures. In some instances, it may be useful to define public variables as part of the interface. It often also specifies the functionality of those procedures and methods, either by comments or (in some experimental languages) by formal logical assertions and preconditions.

The interface of a software module A is deliberately kept separate from the implementation of that module. The latter contains the actual code of the procedures and methods described in the interface, as well as other "private" variables, procedures, etc. Any other software module B (which can be referred to as a client to A) that interacts with A is forced to do so only through the interface. One practical advantage of this arrangement is that replacing the implementation of A by another one that meets the same specifications of the interface should not cause B to fail—as long as its use of A complies with the specifications of the interface.

In object-oriented languages the term "interface" is often used to define an abstract type that contains no data but exposes behaviors defined as methods. A class having all the methods corresponding to that interface is said to implement that interface. Furthermore, a class can implement multiple interfaces, and hence can be of different types at the same time.

An interface is hence a type definition; anywhere an object can be exchanged (in a function or method call) the type of the object to be exchanged can be defined in terms of an interface instead of a specific class. This allows later code to use the same function exchanging different object types; hence such code turns out to be more generic and reusable.

Usually a method in an interface cannot be used directly; there must be a class implementing that object to be used for the method invocation. For example, one can define an interface called "Stack" that has two methods: push() and pop() and later implement it in two different versions, say, FastStack and GenericStack—the first being faster but working with a stack of fixed size, and the second using a data structure that can be resized but at the cost of somewhat lower speed. This approach can be pushed to the limit of defining interfaces with a single method; e.g. the Java language defines the interface Readable that has the single read() method and a collection of implementations to be used for different purposes, among others: BufferedReader, FileReader, InputStreamReader, PipedReader, and StringReader.

In its purest form, an interface (like in Java) must include only method definitions and constant values that make up part of the static interface of a type. Some languages (like C#) also permit the definition to include properties owned by the object, which are treated as methods with syntactic sugar.

Hardware Interfaces

It exist in computing systems between many of the components such as the various buses, storage devices, other I/O devices, etc. A hardware interface is described by the mechanical, electrical and logical signals at the interface and the protocol for sequencing them (sometimes called signaling).A standard interface, such as SCSI, decouples the design and introduction of computing hardware, such as I/O devices, from the design and introduction of other components of a computing system, thereby allowing users and manufacturers great flexibility in the implementation of computing systems.

To work with a system, users have to be able to control and assess the state of the system. For example, when driving an automobile, the driver uses the steering wheel to control the direction of the vehicle, and the accelerator pedal, brake pedal and gearstick to control the speed of the vehicle. The driver perceives the position of the vehicle by looking through the windshield and exact speed of the vehicle by reading the speedometer. The user interface of the automobile is on the whole composed of the instruments the driver can use to accomplish the tasks of driving and maintaining the automobile.

Difference

There is a difference between a user interface and an operator interface or a human–machine interface.

The term "user interface" is often used in the context of (personal) computer systems and electronic devices

- Where a network of equipment or computers are interlinked through an MES (Manufacturing Execution System)-or Host.
- An HMI is typically local to one machine or piece of equipment, and is the interface method between the human and the equipment/machine. An Operator interface is the interface method by which multiple equipment that are linked by a host control system is accessed or controlled.
- The system may expose several user interfaces to serve different kinds of users. For example, a computerized library database might provide two user interfaces, one for library patrons (limited set of functions, optimized for ease of use) and the other for library personnel (wide set of functions, optimized for efficiency).

In some circumstances computers might observe the user, and react according to their actions without specific commands. A means of tracking parts of the body is required, and sensors noting the position of the head, direction of gaze and so on have been used experimentally. This is particularly relevant to immersive interfaces.

Usability

It is the degree to which the design of a particular user interface takes into account the human psychology and physiology of the users, and makes the process of using the system effective, efficient and satisfying.

User interfaces are prime ingredient of Computer user satisfaction. The design of a user interface affects the amount of effort the user must expend to provide input for the system and to interpret the output of the system, and how much effort it takes to learn how to do this.

Usability is mainly a characteristic of the user interface, but is also associated with the functionalities of the product and the process to design it. It describes how well a product can be used for its intended purpose by its target users with efficiency, effectiveness, and satisfaction, also taking into account the requirements from its context of use.

USER INTERFACES : MEANING

In computer world, the user interface of a computer program refers to the pictorial, textual and audio-visual information the program presents to the user, and the control sequences such as keystrokes with the computer keyboard, movements of the computer mouse, and selections with the touchscreen the user employs to control the program.

Types

There are many types of user interface one, the most common are given below :

1. Graphical user interfaces (GUI) accept input via devices such as computer keyboard and mouse and provide articulated graphical output on the computer monitor. There are at least two different principles widely used in

GUI design: Object-oriented user interfaces (OOUIs) and application oriented interfaces.

2. Web-based user interfaces or web user interfaces (WUI) are a subclass of GUIs that accept input and provide output by generating web pages which are transmitted via the Internet and viewed by the user using a web browser program. Newer implementations utilize Java, AJAX, Adobe Flex, Microsoft .NET, or similar technologies to provide real-time control in a separate program, eliminating the need to refresh a traditional HTML based web browser. Administrative web interfaces for web-servers, servers and networked computers are often called control panels.
3. Touchscreens are displays that accept input by touch of fingers or a stylus. Used in a growing amount of mobile devices and many types of point of sale, industrial processes and machines, self-service machines etc.

User interfaces that are common in various fields outside desktop computing:

1. Command line interfaces, where the user provides the input by typing a command string with the computer keyboard and the system provides output by printing text on the computer monitor. Used by programmers and system administrators, in engineering and scientific environments, and by technically advanced personal computer users.
2. Touch user interface are graphical user interfaces using a touchpad or touchscreen display as a combined input and output device. They supplement or replace other forms of output with haptic feedback methods. Used in computerized simulators etc.

Other types of user interfaces are given below :

1. Attentive user interfaces manage the user attention deciding when to interrupt the user, the kind of warnings, and the level of detail of the messages presented to the user.

2. Batch interfaces are non-interactive user interfaces, where the user specifies all the details of the batch job in advance to batch processing, and receives the output when all the processing is done. The computer does not prompt for further input after the processing has started.
3. Conversational Interface Agents attempt to personify the computer interface in the form of an animated person, robot, or other character (such as Microsoft's Clippy the paperclip), and present interactions in a conversational form.
4. Crossing-based interfaces are graphical user interfaces in which the primary task consists in crossing boundaries instead of pointing.
5. Gesture interface are graphical user interfaces which accept input in a form of hand gestures, or mouse gestures sketched with a computer mouse or a stylus.
6. Intelligent user interfaces are human-machine interfaces that aim to improve the efficiency, effectiveness, and naturalness of human-machine interaction by representing, reasoning, and acting on models of the user, domain, task, discourse, and media (e.g., graphics, natural language, gesture).
7. Motion tracking interfaces monitor the user's body motions and translate them into commands, currently being developed by Apple
8. Multi-screen interfaces, employ multiple displays to provide a more flexible interaction. This is often employed in computer game interaction in both the commercial arcades and more recently the handheld markets.
9. Noncommand user interfaces, which observe the user to infer his/her needs and intentions, without requiring that he/she formulate explicit commands.
10. Object-oriented user interface (OOUI)

11. Reflexive user interfaces where the users control and redefine the entire system via the user interface alone, for instance to change its command verbs. Typically this is only possible with very rich graphic user interfaces.
12. Tangible user interfaces, which place a greater emphasis on touch and physical environment or its element.
13. Task-Focused Interfaces are user interfaces which address the information overload problem of the desktop metaphor by making tasks, not files, the primary unit of interaction
14. Text user interfaces are user interfaces which output text, but accept other form of input in addition to or in place of typed command strings.
15. Voice user interfaces, which accept input and provide output by generating voice prompts. The user input is made by pressing keys or buttons, or responding verbally to the interface.
16. Natural-Language interfaces - Used for search engines and on webpages. User types in a question and waits for a response.
17. Zero-Input interfaces get inputs from a set of sensors instead of querying the user with input dialogs.
18. Zooming user interfaces are graphical user interfaces in which information objects are represented at different levels of scale and detail, and where the user can change the scale of the viewed area in order to show more detail.

WordPress Widgets (WPW)

It is like a plugin, but designed to provide a simple way to arrange the various elements of your sidebar content (known as "widgets") without having to change any code. The Widgets SubPanel explains how to use the various Widgets that come delivered with WordPress, and the Widgets page at Automattic explains how to 'widgetize' themes and plugins.

HOW TO SEARCH THE WEB WITH TOOLBARS

Toolbars normally contain buttons, but other components (such as text fields and combo boxes) can be placed in the toolbar as well. The simple words, toolbar is a software application which gives searches the ability to perform quick and convenient access with user-friendly buttons. These are usually distinguished from palettes by their integration into the edges of the screen or larger windows, which results in wasted space if too many underpopulated bars are stacked atop each other (especially horizontal bars on a landscape oriented display) or interface inefficiency if overloaded bars are placed on small windows.

An optional, textured "drag area" on the toolbar indicates that users can drag the toolbar anywhere in the window or into a separate window. The drag area is on the leading edge when the toolbar is horizontal and on the top when it is vertical.

Toolbars implemented as web browser plug-ins have become a popular vulnerability for spyware and malware creators. Browser toolbars are commonly bundled with installers for other "partner" products as an "opt-out" default without the user's explicit consent.

Browser toolbars are supposed to provide additional search fields, form-fill, links back to popular sites, malware detection, etc. However, in many cases their primary purpose is instead to collect anonymous marketing statistics or reinforce a brand (by displaying the logo at the top of each browser window).As plug-ins to the web browser application, toolbars can also degrade computer performance or create compatibility problems

- SEO Toolbar: from SEOInc, a toolbar that is focused on search engine optimization-related information, such as pages indexed, backlinks,etc.
- SearchBliss: Another search engine optimization and webmaster focused toolbar; I like the Google Dance tool especially.
- SEO RX Toolbar:"SEO RX Toolbar auto updates and includes these features: Google Search, Page Rank, Meta

Tag Generator, Search Engine Ranker, Link Popularity Checker, Google Dance Tool, Website Submit to 300 search engines, Radio, Podcast, RSS Feed, Chat room, Dictionary, Plus you can personalize to fit your needs."

Website Toolbar

A website toolbar is a feature which can be found on many modern websites, including Facebook, MySpace and CNET.com.Website toolbars differ from conventional browser toolbars in that they appear only when a user is on a specific site, whilst Browser toolbars appear in a web browser persistently regardless of which site a user is on. A website toolbar serves as a means of persistently presenting visitors to a website with a means of quickly performing many common site functions such as sharing articles of content on a social network, searching through the home website or presenting features which further enhance the community-aspects to a website such as live chat features.

In 2009, a range of free options for everyday site owners to include their own website toolbar on their webpages was made available by companies such as Wibiya and Meebo via an easy to install Wizard or alternatively JavaScript embed code. Custom-made website toolbars are also possible and many open-source plugins are also freely available for this purpose.

1. Google Toolbar for Firefox: Google's Firefox toolbar has some nice features, such as autofill and spellcheck.
2. Dogpile Toolbar: features white and yellow pages search, and a nifty news ticker that you can customize.
3. Yahoo Toolbar for Firefox: add RSS feeds to your My Yahoo page, check your email, and access your favorite sites with the Yahoo Toolbar.
4. MSN Search Toolbar: tabbed browsing, form fill, and one-click access in the MSN Search Toolbar. For Internet Explorer only.
5. Metacrawler Toolbar: Access many search engines at once with the Metacrawler toolbar.

6. Alexa Toolbar: "The Alexa Toolbar offers the unique ability to update in real-time to offer you information about the sites you visit."
7. StumbleUpon Toolbar: Find and share your favorite sites with the StumbleUpon community.
8. A9 Toolbar: Check your search history, get an A9 diary, or get instant site information.
9. Clusty Toolbar: Get clustered results from many search engines at once, Clusty Clips (definitions), and Query Catcher, a way to "easily supplement your favorite search engine with one click."
10. GoogleBar: " The Googlebar project was initially created to address the widespread desire in the mozilla community for the Google toolbar to support the Netscape 7, Mozilla, and Firefox web browsers."
11. Ask Toolbar: Lots of good stuff with the Ask Toolbar, including a way to save notes about particular pages.

Specialized Toolbars

1. eBay Toolbar: For people who really are into eBay; a great way to monitor your buying and selling stats as well as search within eBay.
2. MapQuest Toolbar: instant access to maps and driving directions.
3. Yahoo Toolbar with WorldCat Searching of Library Materials: "Are you a librarian? Use the Toolbar as part of your Web access and online catalog. Are you a library user? Install the Toolbar on your home computer and search for materials no matter where you are on the Web!"
4. Neopets Toolbar: " Can't be without Neopets? Well, now you don't have to... Install the Neopets Toolbar and have your favourite website with you wherever you go on the Internet."

5. Dictionary.com Toolbar: Get instant definitions with the Dictionary.com toolbar.
6. Dealio Toolbar: a comparison shopping toolbar; lets you know when an item you're thinking about buying comes in at a lower price. Also shops eBay stores and listings.
7. Scirus Toolbar: "With the new Scirus Toolbar, finding scientific, technical and medical information on the Web is easier than ever."

(Sources:http://websearch.about.com/od/dailywebsearchtips/qt/dnt0418.htm, http://java.sun.com/products/jlf/ed2/book/HIG.Menus4.html)

Web Widget

It is a software widget for the web. It's a small application that can be installed and executed within a web page by an end user. They are derived from the idea of code reuse. Widgets allow users to turn personal content into dynamic web apps that can be shared on websites where the code can be installed. For example, a "Weather Report Widget" could report today's weather by accessing data from the Weather Channel, it could even be sponsored by the Weather Channel. Widgets come in various shapes and sizes, but most preferred are Web widgets and Desktop widgets. Web widgets are intended for use on (embedding in) webpages and have major implications in areas such as site performance, SEO and even backlink campaigns. Desktop widgets are embedded on local computers, and do not impact SEO or webpage performance. Other terms used to describe web widgets include: portlet, gadget, badge, module, webjit, capsule, snippet, mini and flake. Widgets are typically created in DHTML, JavaScript, or Adobe Flash. Widget management systems offer a method of managing widgets that works on any web page, such as a blog or social networking home page. Many blog systems come with built in widget management systems as plug-ins. Users can obtain widgets and other widget management tools from various widget companies.

A mobile web widget is a web widget that is made or designed for access on mobile device. The W3C is creating a set of standards for web widgets and there are several proprietary standards.A widget is a stand-alone application that can be embedded into third party sites by any user on a page where they have rights of authorship (e.g. a webpage, blog, or profile on a social media site).

Should you want to put that widget on your own Facebook profile, you could do this by copying and pasting the embed code into your profile on Facebook.

Embeddable chunks of code have existed since the early development of the World Wide Web. Web developers have long sought and used third party code chunks in their pages. Early web widgets provided functions such as link counters and advertising banners.

Widgets may be looked upon as downloadable applications which look and act like traditional apps but are implemented using web technologies including JavaScript, Flash, HTML and CSS. Widgets use and depend on web APIs exposed either by the browser or by a widget engine such as Akamai, Clearspring, KickApps, MassPublisher, NewsGator, Plusmo, Widgetbox, Widsets, WebWag and many others. Sites such as MassPublisher, SnackTools and Widgetbox, allow users to easily create widgets from their own content with no coding knowledge necessary.

Widgets often take the form of on-screen tools (clocks, event countdowns, auction-tickers, stock market tickers, flight arrival information, daily weather etc.).

As an example, Widgetbox generate Web widgets that can be used on almost any website. Apple Desktop widgets can only be added to the desktop of your local (Apple) computer.

End users primarily use widgets to enhance their personal web experiences, or the web experiences of visitors to their personal sites.The use of widgets has proven increasingly popular, where users of social media are able to add stand-alone applications to blogs, profiles and community pages. Widgets add utility in the same way that an iPhone application does.

The developers of these widgets are often offering them as a form of sponsored content, which can pay for the cost of the development when the widget's utility maps to the user's needs in a way where both parties gain. (e.g. a sports news brand might gain awareness and increased audience share in exchange for the utility of current game scores being instantly and dynamically available—the blog which posted the Sports score widget might gain in having a stickier site).

Advantage and Satisfaction

One important factor with Widgets is that the host does not control the content. The content or the functionality it provides can not be modified by the host. The content is pre-published by the publisher/author/service provider and the host can either accept that content or not use the widget. The host does however control the placement of the Widget. Because, the host can always take the Widget down, it assures a large degree of mutual advantage and satisfaction with performance and content.

CLIENT-SIDE WIDGETS

As any program code, widgets can be used for malicious purposes. One example is the Facebook "Secret Crush" widget, reported in early 2008 by Fortinet as luring users to install Zango adware. One major consideration in the use of web widgets is how they'll impact the SEO (Search Engine Optimization) of your site. Client-side widgets include pretty much anything rendered in JavaScript or Flash, and are by far the most common types of widgets you'll see today. The content of these widgets is not visible to search engines, and will therefore not be seen as part of the content of your site.

Server-side widget content is visible to search engines, but these are slightly harder to embed. In both cases, search bots can see the embed code for the widget itself, so some of the SEO concern can be alleviated this way—but SEO should be part of your consideration in the use of any widget on your site.

Originally there were two kinds of search services on the Web: directories and engines.

Search Directories

These are systematic and well-arranged databases with references to websites. Included websites are hand picked by experts and classified as per rules of that particular search service.

Yahoo! is the hub of all search directories. In order to search the directory you must go to their special directory page. Their regular search results are not fetched from the directory, but from their search engine.

www.dmoz.org/" >The Open Directory is another popular directory, a catalogue compiled by enthusiasts from all over the world.

Directories are very useful when you have no more than a general notion of what you are looking for.

The first page normally gives you the most general categories (like "Computers and Internet" or "Education"). Click your way down the hierarchy to the right category, select the website you find the most interesting and start reading.

Don't forget that that you are not searching the text of the actual web pages of a particular site while using the search form for exploring a directory. On the contrary, you are searching the text contained in the site title and the description of the site. These are composed by the directory editors, and are often based on suggestions from the site owners themselves.

In addition most directories will also search the words contained in the category titles or descriptions.

Note, however, that some search directories may add data from regular search engines if they cannot find matches to your query. We will tell you more about this below.

SEARCH ENGINES

You can get the required information via searchenginers. Search engines are engines or robots that crawl the Web looking for new webpages. These engines read the webpages and put the text or parts of the text into a large database or index that you may access. None of them cover the whole Net, but some of them are quite large.

As far as the search engines are concerned the most popular are Google, Yahoo! Search (which is not the same as the Yahoo! Directory), Bing (formerly Live Search) and Ask. Search engines should be your first choice when you know exactly what you are looking for. They also cover a much larger part of the Web than the directories.

There are also "metasearch" services like Clusty and Dogpile and Pandia Metasearch engine. They search several search engines and directories at the same time, trying to extract the most relevant hits from all of them.

You might find it useful to start your searching with one of these, just to get a general feeling for what is out there. The search syntax is problematic, however.

It may vary from search engine to search engine, which means that the metasearch engine has to try to "translate" your query into a language that each search engine will understand. More often than not, they will not try to do so.

You should go directly to the relevant search engine for more complex searches. The metasearch engines will give you but a small part of the results from each individual search engine.

Ask any frequent internet surfers, he will tell you that metasearch engines will provide special features not found in the regular search engines.

Clusty, for instance, uses a special clustering technology that sorts the results into different groups or "clusters" that might help you pinpoint the right set of web sites more easily.

Specialized Search Engines

As far as the specialised search engines are concerned, they are basically of two types viz. news search engines and blog search engines. It focus on one type of information which just presents sub-sets of what is found in the regular search engine results, while others may provide information not found there.

It is noteworthy that news sites and blog search engines will rank fresh information much higher than the other search engines. Articles, features, news and other informative material published on news and blog & form the most popular sites and blogs may appear in these search engines less than an hour after they have been published.

So, if you are looking for up to date information on what is happening right now, try search engines like Google News and Google Blog Search. Of these two, Google News works best. Unfortunately so far the various blog search engines haven't managed to handle the spam problem quite well.

Many search sites like google and yahoo indexes billions of webpages. One thing remains true, however: The search engines do not all cover the same parts of the Internet Universe, which gives you every reason to use more than one of them.

References

1. David E. Boundy, A taxonomy of programmers, ACM SIGSOFT Software Engineering Notes 16(4) 23-30 (October 1991)
2. http://codex.wordpress.org/WordPress_Widgets
3. Blaauw, Gerritt A.; Brooks, Jr., Frederick P., "Chapter 8.6, Device Interfaces", Computer Architecture-Concepts and Evolution, Addison-Wesley, pp. 489–493, ISBN 0-201-10557-8 See also: Patterson, David A.; Hennessey, John L., "Chapter 8.5, Interfacing I/O Devices to the Processor, Memory and Operating System", Computer Organization and Design - The Hardware/Software Interface, Third Edition, Morgan Kaufmann, pp. 588–596, ISBN 1-55860-604-1

4. Adamson, Veronica, et al. (2008). JISC & SCONUL Library Management Systems StudyPDF (1 MB). Sheffield, UK: Sero Consulting. p. 51. Retrieved on 21 January 2009. "... a Library Management System (LMS or ILS 'Integrated Library System' in US parlance)."

5. http://websearch.about.com/od/dailywebsearchtips/qt/dnt0418.htm

6. Tennant, Roy (16 April 2008). "Picking When to Jump, Part 2". Library Journal. Reed Business Information. http://blog.libraryjournal.com/tennantdigitallibraries/2008/04/16/picking-when-to-jump-part-2/. Retrieved 20 January 2009. "Across the pond they use the term library management systems (LMS) for what we call the integrated library system (ILS)."

7. It was said to cause "anger and frustration," and "major efforts in time, training and costs." "For one thing, Word 2007 uses the entirely new ribbon interface. ... 'People will get used to the new interface, but at major efforts in time, training and cost,' says [a] director of systems ... When it came time to move [a user] from 2003 to 2007... 'I might as well of hit her over the head with a bat,' he says. 'I could see anger and frustration.'" Power users said it "takes too much time and patience to learn" the new interface. Word 2007: Not Exactly a Must-Have

8. http://www.pandia.com/goalgetter/2.html

9. An online survey by an Excel user group reports that about 80% of respondents had a negative opinion of the change, and within that 80%, the self-estimated reduction in productivity was "about 35%"."Ribbon survey results". http://www.exceluser.com/explore/surveys/ribbon/ribbon-survey-results.htm. Among advanced users, nearly 80% "dislike" or "hate" the new interface, only 20% "like" or "love" it, and of that 80%, the average productivity loss is about 35%.

10. On the other hand, average and less-intensive users who are not as dependent on old user interfaces are less bothered by the change. "'Other readers feel it's worth taking the time to learn the new interface. Once you do, they say, it actually makes creating professional-looking documents much easier for the average user.'" Word 2007: Not Exactly a Must-Have The usual solution in providing a new user interface is to provide a backwards-compatibility mode, so that a product's most intensive users are not forced to bear the costs of the change.

CHAPTER–8

MULTIPLE PROCESSES AND WEB SERVERS

Integrated Technology Processes are used in the aerospace industry to improve efficiency during conception and development phases, by enhancing process automation, information concurrency and avoiding data recopy. It include all the requirements, know-how means pre-requisite for the design office, manufacturing, quality control to define and produce an elementary part or an assembly within a known supply chain. Technology Processes are end-to-end processes aligned with a specific manufacturing or assembly technology.

The Techno process are used for these technologies : Tubing, Sheet Metal, Mechanical Parts, Jigs and Tools, Composites, Electricity, Thermoplastics, Assembly.

The "end-to-end" appellation means Techno Processes address all the activities from design to manufacture and assemble of an elementary part or an assembly.

Concurrent engineering is considered as an accelerator of efficiency and quality on the whole development process. Beside the concurrent use of the geometrical models (DMU), the Integration of Techno Processes is necessary.

Integration of Techno Processes (i.e. "Integrated Techno Processes") corresponds to the optimization of all the requirements (processes), know-how (skill rules, methods), means (organization,

IS tools) necessary for the design office, manufacturing and quality control.

Disruptive Technologies

It refer to a product or service that effect screening, diagnostic, procedural, or medical/drug intervention capabilities can become the standards of care. Minimally invasive surgery (MIS) is a case in point. Using a variety of endoscopic and imaging devices in the operating room (OR), surgeons are able to maneuver around delicate structures and to precisely grasp, dissect, and suture within openings measured in millimeters. High-definition (HD) electronics have measurably enhanced this ability.

Some believes that end-to-end integration of HD devices used in a variety of MIS procedures represents a new era in disruptive technology, one that goes beyond device selection to one of real-time medicine that could engender a sustainable difference in surgical care.

"Obsolescence and potential integration issues abound, as advances in surgical device technologies are introduced every six to nine months," explains Dr. Virginia Cardin, Dr.P.H., senior healthcare consultant with Frost & Sullivan. "To address this, the hospital must select an agile integration partner – one that is vendor-neutral, has its pulse on new technologies, and has the ability to customize a system to accommodate choices in equipment from several manufacturers."

The hospital evaluation process extended over 18 months. A "defining moment" question revolved around the idea that monitors in the OR should be HD, much like the rapid adoption of HD viewing of TV at home. The Penn SurgiCentre/Penn Endoscopy Center believed that the enhancement in visualization and clarity available in a home HD TV should be available during a medical procedure, consultations, or education.

The Penn SurgiCentre/Penn Endoscopy Center eventually selected VTS Medical Systems, for the company's understanding of the needs of surgeons and the functionalities of open and MIS procedures. VTS' staff designed, engineered, programmed and tested a portfolio of products and services specifically for Penn Medicine, employing a structured methodology throughout the process for user validation of the functionality of the integrated Operating Rooms and Endoscopy rooms.

"Medical electronics is an art and a science," adds Dr. Cardin.

In operation for close to six months, the HD-integrated operating rooms at the Penn SurgiCentre have received considerable praise and support from the local medical community, pointing to the goal that end-to-end HD integration in each of the 8 OR room and 8 GI Endoscopy rooms have contributed to the Centre's goal to provide real-time medicine and multidisciplinary collaboration among healthcare providers.

MIDDLEWARE

Middleware is software glue. Middleware is the slash in Client/ Server. That's fine as far as it goes, but is deceptively simplistic. This definition concentrates the term on one computing paradigm and masks the complexity of what middleware as a broad category is and does.

The Free On-line Dictionary of Computing, by Denis Howe offers this definition. Software that mediates between an application program and a network. It manages the interaction between disparate applications across the heterogeneous computing platforms. The Object Request Broker (ORB), software that manages communication between objects, is an example of a middleware program.

This is actually a reasonably good definition. I would change "application program" to "piece of software" and remove the reference to a network. Middleware can be used between application programs and other software facilities such as database managers. The term "mediate" is a good one. That is exactly what middleware does.

Middleware is especially integral to modern information technology based on XML, SOAP, Web services, and service-oriented architecture. It is computer software that connects software components or applications. It is used most often to support complex, distributed applications. It includes web servers, application servers, content management systems, and similar tools that support application development and delivery. It goes on to say that it describes a piece of software that connects two or more software applications so that they can exchange data. Middleware is an "intermediary." This type of software is used in complex environments and it doesn't necessarily represent one-to-one interactions between software agents. Middleware is essential to Enterprise Application Integration or EAI.

That brings the definition close to home, because as we pointed out earlier, the Middleware Resource Center concentrates on application integration middleware.

At the Middleware Resource Center, we tend to use this definition. Middleware is any software that allows other software to interact. Again, it isn't complete, but it is accurate. Completeness, however, may tax the patience of you, the reader.

The middleware can be classified as below :

1. *Message Oriented Middleware* : This is a large category and includes asynchronous store and forward application messaging capabilities as well as integration brokers that perform message transformation and routing or even business process coordination.
2. *Object Middleware* : This category consists largely of Object Request Brokers that were mentioned on one of the earlier definitions.
3. *RPC Middleware* : This type of middleware provides for calling procedures on remote systems, hence the name Remote Procedure Call. Unlike message oriented middleware, RPC middleware represents synchronous interactions between systems and is commonly used within an application.

4. *Database Middleware* : Database middleware allows direct access to data structures and provides interaction directly with databases. There are database gateways and a variety of connectivity options. Extract, Transform, and Load (ETL) packages are included in this category.
5. *Transaction Middleware* : This category as used in the Middleware Resource Center includes traditional transaction processing monitors (TPM) and web application servers. One could make the case for splitting the category.
6. *Portals* : We include enterprise portal servers as middleware largely because they facilitate what we refer to as "front end" integration. They allow interaction between the user's desktop and back end systems and services.

Good Website Do Wonders

Your website is the mirror of your online business, it is the virtual representation of your company whether your company is a traditional "brick and mortar" location, or exists solely on the Internet. When you are doing business online, people cannot see you in person as they are able to if they are dealing with a physical location. Therefore, people do judge you by your cover. This is why a good design is important.

Imagine if you were in charge of an actual physical store. Would you allow your salespeople to be dressed in shabby or casual clothes when they are dealing with your customers? By having your staff dress professionally, you are telling your customers that you do care about quality. This works simply because first impressions do matter.

Your website works the same way. If your website is shabby or looks stock, with no personalization, you're telling your visitors that you are not professional and you do not care for quality.

Only organized, genuine and result-oriented companies can be serious about making their excellent website layout. The visitors will attract to your Website as nails to magnet.

Displays, brochures, business cards, its all there. The better it looks, the better your visitors will feel about doing business with you. No doubt, the Internet is by far the most attractive and effective medium of communication one can come across since the birth of paper. People are doing risk business through Internet.

It is important to practice good design principles to make sure your site appeals to the maximum number of visitors and sells to as many people as possible.

A good hosting company will have tools and templates for you to start out with, but as you learn more and take control of your own design, keep these things in mind.

Be sure you have clear directions for the navigation of your site. The navigation menu should be uncluttered and easy to read in order for your visitors to know how to navigate around your website without confusion.

More images means more downloading. So keep the no. of pages on your website at a minimum. If you think any images are essential for your site, make sure you optimize them using an image editing program so that they have a minimum file size. Small is beautiful. Short paragraphs always catches the attention of readers while long one detach him. This is important because blocks of text that are too big will discourage visitors from reading all your content.

Make certain that your website pages match with to the web standards at www.w3.org and be sure they're cross-browser compatible. If your website looks great in Internet Explorer but is hard to read in Firefox or Opera, you'll lose out on many prospective customers.

If you serious in saving your precious time, then don't forget to use Cascading Style Sheets (CSS). It styles all elements on the website simultaneously. By using CSS, one can make future changes instead of making individual changed to the HTML of each sheet.

Script language can endanger your security system of your computer, so it is advisable to avoid it. Use scripting languages to handle or manipulate data, not to create visual effects on your website. Heavy scripts will slow down the loading time of your site and even crash some browsers. Scripts arn't always supported across all browsers, so some visitors might miss important information because of that.

Use Cascading Style Sheets (CSS) to save a lot of work in the long run by styling all elements on your website at the same time. Many future changes you may need to do can be done easily via CSS rather than making individual changed to the HTML of each page.

CHAPTER–9

INFORMATION TECHNOLOGY SYSTEM

People use Internet for different purposes, but how to get the desired result with minimum time is the hallmark of Internet Experts. Internet has become user-friendly so that even semi-illiterate person can also handle it conveniently. Practice makes the man perfect. It is also applicable for Internet-users too.

Where the data is stored in Internal and how we can access required data is the burning question before many net-users. All of these different parameters could conceivably be used to address the sheer size of the Internet, but all are very different. Perhaps, the simplest metric is simply how many people use the Internet. This can be viewed as the population of the Internet, and so would seem to be a decent gauge of its size. Many different companies try to measure Internet usage, ranging from Nielsen Ratings to the Office of the CIA to Serverwatch. The general answer seems to be that just over a billion people used the Internet in 2008. Of these, about 500 million use the Internet at least once a week, making them more-or-less permanent citizens of the Internet population.

It may be that what most people mean when they ask the size of the Internet is how many bytes it takes up. Estimating that is a fairly difficult task, but one person made an estimate not so long ago who can probably be trusted to have a good idea. Eric Schmidt, the CEO of Google, the world's largest index of the Internet, estimated the size at roughly 5 million terabytes of data.

That's over 5 billion gigabytes of data, or 5 trillion megabytes. Schmidt further noted that in its seven years of operations, Google has indexed roughly 200 terabytes of that, or .004% of the total size. There are thought to be some 155 million websites on the Internet, but this number fluctuates wildly from month to month, and one runs into a problem of what exactly constitutes a website. Is a person's individual Facebook page its own website? How about their LiveJournal or blog? What if the blog is hosted by a blog service?

According to a survey, there are nearly 75 million servers worldwide. The traffic that runs through the Internet in a single day might seem like it would be easily measured, but in fact it is very hard to find a reliable collection of this data, because of the sheer amount of computers, servers, and nations involved.

Russes Seitz

Perhaps the best way to conceive of something as inconceivable as the size of the Internet is to follow the lead of Russel Seitz. He took estimates for size and traffic of the entire Internet, and used this with the weight of the energy used to move a byte of information around. Although minuscule individually, over trillions and trillions of bytes it slowly added up. How large is the Internet? According to Russel Seitz: two ounces.

A program written for .NET requires that the .NET framework must be installed before the new program can run.

The .NET Framework is a software framework (an operating system within an operating system) that runs on Microsoft Windows..NET not only works on Windows computers, but is also available for other platforms like Linux and Mac OS.It is not specific to computers , Compact .NET also runs on PDA, Smartphones etc.

Programs written for the .NET Framework execute in a software environment (as contrasted to hardware environment), known as the Common Language Runtime (CLR). The CLR is an application virtual machine.

To an end user, the promise of .NET is more programs available more quickly, on more platforms, with fewer problems.

With a CLR like .NET, programmers need not consider the capabilities of the specific CPU that will execute the program. The CLR also provides other important services such as security, memory management, and exception handling.

Language Interoperability

The .NET Framework includes a large library. It supports several programming languages which allows language interoperability (each language can use code written in other languages). The .NET library is available to all the programming languages that .NET supports. The class library and the CLR together constitute the .NET Framework.

The .NET framework's Base Class Library provides user interface, data access, database connectivity, cryptography, web application development, numeric algorithms, and network communications. The class library is used by programmers, who combine it with their own code to produce applications. The .NET Framework is intended to be used by most new applications created for the Windows platform. To develop new applications, software developers can also use Microsoft's SDK for Windows 7 or .NET Framework 4 (or newer) or Visual Studio 2010 on top of the .NET Framework.

Because computer systems commonly require interaction between new and older applications, the .NET Framework provides means to access functionality that is implemented in programs that execute outside the .NET environment. Access to COM components is provided in the System.Runtime .InteropServices and System.EnterpriseServices namespaces of the framework; access to other functionality is provided using the P/Invoke feature.

The Common Language Runtime (CLR) is the execution engine of the .NET Framework. All .NET programs execute under the supervision of the CLR, guaranteeing certain properties and behaviors in the areas of memory management, security, and exception handling.

The .NET Framework introduces a Common Type System, or CTS. The CTS specification defines all possible datatypes and programming constructs supported by the CLR and how they may or may not interact with each other conforming to the Common Language Infrastructure (CLI) specification. Because of this feature, the .NET Framework supports the exchange of types and object instances between libraries and applications written using any conforming .NET language.

The Base Class Library (BCL) is a part of the Framework Class Library (FCL). It is a library of functionality available to all languages using the .NET Framework. The BCL provides classes which encapsulate a number of common functions, including file reading and writing, graphic rendering, database interaction, XML document manipulation and so on.

DESIGN FEATURES AND TOOLS

The .NET Framework includes design features and tools that help manage the installation of computer software to ensure that it does not interfere with previously installed software, and that it conforms to security requirements.

Common Security Model

The design is meant to address some of the vulnerabilities, such as buffer overflows, that have been exploited by malicious software. Additionally, .NET provides a common security model for all applications.

A program written to use the framework should run without change on any type of system for which the framework is implemented. While Microsoft has never implemented the full framework on any system except Microsoft Windows, the framework is engineered to be platform agnostic,and cross-platform implementations are available for other operating systems.

Architecture

Common Language Infrastructure (CLI)

Microsoft's implementation of the CLI is called the Common Language Runtime, or CLR. The main function of the Common Language Infrastructure, is to provide a language-neutral platform for application development and execution, including functions for Exception handling, Garbage Collection, security, and interoperability. By implementing the core aspects of the .NET Framework within the scope of the CLI, this functionality will not be tied to a single language but will be available across the many languages supported by the framework.

Assemblies

The CIL code is housed in .NET assemblies. As mandated by specification, assemblies are stored in the Portable Executable (PE) format, common on the Windows platform for all DLL and EXE files. The assembly consists of one or more files, one of which must contain the manifest, which has the metadata for the assembly. The complete name of an assembly (not to be confused with the filename on disk) contains its simple text name, version number, culture, and public key token.

The public key token is a unique hash generated when the assembly is compiled, thus two assemblies with the same public key token are guaranteed to be identical from the point of view of the framework.A private key can also be specified known only to the creator of the assembly and can be used for strong naming and to guarantee that the assembly is from the same author when a new version of the assembly is compiled (required to add an assembly to the Global Assembly Cache).

Security Mechanism

.NET has its own security mechanism with two general features: Code Access Security (CAS), and validation and verification. Code Access Security is based on evidence that is associated with a specific assembly. Typically the evidence is the source of the assembly (whether it is installed on the local machine or has been downloaded from the intranet or Internet). Code Access Security uses evidence to determine the permissions granted to the code. Other code can demand that calling code is granted a specified permission.

The demand causes the CLR to perform a call stack walk: every assembly of each method in the call stack is checked for the required permission; if any assembly is not granted the permission a security exception is thrown. however, has to split the application into subdomains; it is not done by the CLR.

Class Library

Namespaces in the BCL

System

System. CodeDom

System. Collections

System. Diagnostics

System. Globalization

System. IO

System. Resources

System. Text

System. Text.RegularExpressions

The .NET Framework includes a set of standard class libraries. The class library is organized in a hierarchy of namespaces. Most of the built in APIs are part of either System.* or Microsoft.* namespaces. These class libraries implement a large number of common functions, such as file reading and writing, graphic rendering, database interaction, and XML document manipulation, among others. The .NET class libraries are available to all CLI compliant languages. The .NET Framework class library is divided into two parts: the Base Class Library and the Framework Class Library.

The Base Class Library (BCL) includes a small subset of the entire class library and is the core set of classes that serve as the basic API of the Common Language Runtime. The classes in mscorlib.dll and some of the classes in System.dll and System.core.dll are considered to be a part of the BCL. The BCL classes are available in both .NET Framework as well as its alternative implementations including .NET Compact Framework, Microsoft Silverlight and Mono.

The Framework Class Library (FCL) is a superset of the BCL classes and refers to the entire class library that ships with .NET Framework. It includes an expanded set of libraries, including Windows Forms, ADO.NET, ASP.NET, Language Integrated Query, Windows Presentation Foundation, Windows Communication Foundation among others. The FCL is much larger in scope than standard libraries for languages like C++, and comparable in scope to the standard libraries of Java.

The .NET Framework CLR frees the developer from the burden of managing memory (allocating and freeing up when done); instead it does the memory management itself even though there are no actual guarantees as to when the Garbage Collector will perform its work, unless an explicit double-call is issued. To this end, the memory allocated to instantiations of .NET types (objects) is done contiguously from the managed heap, a pool of memory managed by the CLR.

As long as there exists a reference to an object, which might be either a direct reference to an object or via a graph of objects, the object is considered to be in use by the CLR. When there is no reference to an object, and it cannot be reached or used, it becomes garbage. However, it still holds on to the memory allocated to it. .NET Framework includes a garbage collector which runs periodically, on a separate thread from the application's thread, that enumerates all the unusable objects and reclaims the memory allocated to them.

It .NET Garbage Collector (GC) is a non-deterministic, compacting, mark-and-sweep garbage collector. It runs only when a certain amount of memory has been used or there is enough pressure for memory on the system. Since it is not guaranteed when the conditions to reclaim memory are reached, the GC runs are non-deterministic. Each .NET application has a set of roots, which are pointers to objects on the managed heap (managed objects). These include references to static objects and objects defined as local variables or method parameters currently in scope, as well as objects referred to by CPU registers.

When the GC runs, it pauses the application, and for each object referred to in the root, it recursively enumerates all the objects reachable from the root objects and marks them as reachable. It uses .NET metadata and reflection to discover the objects encapsulated by an object, and then recursively walk them. It then enumerates all the objects on the heap (which were initially allocated contiguously) using reflection. All objects not marked as reachable are garbage. This is the mark phase.

Free Space

Since the memory held by garbage is not of any consequence, it is considered free space. However, this leaves chunks of free space between objects which were initially contiguous. The objects are then compacted together to make used memory contiguous again. Any reference to an object invalidated by moving the object is updated to reflect the new location by the GC. The application is resumed after the garbage collection is over.

The GC used by .NET Framework is actually generational. Objects are assigned a generation; newly created objects belong to Generation 0. The objects that survive a garbage collection are tagged as Generation 1, and the Generation 1 objects that survive another collection are Generation 2 objects. The .NET Framework uses up to Generation 2 objects. Higher generation objects are garbage collected less frequently than lower generation objects. This helps increase the efficiency of garbage collection, as older objects tend to have a larger lifetime than newer objects. Thus, by removing older (and thus more likely to survive a collection) objects from the scope of a collection run, fewer objects need to be checked and compacted.

In August 2000, Microsoft, Hewlett-Packard, and Intel worked to standardize CLI and the C# programming language. By December 2001, both were ratified ECMA standards (ECMA 335 and ECMA 334). ISO followed in April 2003 - the current version of the ISO standards are ISO/IEC 23271:2006 and ISO/IEC 23270:2006.

While Microsoft and their partners hold patents for the CLI and C#, ECMA and ISO require that all patents essential to implementation be made available under "reasonable and non-discriminatory terms". In addition to meeting these terms, the companies have agreed to make the patents available royalty-free. However, this does not apply for the part of the .NET Framework which is not covered by the ECMA/ISO standard, which includes Windows Forms, ADO.NET, and ASP.NET. Patents that Microsoft holds in these areas may deter non-Microsoft implementations of the full framework.

On 3 October 2007, Microsoft announced that much of the source code for the .NET Framework Base Class Library (including ASP.NET, ADO.NET, and Windows Presentation Foundation) was to have been made available with the final release of Visual Studio 2008 towards the end of 2007 under the shared source Microsoft Reference License.The source code for other libraries including Windows Communication Foundation (WCF), Windows Workflow Foundation (WF), and Language Integrated Query (LINQ) were to be added in future releases. Being released under the non-open source Microsoft Reference License means this source code is made available for debugging purpose only, primarily to support integrated debugging of the BCL in Visual Studio.

Next Generation Windows Services

Microsoft started development on the .NET Framework in the late 1990s originally under the name of Next Generation Windows Services (NGWS). By late 2000 the first beta versions of .NET 1.0 were released.

Version 3.0 of the .NET Framework is included with Windows Server 2008 and Windows Vista. Version 3.5 is included with Windows 7, and can also be installed on Windows XP and the Windows Server 2003 family of operating systems. On April 12, 2010, .NET Framework 4 was released alongside Visual Studio 2010. The .NET Framework family also includes two versions for mobile or embedded device use. A reduced version of the framework, the .NET Compact Framework, is available on Windows CE platforms, including Windows Mobile devices such as smartphones. Additionally, the .NET Micro Framework is targeted at severely resource-constrained devices.

Version	Version Number	Release Date	Visual Studio	Default in Windows
1.0	1.0.3705.0	2002-02-13	Visual Studio .NET	
1.1	1.1.4322.573	2003-04-24	Visual Studio .NET 2003	Windows Server 2003
2.0	2.0.50727.42	2005-11-07	Visual Studio 2005	Windows Server 2003 R2
3.0	3.0.4506.30	2006-11-06		Windows Vista, Windows Server 2008
3.5	3.5.21022.8	2007-11-19	Visual Studio 2008	Windows 7, Windows Server 2008 R2
4.0	4.0.30319.1	2010-04-12	Visual Studio 2010	

A more complete listing of the releases of the .NET Framework may be found on the List of .NET Framework versions.

Some concerns and criticism relating to .NET include:

Applications running in a managed environment tend to require more system resources than similar applications that access machine resources more directly.

Unobfuscated managed CIL bytecode can often be easier to reverse-engineer than native code. One concern is over possible loss of trade secrets and the bypassing of license control mechanisms. Since Visual Studio .NET (2002), Microsoft has included a tool to obfuscate code (Dotfuscator Community Edition).

Newer versions of the framework (3.5 and up) are not pre-installed in versions of Windows below Windows 7 (although newer versions are available via Windows Updates). For this reason, applications must lead users without the framework through a procedure to install it. Some developers have expressed concerns about the large size of the .NET Framework runtime installers for end-users. The size is around 54 MB for .NET 3.0, 197 MB for .NET 3.5, and 250 MB for .NET 3.5 SP1 (while using web installer the typical download for Windows XP is around 50 MB, for Windows Vista - 20 MB). The size issue is partially solved with .NET 4 installer (x86 + x64) being 54 MB and not embedding full runtime installation packages for previous versions. The .NET 3.5 SP1 full installation package includes the full runtime installation packages for .NET 2.0 SP2 as well as .NET 3.0 SP2 for multiple operating systems (Windows XP/Server 2003 and Windows Vista/Server 2008) and for multiple CPU architectures (x86, x86-64, and IA-64).

The first service pack for version 3.5 mitigates this concern by offering a lighter-weight client-only subset of the .NET Framework. Two significant limitations should be noted, though. Firstly, the client-only subset is only an option on an existing Windows XP SP2 system that currently has no other version of the .NET Framework installed. In all other scenarios, the client-only installer will install the full version of the .NET Framework 3.5 SP1. Secondly, the client-only framework does not have a 64-bit option. However, the 4 release of the .NET Framework Client Profile will be available on all operating systems and all architectures (excluding Itanium) supported by the full .NET Framework. The .NET Framework currently does not provide support for calling Streaming SIMD Extensions (SSE) via managed code. However, Mono has provided support for SIMD Extensions as of version 2.2

within the Mono.Simd namespace; Mono's lead developer Miguel de Icaza has expressed hope that this SIMD support will be adopted by the CLR ECMA standard. Streaming SIMD Extensions have been available in x86 CPUs since the introduction of the Pentium III. Some other architectures such as ARM and MIPS also have SIMD extensions. In case the CPU lacks support for those extensions, the instructions are simulated in software.

While the standards that make up .NET are inherently cross platform, Microsoft's full implementation of .NET is only supported on Windows. Microsoft does provide limited .NET subsets for other platforms such as XNA for Windows, XBOX 360 and Windows Phone 7, Silverlight for Windows and Mac OS X. Alternative implementations of the CLR, base class libraries, and compilers also exist (sometimes from other vendors). While all of these implementations are based on the same standards, they are still different implementations with varying levels of completeness in comparison to the full .NET version Microsoft ships for Windows and are on occasion incompatible.

The Microsoft .NET Framework is the predominant implementation of .NET technologies. Other implementations for parts of the framework exist. Although the runtime engine is described by an ECMA/ISO specification, other implementations of it may be encumbered by patent issues; ISO standards may include the disclaimer, "Attention is drawn to the possibility that some of the elements of this document may be the subject of patent rights. ISO shall not be held responsible for identifying any or all such patent rights."

Alternative Implementation

It is more difficult to develop alternatives to the base class library (BCL), which is not described by an open standard and may be subject to copyright restrictions. Additionally, parts of the BCL have Windows-specific functionality and behavior, so implementation on non-Windows platforms can be problematic.

Few alternative implementations of parts of the framework are :

- Microsoft's Shared Source Common Language Infrastructure is a shared source implementation of the CLR component of the .NET Framework. However, the last version only runs on Microsoft Windows XP SP2, and does not contain all features of version 2.0 of the .NET Framework.
- Microsoft's .NET Micro Framework is a .NET platform for extremely resource-constrained devices. It includes a small version of the .NET CLR and supports development in C# (with unofficial support for VB.NET and other languages) and debugging (in an emulator or on hardware), both using Microsoft Visual Studio. It also features a subset of the .NET base class libraries (about 70 classes with about 420 methods), a GUI framework loosely based on Windows Presentation Foundation, and additional libraries specific to embedded applications.
- Mono is an up-to-date implementation of the CLI and the .NET Base Class Library (BCL), and provides additional functionality. It is dual-licensed under free software and proprietary software licenses. Mono is actively being developed by Novell, Inc. It includes support for ASP.NET, ADO.NET, and Windows Forms libraries for a wide range of architectures (including iPhone, Wii and others) and operating systems. It also includes C# and VB.NET compilers.
- CrossNet is an implementation of the CLI and portions of the .NET Base Class Library (BCL). It is free software using the open source MIT License. It parses .NET assemblies and generates standard C++ code, compilable with any ANSI C++ compiler on any platform.
- Portable.NET (part of DotGNU) provides an implementation of the Common Language Infrastructure (CLI), portions of the .NET Base Class Library (BCL), and a C# compiler. It supports a variety of CPUs and operating systems.

Ways to Internet Sharing

If you want to share one Internet connection among several users there are two options :

- Use Internet Connection Sharing (ICS).
- Use a router.

On the priority list, you need a good running computer or laptop, called the host computer. It must be is connected to the Internet and that has a separate connection to the other computers on your network. You enable ICS on the Internet connection. The other computers on your network then connect to the host computer, and from there to the Internet through the host computer's shared Internet connection.

To enable ICS on your host computer. Firstly, Open Network Connections by clicking the Start button, clicking Control Panel, clicking Network and Internet, clicking Network and Sharing Center, and then clicking Manage network connections. Secondly, Right-click the connection that you want to share, and then click Properties. If you are prompted for an administrator password or confirmation, type the password or provide confirmation. Thirdly, Activate the sharing tab and then select the Allow other network users to connect through host computer's Internet connection check box. Fourthly, One can also select the Allow other network users to control or disable the shared Internet connection check box. Optionally, to allow other network users to use services running on your network, click Settings and select the services you want to allow.

When you enable ICS, your local area network (LAN) connection gets a new static IP address and configuration, so you'll need to reestablish any TCP/IP connections between your host computer and the other network computers.

To test your network and Internet connection, see if you can share files between computers and make sure each computer can reach a website.

To use ICS, make sure the local area network (LAN) connection on each network computer is configured to get an IP address automatically. To do this:

1. Open Network Connections by clicking the Start button , clicking Control Panel, clicking Network and Internet, clicking Network and Sharing Center, and then clicking Manage network connections.
2. Right-click the LAN connection, and then click Properties. If you are prompted for an administrator password or confirmation, type the password or provide confirmation.
3. Click Internet Protocol Version 4 (TCP/IPv4) or Internet Protocol Version 6 (TCP/IPv6), and then click Properties.
4. Click Obtain an IP address automatically or Obtain an IPv6 address automatically.

The Internet options on your network computers should also be configured for ICS.

Do not use ICS on a network with domain controllers, DNS servers, gateways, or DHCP servers. And don't use ICS on systems configured for static IP addresses.

Sharing a Single Internet Connection

Users on both Windows and Mac computers can configure their systems to share a single Internet connection among several users on the same local network. First, users must priortize which computer will host the network connection and then set up that machine with the active Internet signal. Via Ethernet or wireless connection the host computer needs to be directly connected to the Internet. Then the host system can be configured to share the connection, using the Internet control panel on the computer.

Remote Set Up

Remote systems can be set up to locate and connect to the newly created network. Once the host computer has been set up to share an Internet connection. If the host computer is sharing the connection through an Ethernet port, then an Ethernet cable must be connected from the host to the remote system. On the other hand, if the host computer is sharing the network connection through a wireless card, then the remote system's wireless scanner must be enabled. The name of the host computer should appear in the list of available devices to connect from the remote system.

Remote Connection

One can receive or send data while working on computer with Internet facility. One can Once Internet sharing is set up with remote systems, the host computer begins transferring those packets of network data to the other machines on the local network. Each computer on the shared network receives a distinct IP address from the host system, but these addresses are not seen on the Internet. It is interesting to note that All actions from the remote computers go through the host system, so all of the machines are actually sharing the host's IP address.

References

1. http://www.wisegeek.com/how-big-is-the-internet.htm
2. http://www.ehow.com/how-does_4691891_internet-connection-sharing-work.html
3. Scott Guthrie (3 October 2007). "Releasing the Source Code for the NET Framework". http://weblogs.asp.net/scottgu/archive/2007/10/03/releasing-the-source-code-for-the-net-framework-libraries.aspx. Retrieved 15 September 2010.
4. "Scott Guthrie: Silverlight and the Cross-Platform CLR". Channel 9. 30 April 2007. http://channel9.msdn.com/shows/Going+Deep/Scott-Guthrie-Silverlight-and-the-Cross-Platform-CLR.
5. "Garbage Collection: Automatic Memory Management in the Microsoft .NET Framework". Archived from the original on 3 July 2007. http://web.archive.org/web/20070703083608/http://msdn.microsoft.com/msdnmag/issues/1100/GCI/. Retrieved 1 June 2008.
6. "Garbage collection in .NET". http://www.csharphelp.com/archives2/archive297.html. Retrieved 1 June 2008.

7. "Garbage Collection—Part 2: Automatic Memory Management in the Microsoft .NET Framework". Archived from the original on 26 June 2007. http://web.archive.org/web/20070626080134/http://msdn.microsoft.com/msdnmag/issues/1200/GCI2/default.aspx. Retrieved 1 June 2008.
8. ISO/IEC 23271:2006 - Information technology - Common Language Infrastructure (CLI) Partitions I to VI
9. ISO/IEC 23270:2006 - Information technology - Programming languages - C#
10. "Microsoft's Empty Promise". Free Software Foundation. 16 July 2009. Archived from the original on 5 August 2009. http://www.webcitation.org/5io4tT8mO. Retrieved 3 August 2009. "However, there are several libraries that are included with Mono, and commonly used by applications like Tomboy, that are not required by the standard. And just to be clear, we're not talking about Windows-specific libraries like ASP.NET and Windows Forms. Instead, we're talking about libraries under the System namespace that provide common functionality programmers expect in modern programming languages"
11. "Framework Versions". http://ben.skyiv.com/clrversion.html.
12. Microsoft. "Microsoft .NET Framework 3.5 Administrator Deployment Guide". http://msdn.microsoft.com/library/cc160717.aspx. Retrieved 26 June 2008.
13. "Reverse Engineering Risk Assessment". http://www.preemptive.com/images/documentation/Reverse_Engineering_Risk_Assessment.pdf.

CHAPTER–10

METHODS OF COMMUNICATION VIA WEB SERVICES

The Application Services Library (ASL) is a public domain standard, which describes a standard for processes within Application Management (the discipline of producing and maintaining information systems and applications). The term "library" is used because the ASL standard is based on the descriptions of best practices from the industry. ASL is a methodology used in the IT industry.

TIES (Telecommunication Information Exchange Service) is a set of networked information resources and services offered by ITU to its Members (ITU Member States, Sector Members and Associates) to support their participation in the activities of the Union.

TIES is available without any charge to ITU Member States (including Geneva-based Permanent Missions), ITU Sector Members and Associates.

TIES Focal Point

In each organization/company, there is a TIES Focal Point responsible for:

- accepting/refusing requests to create TIES Accounts in the organization/company;

- maintaining the list of TIES Accounts in the organization/ company updated;
- deleting TIES Accounts.

The TIES Focal Point has a dedicated Web page, which is accessible with an Access Code.

This standard was developed in the late nineties in the Netherlands, originally as the proprietary R2C model, which evolved into ASL in 2000. In 2001 it was donated by the IT Service Provider PinkRoccade to the ASL Foundation, now the ASL BiSL Foundation.

ASL is closely related to ITIL, BiSL and CMM. It is described in several books and articles (most of them only available in Dutch), as well as on the official website of the ASL BiSL Foundation.

The standard was developed because of the inability to structure the way of working within the Application Management departments by only using the ITIL framework, an older library embraced by the IT infrastructure departments for structuring their way of working. At the time of development, ITIL was very useful for infrastructure management but lacked specific guidance for application design, development, maintenance and support. Newer ITIL versions, particularly V3, have increasingly addressed the Application Development and Application Management domains. A reference to a white paper comparing ITIL V3 and ASL is included.

ASL was defined in order to fill this gap for Application Management. A similar development has led to the definition of the BiSL-standard for Information Management / Functional Management.

The ASL is intended to support Application Management by providing tools. Two main categories of aids are defined:

- Descriptions of the processes for Application Management. Plus the use of best-practises
- Standard terminology, avoiding the pitfall of talking about different topics while using the same words.

The aim of ASL is to assist in the professionalization of Application Management.

STRUCTURE OF ASL

ASL contains six clusters of processes, three on the operational level, one on the tactical level and two on the strategic level.

Operational Level

Service Organisation

There are five processes within the cluster Service Organisation. The processes in the Service Organisation cluster support the daily use of the information systems. The following given processes in this cluster are as follows :

1. incident management
2. continuity management
3. capacity management
4. availability management
5. configuration management

These processes have as well been defined in the ITIL framework. The processes are similar, but are viewed from another point of view, therefore the activities in each of these processes may differ from the activities in an ITIL-environment.

Development and Maintenance

Within this cluster the majority of the work of Application Development is done. A major part of the work of Application Management deals with designing, programming and testing applications and information systems. Processes are given below :

1. impact analysis
2. design
3. realization
4. testing
5. implementation

These processes are not described at all in the ITIL V1 framework, but do have their counterparts in BiSL, the model for Information management / Functional Management.

Connecting Processes

The connecting processes aim at the synchronisation of the activities between Service Organisation/operations (using the applications) and development and maintenance (changing the applications). The two processes included are given below :

1. change management
2. release management.

Tactical Level

Management Processes

The processes in this cluster are used in the management of the activities within the clusters on the operational level. The processes are located on the tactical level, are used for steering the operational processes. The processes included are given below:

1. quality management
2. service level management
3. cost management
4. planning & control.

Strategic Level

Application Cycle Management

Applications live for longer than expected. Systems, functionality, concepts and structure of information systems remain stable over many years. This knowledge is rarely used. It is important that, while maintaining and enhancing systems, there is a clear view needed what the demands are in the future, and based on that, what and how the future of these applications should look like. This view, the application management strategies, is created within the cluster application cycle management. The processes in this cluster are as follow :

1. life cycle management
2. information portfolio management
3. customer organisation strategy
4. customer environment strategy
5. ICT development strategy.

Organisation Cycle Management

Also the future of the Application Management organisation, with aspects as skills and capabilities, markets and customers, is very important. Creating the organisation management strategies for this is the aim of Organization Cycle Management. The main Processes in this cluster include are given under :

1. account definition
2. market definition
3. skills definition
4. technology definition
5. service delivery definition

Public Domain

Works are in the public domain if they are not covered by intellectual property rights at all, if the intellectual property rights have expired,and/or if the intellectual property rights are forfeited.Examples include the English language, the formulae of Newtonian physics, the works of Shakespeare and Beethoven, and the patents on powered flight. In a general context public domain may refer to ideas, information, and works that are "publicly available", but in the context of intellectual property law, which includes copyright, patents, and trademarks, public domain refers to works, ideas, and information which are intangible to private ownership and/or which are available for use by members of the public.

The term public domain did not appear in early copyright law, which was first established in Britain with the Statute of Anne

1710. Though the concept did exist and 18th Century British and French jurists used terms such as publici juris or propriété publique to describe works that were not covered by copyright law.The phrase "fall in the public domain" can be traced to mid 19th Century France to describe the end of copyright term. The French poet Alfred de Vigny equated the expiration of copyright with a work falling "into the sink hole of the public domain"and if the public domain receives any attention from intellectual property lawyers it is still treated as little more than that which is left when intellectual property rights, such as copyright, patents, and trademarks, expire or are abandoned.

Copyright law was created by statute and all works created and published before copyright law was first established are in the public domain. In this historical context Paul Torremans describes copyright as a "little coral reef of private right jutting up from the ocean of the public domain." Because copyright law is different from country to country, Pamela Samuelson has described the public domain as being "different sizes at different times in different countries".

Definitions of the boundaries of the public domain in relation to copyright, or intellectual property more generally, regard the public domain as a negative space, that is, it consists of works that are no longer in copyright term or were never protected by copyright law. More subtle definitions of the public domain move beyond those works that no longer receive legal protection under intellectual property law and incorporates all aspects of works which are not covered by the intellectual property doctrine, such as insubstantial parts of a copyrighted work or the statutory defined permitted acts and exceptions to copyright.

A less legalistic definition of the public domain comes from Lange, who focused on what the public domain should be: "it should be a place of sanctuary for individual creative expression, a sanctuary conferring affirmative protection against the forces of private appropriation that threatened such expression".

Patterson and Lindberg described the public domain not as a "territory", but rather as a concept: "There are certain materials - the air we breathe, sunlight, rain, space, life, creations, thoughts, feelings, ideas, words, numbers - not subject to private ownership. The materials that compose our cultural heritage must be free for all to use no less than matter necessary for biological survival." The term public domain may also be interchangeably used with other imprecise and/or undefined terms such as the "public sphere" or "commons", including concepts such as "commons of the mind", the "intellectual commons", and the "information commons".

Value of the public domain

In attempting to map the public domain Pamela Samuelson has identified eight "values" that can arise from information and works in the public domain, though not every idea or work that is in the public domain necessarily has a value. Possible values include are given below:

1. Building blocks for the creation of new knowledge, examples include data, facts, ideas, theories, and scientific principle.
2. Access to cultural heritage through information resources such as ancient Greek texts and Mozart's symphonies.
3. Promoting education, through the spread of information, ideas, and scientific principles.
4. Enabling follow-on innovation, through for example expired patents and copyright.
5. Enabling low cost access to information without the need to locate the owner or negotiate rights clearance and pay royalties, through for example expired copyrighted works or patents, and non-original data compilation.
6. Promoting public health and safety, through information and scientific principles.
7. Promoting the democratic process and values, through news, laws, regulation, and judicial opinion.

8. Enabling competitive imitation, through for example expired patents and copyright, or publicly disclosed technologies that do not qualify for patent protection.

Public Domain and Derivative Works

Derivative works include translations, musical arrangements, and dramatizations of a work, as well as other forms of transformation or adaptation. Copyrighted works may not be used for derivative works without permission from the copyright owner, while public domain works can be freely used for derivative works without permission. Artworks that are public domain may also be reproduced photographically or artistically or used as the basis of new, interpretive works. Once works enter into the public domain, derivative works such as adaptations in book and film may increase noticeably, as happened with Frances Hodgson Burnett's novel The Secret Garden, which became public domain in 1987.

As of 1999, the plays of Shakespeare, all public domain, had been used in more than 420 feature-length films. In addition to straightforward adaptation, they have been used as the launching point for transformative retellings such as Tom Stoppard's Rosencrantz and Guildenstern Are Dead and Troma Entertainment's Tromeo and Juliet. Marcel Duchamp's L.H.O.O.Q. is a derivative of Leonardo Da Vinci's Mona Lisa, one of thousands of derivative works based on the public domain painting.

According to Bernt Hugenholtz and Lucie Guibault the public domain is under pressure from the "commodification of information" as items of information that previously had little or no economic value have acquired independent economic value in the information age, such as factual data, personal data, genetic information, and pure ideas.

The commodification of information is taking place through intellectual property law, contract law, as well as broadcasting and telecommunications law. The undermining of the public domain, and in particular limitations and exceptions to copyright by contract law is also an issue frequently raised by libraries, and library groups such as International Federation of Library Associations and Institutions.

Perpetual Copyright

Some works may never fully lapse into the public domain. A perpetual crown copyright is held for the Authorized King James Version of the Bible in the UK. While the copyright of the play Peter Pan, or the Boy Who Wouldn't Grow Up by J. M. Barrie has expired in the United Kingdom, it was granted a special exception under the Copyright, Designs, and Patents Act 1988 (Schedule 6) that requires royalties to be paid for performances within the UK, so long as Great Ormond Street Hospital (to whom Barrie gave the rights) continues to exist.

Public Domain in Copyrightable Works

Works not Covered by Copyright Law

The underlying idea that is expressed or manifested in the creation of a work generally cannot be the subject of copyright law (see idea-expression divide). Mathematical formulae will therefore generally form part of the public domain, to the extent that their expression in the form of software is not covered by copyright; however, algorithms can be the subject of a software patent in some jurisdictions.

Works created before the existence of copyright and patent laws also form part of the public domain. For example, the Bible and the inventions of Archimedes are in the public domain, but copyright may exist in translations or new formulations of these works.

Expiration of Copyright

The expiration of a copyright is more complex than that of a patent. Historically the United States has specified terms of a number of years following creation or publication; this number has been increased several times. Most other countries specify terms of a number of years following the death of the last surviving creator; this number varies from one country to another (50 years and 70 years are the most common), and has also been increased in many of them.

Legal traditions differ on whether a work in the public domain can have its copyright restored. Term extensions by the U.S. and Australia generally have not removed works from the public domain, but merely delayed the addition of works to it. By contrast, a European Union directive harmonizing the term of copyright protection was applied retroactively, restoring and extending the terms of copyright on material previously in the public domain.

Government Work

Works of the United States Government and various other governments are excluded from copyright law and may therefore be considered to be in the public domain in their respective countries. In the United States, when copyrighted material is enacted into the law, it enters the public domain. Thus, the building codes, when enacted, are in the public domain. They may also be in the public domain in other countries as well. "It is axiomatic that material in the public domain is not protected by copyright, even when incorporated into a copyrighted work."

Main Definition

The definition of public domain is not uniform and may not only include completed works, but also permitted uses of works still covered by intellectual property rights, such as for example the right to excerpt short quotations in a review. This definition divides areas of private property from areas of the public domain. For example, Mozart's music is public property, and Britney Spears' music is private property.

Public Domain in Trademarks

A trademark registration may remain in force indefinitely, or expire without specific regard to its age. For a trademark registration to remain valid, the owner must continue to use it. In some circumstances, such as disuse, failure to assert trademark rights, or common usage by the public without regard for its intended use, it could become generic, and therefore part of the public domain.

Because trademarks are registered with governments, some countries or trademark registries may recognize a mark, while others may have determined that it is generic and not allowable as a trademark in that registry. For example, the drug "acetylsalicylic acid" (2-acetoxybenzoic acid) is better known as aspirin in the United States—a generic term. In Canada, however, "aspirin" is still a trademark of the German company Bayer. Bayer lost the trademark after World War I, when the mark was sold to an American firm. So many copy-cat products entered the marketplace during the war that it was deemed generic just three years later.

Generic Trademarks

Trademarks currently thought to be in danger of being generic include Kleenex, iPod, Jell-O, Band-Aid, Rollerblade, Frisbee, Google, Spam, Hoover, Xerox, Velcro, and Sheetrock. Google vigorously defends its trademark rights. Although Hormel resigned itself to genericide, it has fought attempts by other companies to register "spam" as a trademark in relation to computer products.

WEB SERVICE

A web service is a method of communication between two electronic devices over a network. The W3C defines a "web service" as "a software system designed to support interoperable machine-to-machine interaction over a network. It has an interface described in a machine-processable format (specifically Web Services Description Language WSDL). Other systems interact with the web service in a manner prescribed by its description using SOAP messages, typically conveyed using HTTP with an XML serialization in conjunction with other Web-related standards."

The W3C also states, "We can identify two major classes of web services, REST-compliant Web services, in which the primary purpose of the service is to manipulate XML representations of Web resources using a uniform set of "stateless" operations; and arbitrary Web services, in which the service may expose an arbitrary set of operations."

"Big Web services" use Extensible Markup Language (XML) messages that follow the SOAP standard and have been popular with traditional enterprises. In such systems, there is often a machine-readable description of the operations offered by the service written in the Web Services Description Language (WSDL). The latter is not a requirement of a SOAP endpoint, but it is a prerequisite for automated client-side code generation in many Java and .NET SOAP frameworks (frameworks such as Apache Axis2, Apache CXF, and Spring being notable exceptions). Some industry organizations, such as the WS-I, mandate both SOAP and WSDL in their definition of a Web service.

Web API is a development in Web services (in a movement called Web 2.0) where emphasis has been moving away from SOAP based services towards Representational State Transfer (REST) based communications.REST services do not require XML, SOAP, or WSDL service-API definitions. Web APIs allow the combination of multiple Web services into new applications known as mashups.

When used in the context of Web development, Web API is typically a defined set of Hypertext Transfer Protocol (HTTP) request messages along with a definition of the structure of response messages, usually expressed in an Extensible Markup Language (XML) or JavaScript Object Notation (JSON) format.

When running composite Web services, each sub service can be considered autonomous. The user has no control over these services. Also the Web services themselves are not reliable; the service provider may remove, change or update their services without giving notice to users. The reliability and fault tolerance is not well supported; faults may happen during the execution. Exception handling in the context of Web services is still an open research issue. Still it can be handled by responding with an error object to the client.

Using Style

Web services are a set of tools that can be used in a number of ways. The three most common styles of use are RPC, SOAP and REST.

Remote Procedure Calls

RPC Web services present a distributed function (or method) call interface that is familiar to many developers. Typically, the basic unit of RPC Web services is the WSDL operation.

The first Web services tools were focused on RPC, and as a result this style is widely deployed and supported. However, it is sometimes criticized for not being loosely coupled, because it was often implemented by mapping services directly to language-specific functions or method calls. Many vendors felt this approach to be a dead end, and pushed for RPC to be disallowed in the WS-I Basic Profile.

Other approaches with nearly the same functionality as RPC are Object Management Group's (OMG) Common Object Request Broker Architecture (CORBA), Microsoft's Distributed Component Object Model (DCOM) or Sun Microsystems's Java/Remote Method Invocation (RMI).

Service-oriented Architecture

Web services can also be used to implement an architecture according to service-oriented architecture (SOA) concepts, where the basic unit of communication is a message, rather than an operation. This is often referred to as "message-oriented" services.

SOA Web services are supported by most major software vendors and industry analysts. Unlike RPC Web services, loose coupling is more likely, because the focus is on the "contract" that WSDL provides, rather than the underlying implementation details.

Middleware analysts use enterprise service buses that combine message-oriented processing and Web services to create an event-driven SOA. One example of an open-source ESB is Mule, another one is Open ESB.

Representational State Transfer (REST)

REST attempts to describe architectures that use HTTP or similar protocols by constraining the interface to a set of well-known, standard operations (like GET, POST, PUT, DELETE for HTTP). Here, the focus is on interacting with stateful resources, rather than messages or operations.

An architecture based on REST (one that is 'RESTful') can use WSDL to describe SOAP messaging over HTTP, can be implemented as an abstraction purely on top of SOAP (e.g., WS-Transfer), or can be created without using SOAP at all.

WSDL version 2.0 offers support for binding to all the HTTP request methods (not only GET and POST as in version 1.1) so it enables a better implementation of RESTful Web services. However, support for this specification is still poor in software development kits, which often offer tools only for WSDL 1.1.

Automated Tools

Automated tools can aid in the creation of a Web service. For services using WSDL it is possible to either automatically generate WSDL for existing classes (a bottom-up strategy) or to generate a class skeleton given existing WSDL (a top-down strategy).

- A developer using a bottom up method writes implementing classes first (in some programming language), and then uses a WSDL generating tool to expose methods from these classes as a Web service. This is often the simpler approach.
- A developer using a top down method writes the WSDL document first and then uses a code generating tool to produce the class skeleton, to be completed as necessary. This way is generally considered more difficult but can produce cleaner designs.

Criticisms

Critics of non-RESTful Web services often complain that they are too complex and based upon large software vendors or integrators, rather than typical open source implementations. There are open source implementations like Apache Axis and Apache CXF.

One key concern of the REST Web service developers is that the SOAP WS toolkits make it easy to define new interfaces for remote interaction, often relying on introspection to extract the WSDL, since a minor change on the server (even an upgrade of the SOAP stack) can result in different WSDL and a different service interface.

The client-side classes that can be generater from WSDL and XSD descriptions of the service are often similarly tied to a particular version of the SOAP endpoint and can break, if the endpoint changes or the client-side SOAP stack is upgraded. Well-designed SOAP endpoints (with handwritten XSD and WSDL) do not suffer from this but there is still the problem that a custom interface for every service requires a custom client for every service.

There are also concerns about performance due to Web services' use of XML as a message format and SOAP/HTTP in enveloping and transport, such as that published by the University of Wollongong in 2005 by N.A.B.Gray.

References

1. "Web Services Glossary". W3C. February 11, 2004. http://www.w3.org/TR/2004/NOTE-ws-gloss-20040211/. Retrieved 2011-04-22.
2. "Relationship to the World Wide Web and REST Architectures". Web Services Architecture. W3C. http://www.w3.org/TR/ws-arch/#relwwwrest. Retrieved 2011-04-22.
3. Benslimane, Djamal; Schahram Dustdar, and Amit Sheth (2008). "Services Mashups: The New Generation of Web Applications". IEEE Internet Computing, vol. 12, no. 5. Institute of Electrical and Electronics Engineers. pp. 13–15. http://dsonline.computer.org/portal/site/dsonline/

menuitem.9ed3d9924aeb0dcd82ccc6716bbe36ec/index.jsp?&pName=dso_level1&path=dsonline/2008/09&file=w5gei.xml&xsl=article.xsl.

4. "Mashup Dashboard". ProgrammableWeb.com. 2009. http://www.programmableweb.com/mashups.
5. "Web Services Description Language (WSDL) Version 2.0 Part 2: Adjuncts". W3C. http://www.w3.org/TR/2007/REC-wsdl20 -adjuncts-20070626/#_http_binding_default_rule_method.
6. "Help - Creating bottom-up Web services". Eclipse. http://help.eclipse.org/help33/index.jsp?topic=/org.eclipse.jst.ws.doc.user/concepts/cwsbtmup.html. Retrieved 2011-04-22.
7. "Help - Creating top-down Web services". Eclipse. http://help.eclipse.org/help33/index.jsp?topic=/org.eclipse.jst.ws.doc.user/concepts/cwstopdown.html. Retrieved 2011-04-22.
8. Bray, Tim (October 28, 2004). "WS-Pagecount". TBray.org. http://www.tbray.org/ongoing/When/200x/2004/09/21/WS-Research. Retrieved 2011-04-22.
9. "Rethinking the Java SOAP Stack". HP. http://www.hpl.hp.com/techreports/2005/HPL-2005-83.html. Retrieved 2011-04-22.
10. Gray, N. A. B. (2005). "Performance of Java Middleware - Java RMI, JAXRPC, and CORBA". University of Wollongong. pp. 31–39. http://ro.uow.edu.au/infopapers/676/. Retrieved January 11, 2011. "The results presented in this paper show that the nature of response data has a greater impact on relative performance than has been allowed for in most previous studies."

Chapter–11

Applications of the Integrated Information Systems

The term modularity is widely used in studies of technological and organizational systems. Product systems are deemed "modular", for example, when they can be decomposed into a number of components that may be mixed and matched in a variety of configurations. Modularity is a general systems concept, typically defined as a continuum describing the degree to which a system's components may be separated and recombined.It refers to both the tightness of coupling between components, and the degree to which the "rules" of the system architecture enable (or prohibit) the mixing and matching of components.

The components are able to connect, interact, or exchange resources (such as energy or data) in some way, by adhering to a standardized interface. Unlike a tightly integrated product whereby each component is designed to work specifically (and often exclusively) with other particular components in a tightly coupled system, modular products are systems of components that are "loosely coupled."

The five principles given by Lev Manovich in The Language ofNew Media are numerical representation, modularity, automation, variability,and transcoding. Modularity within new media represents new media as being composed of several separate self-sufficient modules that can act independently or together in synchronisation to complete the new media object. In Photoshop, modularity is most evident in layers; a single image can be composed of many layers, each of which can be treated as an entirely independent and separate entity.

The entire Web, Manovich notes, has a modular structure, composed of independent sites and pages, and each webpage itself is composed of elements and code that can be independently modified. Their structure is formed in a format that allows their contents to be changed, removed or edited whilst still retaining the structure of the website, this is because the websites content operates separately to the website and does not define the structure of the site.

Organizational systems are said to become increasingly modular when they begin to substitute loosely coupled forms for tightly integrated, hierarchical structures. As an examples, when the firm utilizes contract manufacturing rather than in-house manufacturing, it is using an organizational component that is more independent than building such capabilities in-house: the firm can switch between contract manufacturers that perform different functions, and the contract manufacturer can similarly work for different firms. As firms in a given industry begin to substitute loose coupling with organizational components that lie outside of firm boundaries for activities that were once conducted in-house, the entire production system which may encompass many firms becomes increasingly modular. The firms themselves become more specialized components. Using loosely-coupled structures enables firms to achieve greater scope flexibility and scale flexibility. The firm can switch easily between different providers of these activities compared to building the capabilities for all activities in house, thus responding to different market needs more quickly. However, these flexibility gains come with a price. Therefore, the organization must assess the flexibility gains achievable, and any accompanying loss of performance, with each of these forms.

Views ofJerry Fodor

It is valuable work on modularity in psychology. The Modularity of Mind (1996/1983). In the book, Jerry Fodor proposes a 'modified' modularity theory of cognitive processes. His theory builds on the premise of faculty psychology that there are certain faculties innate in the mind, and mental "organs" that are biologically predisposed to perform certain types of computational processes. Fodor does not argue that the entire mind is modular; rather he proposes that the central cognitive system responsible for complex cognitive activities (such as analogical reasoning) is not modular, but that input systems (which interpret the neural signals from physical stimuli, and are responsible for basic cognitive activities such as language and vision) are likely to be modular.

Input systems, or "domain specific computational mechanisms" (such as the ability to perceive spoken language) are termed vertical faculties, and according to Fodor they are modular in that they possess a number of characteristics Fodor argues constitute modularity. His list of features characterizing modules includes the following:

1. Domain specific (modules only respond to inputs of a specific class, and thus a "species of vertical faculty".
2. Innately specified (the structure is inherent and is not formed by a learning process)
3. Not assembled (modules are not put together from a stock of more elementary subprocesses but rather their virtual architecture maps directly onto their neural implementation)
4. Neurologically hardwired (modules are associated with specific, localized, and elaborately structured neural systems rather than fungible neural mechanisms)
5. Autonomous (modules are independent of other modules)

He argues only that cognitive systems characterized by some of the features above are likely to be characterized by them all, and that such systems can be considered modular. He also notes that the characteristics are not an all-or-nothing proposition, but rather each of the characteristics may be manifest in some degree, and that modularity itself is also not a dichotomous construct—

something may be more or less modular: "One would thus expect—what anyhow seems to be desirable—that the notion of modularity ought to admit of degrees".

Notably, Fodor's "not assembled" feature contrasts sharply with the use of modularity in other fields in which modular systems are seen to be hierarchically nested (that is, modules are themselves composed of modules, which in turn are composed of modules, etc.) However, Coltheart notes that Fodor's commitment to the non-assembled feature appears weak, and other scholars (e.g., Block) have proposed that Fodor's modules could be decomposed into finer modules. For instance, while Fodor distinguishes between separate modules for spoken and written language, Block might further decompose the spoken language module into modules for phonetic analysis and lexical forms: "Decomposition stops when all the components are primitive processors—because the operation of a primitive processor cannot be further decomposed into suboperations"

Though Fodor's work on modularity is one of the most extensive, there is other work in psychology on modularity worth noting for its symmetry with modularity in other disciplines. For instance, while Fodor focused on cognitive input systems as modules, Coltheart proposes that there may be many different kinds of cognitive modules, and distinguishes between, for example, knowledge modules and processing modules. The former is a body of knowledge that is independent of other bodies of knowledge, while the latter is a mental information-processing system independent from other such systems.

Modularity in Biology

The term has also been used in a broader sense in biology to refer to the reuse of homologous structures across individuals and species. As in some of the other disciplines, the term modularity may be used in multiple ways in biology. Many plants and sessile benthic invertebrates demonstrate this type of modularity (by contrast, many other organisms have a determinate structure that is predefined in embryogenesis).

Even within this latter category, there may be differences in how a module is perceived. Evolutionary biologists may focus on the module as a morphological component (subunit) of a whole organism, while developmental biologists may use the term module to refer to some combination of lower-level components (e.g., genes) that are able to act in a unified way to perform a function. In the former, the module is perceived a basic component, while in the latter the emphasis is on the module as a collective.

Biology scholars have provided a list of features that should characterize a module (much as Fodor did in The Modularity of Mind). Here Raff gives the following list of characteristics that developmental modules should possess:

1. discrete genetic specification
2. hierarchical organization
3. interactions with other modules
4. a particular physical location within a developing organism
5. the ability to undergo transformations on both developmental and evolutionary time scales

To Raff's mind, developmental modules are "dynamic entities representing localized processes (as in morphogenetic fields) rather than simply incipient structures ... (... such as organ rudiments)." Bolker, however, attempts to construct a definitional list of characteristics that is more abstract, and thus more suited to multiple levels of study in biology. She argues that:

1. A module is a biological entity (a structure, a process, or a pathway) characterized by more internal than external integration
2. Modules are biological individuals that can be delineated from their surroundings or context, and whose behavior or function reflects the integration of their parts, not simply the arithmetical sum. That is, as a whole, the module can perform tasks that its constituent parts could not perform if dissociated.

3. In addition to their internal integration, modules have external connectivity, yet they can also be delineated from the other entities with which they interact in some way.

Another stream of research on modularity in biology that should be of particular interest to scholars in other disciplines is that of Gunter Wagner. Wagner's work explores how natural selection may have resulted in modular organisms, and the roles modularity plays in evolution. Wagner's work suggests that modularity is both the result of evolution, and facilitates evolution—an idea that shares a marked resemblance to work on modularity in technological and organizational domains.

Modularity in the Arts

Modularity as a means of measurement is intrinsic to certain types of building; for example, brick construction is by its nature modular insofar as the fixed dimensions of a brick necessarily yield dimensions that are multiples of the original unit. Attaching bricks to one another to form walls and surfaces also reflects a second definition of modularity: namely, the use of standardized units that physically connect to each other to form larger compositions.

The use of modules in the fine arts has a long pedigree among diverse cultures. In the classical architecture of Greco-Roman antiquity, the module was utilized as a standardized unit of measurement for proportioning the elements of a building.

Typically the module was established as one-half the diameter of the lower shaft of a classical column; all the other components in the syntax of the classical system were expressed as a fraction or multiple of that module.

In traditional Japanese construction, room sizes were often determined by combinations of standard rice mats called tatami; the standard dimension of a mat was around 3 feet by 6 feet, which approximate the overall proportions of a reclining human figure. The module thus becomes not only a proportional device for use with three-dimensional vertical elements but a two-dimensional planning tool as well.

With the advent of modernism and advanced construction techniques in the 20th century this latter definition transforms modularity from a compositional attribute to a thematic concern in its own right. A school of Modular Constructivism develops in the 1950s among a circle of sculptors who create sculpture and architectural features out of repetitive units cast in concrete. A decade later modularity becomes an autonomous artistic concern of its own, as several important Minimalist artists adopt it as their central theme. Modular building as both an industrial production model and an object of advanced architectural investigation develops from this same period.

Modularity has found renewed interest among proponents of ModulArt, a form of modular art in which the constituent parts can be physically reconfigured, removed and/or added to. After a few isolated experiments in ModulArt starting in the 1950s, several artists since the 1990s have explored this flexible, customizable and co-creative form of art.

Modularity in American Studies

Blair defines a modular system as "one that gives more importance to parts than to wholes. Parts are conceived as equivalent and hence, in one or more senses, interchangeable and/ or cumulative and/or recombinable".

In Blair's Modular America, he argues that as American's began to replace social structures inherited from Europe (predominantly England and France), they evolved a uniquely American tendency towards modularity, in fields as diverse as education, music, and architecture.

Blair observes that when the word module first emerged in the sixteenth and seventeenth centuries, it meant something very close to model. It implied a small-scale representation or example. By the eighteenth and nineteenth centuries, the word had come to imply a standard measure of fixed ratios and proportions. For example, in architecture, the proportions of a column could be stated in modules (i.e., " a height of fourteen modules equaled seven times the diameter measured at the base") and thus multiplied to any size while still retaining the desired proportions.

However in America the meaning and usage of the word shifted considerably:"Starting with architectural terminology in the 1930s, the new emphasis was on any entity or system designed in terms of modules as subcomponents. As applications broadened after World War II to furniture, hi-fi equipment, computer programs and beyond, modular construction came to refer to any whole made up of self-contained units designed to be equivalent parts of a system, hence, we might say, "systemically equivalent." Modular parts are implicitly interchangeable and/or recombinable in one or another of several senses"

Blair describes the emergence of modular structures in education (the college curriculum), industry (modular product assembly), architecture (skyscrapers), music (blues and jazz), and more. In his concluding chapter, Blair does not commit to a firm view of what causes Americans to pursue more modular structures in the diverse domains in which it has appeared, but he does suggest that it may in some way be related to the American ideology of liberal individualism, and a preference for anti-hierarchical organization.

Consistent Themes

Comparing the use of modularity across these disciplines reveals several themes:

One theme that shows up in psychology and biology study is innately specified. Innately specified (as used here) implies that the purpose or structure of the module is predetermined by some biological mandate.

Domain specificity, that modules respond only to inputs of a specific class (or perform functions only of a specific class) is a theme that clearly spans psychology and biology, and it can be argued that it also spans technological and organizational systems. Domain specificity would be seen in the latter disciplines as specialization of function.

Hierarchically nested is a theme that recurs in most disciplines. Though originally disavowed by Fodor, other psychologists have embraced it, and it is readily apparent in the use of modularity in biology (e.g., each module of an organism can be decomposed into finer modules), social processes and artifacts (e.g., we can think of a skyscraper in terms of blocks of floors, a single floor, elements of a floor, etc.), mathematics (e.g., the modulus 6 may be further divided into the moduli 1, 2 and 3), and technological and organizational systems (e.g., an organization may be composed of divisions, which are composed of teams, which are composed of individuals)

Greater internal than external integration is a theme that showed up in every discipline but mathematics. Often referred to as autonomy, this theme acknowledged that there may be interaction or integration between modules, but the greater interaction and integration occurs within the module. This theme is very closely related to information encapsulation, which shows up explicitly in both the psychology and technology research.

Near decomposability (as termed by Simon, 1962) shows up in all of the disciplines, but is manifest in a matter of degrees. For instance, in psychology and biology it may refer merely to the ability to delineate one module from another (recognizing the boundaries of the module). In several of the social artifacts, mathematics, and technological or organizational systems, however, it refers to the ability to actually separate components from one another.

In several of the disciplines this decomposability also enables the complexity of a system (or process) to be reduced. This is aptly captured in a quote from Marr about psychological processes where he notes that, "any large computation should be split up into a collection of small, nearly independent, specialized sub-processes." Reducing complexity is also the express purpose of casting out nines in mathematics.

Substitutability and recombinability are closely related constructs. The former refers to the ability to substitute one component for another as in Blair's "systemic equivalence" while the latter may refer both to the indeterminate form of the system and the indeterminate use of the component. In college curricula, for example, each course is designed with a credit system that ensures a uniform number of contact hours, and approximately uniform educational content, yielding substitutability.

By virtue of their substitutability, each student may create their own curricula (recombinability of the curriculum as a system) and each course may be said to be recombinable with a variety of students' curricula (recombinability of the component within multiple systems). Both substitutability and recombinability are immediately recognizable in Blair's social processes and artifacts, and are also well captured in Garud and Kumaraswamy's discussion of economies of substitution in technological systems.

Blair's systemic equivalence also demonstrates the relationship between substitutability and the module as a homologue. Blair's systemic equivalence refers to the ability for multiple modules to perform approximately the same function within a system, while in biology a module as a homologue refers to different modules sharing approximately the same form or function in different organisms. The extreme of the module as homologue is found in mathematics, where (in the simplest case) the modules refer to the reuse of a particular number and thus each module is exactly alike. In all but mathematics, there has been an emphasis that modules may be different in kind. In Fodor's discussion of modular cognitive system, each module performs a unique task. In biology, even modules that are considered homologous may be somewhat different in form and function (e.g., a whale's fin versus a human's hand). In Blair's book, he points out that while jazz music may be composed of structural units that conform to the same underlying rules, those components vary significantly. Similarly in studies of technology and organization, modular systems may be composed of modules that are very similar (as in shelving units that may be piled one atop the other) or very different (as in a stereo system where each component performs unique functions) or any combination in between.

OPEN SOURCE

It explains practices in production and development that promote access to the end product's source materials. Some consider open source a philosophy, others consider it a pragmatic methodology. Before the term open source became widely adopted, developers and producers used a variety of phrases to describe the concept; open source gained hold with the rise of the Internet, and the attendant need for massive retooling of the computing source code. Opening the source code enabled a self-enhancing diversity of production models, communication paths, and interactive communities.Subsequently, the new phrase "open-source software" was born to describe the environment that the new copyright, licensing, domain, and consumer issues created.

The open source model includes the concept of concurrent yet different agendas and differing approaches in production, in contrast with more centralized models of development such as those typically used in commercial software companies.A main principle and practice of open source software development is peer production by bartering and collaboration, with the end-product, source-material, "blueprints," and documentation available at no cost to the public. This is increasingly being applied in other fields of endeavor, such as biotechnology.

History

The concept of open source and free sharing of technological information existed long before computers. For example, cooking recipes have been shared since the beginning of human culture. Open source can pertain to businesses and to computers, software and technology.

In the early years of automobile development, a group of capital monopolists owned the rights to a 2 cycle gasoline engine patent originally filed by George B. Selden. By controlling this patent, they were able to monopolize the industry and force car manufacturers to adhere to their demands, or risk a lawsuit. In 1911, world-fame automaker Henry Ford won a challenge to the

Selden patent. The result was that the Selden patent became virtually worthless and a new association (which would eventually become the Motor Vehicle Manufacturers Association) was formed.The new association instituted a cross-licensing agreement among all US auto manufacturers: although each company would develop technology and file patents, these patents were shared openly and without the exchange of money between all the manufacturers.Until the US entered World War 2, 92 Ford patents were being used freely by other manufacturers who were in turn making use of 515 patents from other companies, all without lawsuits or the exchange of money.

Very similar to open standards, researchers with access to Advanced Research Projects Agency Network (ARPANET) used a process called Request for Comments to develop telecommunication network protocols. This collaborative process of the 1960s led to the birth of the Internet in 1969.

Early instances of open source and free software include IBM's source releases of its operating systems and other programs in the 1950s and 1960s, and the SHARE user group that formed to facilitate the exchange of software. Open source on the Internet began when the Internet was just a message board, and progressed to more advanced presentation and sharing forms like a Web site. There are now many Web sites, organizations and businesses that promote open source sharing of everything from computer code to mechanics of improving a product, technique, or medical advancement.

The label "open source" was adopted by some people in the free software movement at a strategy session held at Palo Alto, California, in reaction to Netscape's January 1998 announcement of a source code release for Navigator. The group of individuals at the session included Christine Peterson who suggested "open source", Todd Anderson, Larry Augustin, Jon Hall, Sam Ockman, Michael Tiemann and Eric S. Raymond. Over the next week, Raymond and others worked on spreading the word. Linus Torvalds gave an all-important sanction the following day. Phil Hughes offered a pulpit in Linux Journal. Richard Stallman, pioneer of the free software movement, flirted with adopting the term, but changed his mind. Those people who adopted the term used the opportunity before the release of Navigator's source code to free themselves of the ideological and confrontational connotations of the term "free software". Netscape released its source code under the Netscape Public License and later under the Mozilla Public License.

The term was given a big boost at an event organized in April 1998 by technology publisher Tim O'Reilly. Originally titled the "Freeware Summit" and later known as the "Open Source Summit", The event brought together the leaders of many of the most important free and open source projects, including Linus Torvalds, Larry Wall, Brian Behlendorf, Eric Allman, Guido van Rossum, Michael Tiemann, Paul Vixie, Jamie Zawinski of Netscape, and Eric Raymond. At that meeting, the confusion caused by the name free software was brought up. Tiemann argued for "sourceware" as a new term, while Raymond argued for "open source." The assembled developers took a vote, and the winner was announced at a press conference that evening. Five days later, Raymond made the first public call to the free software community to adopt the new term. The Open Source Initiative was formed shortly thereafter.

Starting in the early 2000s, a number of companies began to publish a portion of their source code to claim they were open source, while keeping key parts closed. This led to the development of the now widely used terms free open source software and commercial open source software to distinguish between truly open and hybrid forms of open source.

Economic Analysis

Most economists agree that open source candidates have an information good (also termed 'knowledge good') aspect. In general, this suggests that the original work involves a great deal of time, money, and effort. However, the cost of reproducing the work is very low, so that additional users may be added at zero or near zero cost — this is referred to as the marginal cost of a product. At this point, it is necessary to consider a copyright. The idea of copyright for works of authorship is to protect the incentive of making these original works. Copyright restriction then creates access costs on consumers who value the original more than making an additional copy but value the original less than its price. Thus, they will pay an access cost of this difference. Access costs also pose problems for authors who wish to create something based on another work but are not willing to pay the copyright holder for the rights to the copyrighted work. The second type of cost incurred with a copyright system is the cost of administration and enforcement of the copyright.

Being organised effectively as a consumers' cooperative, the idea of open source is then to eliminate the access costs of the consumer and the creator by reducing the restrictions of copyright. This will lead to creation of additional works, which build upon previous work and add to greater social benefit. Additionally some proponents argue that open source also relieves society of the administration and enforcement costs of copyright. Organizations such as Creative Commons have websites where individuals can file for alternative "licenses", or levels of restriction, for their works. These self-made protections free the general society of the costs of policing copyright infringement. Thus, on several fronts, there is an efficiency argument to be made on behalf of open sourced goods.

Others argue that society loses through open sourced goods. As there is a loss in monetary incentive to the creation of new goods some argue that new products will not be created. This argument seems to apply particularly well to the business model where extensive research and development is done, e.g. pharmaceuticals. However, this argument ignores the fact that cost reduction for all concerned is perhaps an even better monetary incentive than is a price increase. Moreover, others argue that visual art and other works of authorship should be free. These proponents of extensive open source ideals argue that monetary incentive for artists would perhaps better be derived from performances or exhibitions, in a similar fashion to the funding of provision of other types of services.

Case Study

An investigation of open source industrial symbiosis was performed by Doyle and Pearce using Google Earth. Their research reveal that virtual globes coupled with open source waste information can be used to:

1. Control embodied energy of transport by reducing distances to recycling facilities,
2. Prefer end of life at recycling facilities rather than landfills, and
3. Cooperate industrial symbiosis and eco-industrial parks on known by-product synergies.

Ultimately, open source sharing of information in virtual globes provide a means to identify economically and environmentally beneficial opportunities for waste management if the data have been made available.

Open Source Movement

Many fields of study and social and political views have been affected by the growth of the concept of open source. Advocates in one field often support the expansion of open source in other fields. For example, Linus Torvalds said, "the future is open source everything." But Eric Raymond and other founders of the open source movement have sometimes publicly argued against speculation about applications outside software, saying that strong arguments for software openness should not be weakened by overreaching into areas where the story is less compelling. The broader impacts of the open source movement, and the extent of its role in the development of new information sharing procedures, remain to be seen.

The open source movement has inspired increased transparency and liberty in other fields, including the release of biotechnology research by CAMBIA, Wikipedia, and other projects. The open-source concept has also been applied to media other than computer programs, e.g., by Creative Commons. It also constitutes an example of user innovation (see for example the book Democratizing Innovation). Often, open source is an expression where it simply means that a system is available to all who wish to work on it. The difference between crowdsourcing and open source is that open source production is a cooperative activity initiated and voluntarily undertaken by members of the public

Computer Software

Open source software is software whose source code is published and made available to the public, enabling anyone to copy, modify and redistribute the source code without paying royalties or fees. Open source code evolves through community cooperation. These communities are composed of individual programmers as well as very large companies. Examples of open-source software products are:

Programming Language

- PHP - Scripting language suited for the web
- Python - General purpose programming language

OS

- GNU Project — "a sufficient body of free software"
- Linux — operating system kernel based on Unix
- NetBSD — operating system derived from Unix
- OpenBSD — operating system derived from Unix
- FreeBSD — operating system derived from Unix
- OpenSolaris — Unix Operating System from Sun Microsystems
- Symbian — real-time mobile operating system

Server

- Apache — HTTP web server
- Tomcat web server — web container
- MediaWiki — wiki server software, the software that runs Wikipedia

- Alfresco — content management system
- RenovatioCMS — content management system
- Joomla — content management system
- Drupal — content management system
- TYPO3 — content management system
- WordPress — blog software
- MongoDB — document-oriented, non-relational database
- Eclipse — software development environment comprising an integrated development environment (IDE)
- Moodle — course management system or virtual learning environment
- openSIS — open source Student Information System

Client Software

- osCommerce — ecommerce
- PeaZip — File archiver
- NASA World Wind — virtual globe, geobrowser
- Mozilla Firefox — web browser
- Mozilla Thunderbird — e-mail client
- OpenOffice.org — office suite
- Stockfish — chess engine series, considered to be one of the strongest chess programs of the world
- 7-Zip — File archiver

Electronics

Open-source hardware is hardware whose initial specification, usually in a software format, are published and made available to the public, enabling anyone to copy, modify and redistribute the hardware and source code without paying royalties or fees. Open source hardware evolves through community cooperation. These communities are composed of individual hardware/software developers, hobbyists, as well as very large companies. Examples of open source hardware initiatives are given below :

1. Openmoko: a family of open source mobile phones, including the hardware specification and the operating system.
2. OpenRISC: an open source microprocessor family, with architecture specification licensed under GNU GPL and implementation under LGPL.
3. Sun Microsystems's OpenSPARC T1 Multicore processor. Sun has released it under GPL.
4. Arduino, a microcontroller platform for hobbyists, artists and designers.
5. Simputer, an open hardware handheld computer, designed in India for use in environments where computing devices such as personal computers are deemed inappropriate.
6. LEON: A family of open source microprocessors distributed in a library with peripheral IP cores, open SPARC V8 specification, implementation available under GNU GPL.

Beverages

1. OpenCola — a cola soft drink, similar to Coca-Cola and Pepsi, whose recipies open source and developed by volunteers. The taste is said to be comparable to that of the standard beverages. Most corporations producing beverages hold their formulas as closely guarded secrets.
2. Vores Øl beer — a beer created by students at the IT-University in Copenhagen together with Superflex, a Copenhagen-based artist collective, to illustrate how open source concepts might be applied outside the digital world.
3. In 2002, the beer company Brewtopia in Australia started an open source brewery and invited the general population to be involved in the development and

ownership of the brewery, and to vote on the development of every aspect of its beer, Blowfly, and its road to market. In return for their feedback and input, individuals received shares in the company, which is now publicly traded on a stock exchange in Australia. The company has always adhered to its Open Source roots and is the only beer company in the world that allows the public to design, customise and develop its own beers online.

4. Coffee — capsule-based beverage systems such as Nestle's Nespresso or Krups' Tassimo turn home-brewed coffee from an inherently "open-source" beverage into a product limited by the specific range of capsules made available by the system manufacturers.

Digital Content

- Open-content projects organized by the Wikimedia Foundation — Sites such as Wikipedia and Wiktionary have embraced the open-content GFDL and Creative Commons content licenses. These licenses were designed to adhere to principles similar to various open-source software development licenses. Many of these licenses ensure that content remains free for re-use, that source documents are made readily available to interested parties, and that changes to content are accepted easily back into the system. An important site embracing open source-like ideals is Project Gutenberg, which posts many books on which the copyright has expired and are thus in the Public Domain, ensuring that anyone can use that content for any purpose whatsoever.

Health and Science

Medicine

- Pharmaceuticals — There have been several proposals for open-source pharmaceutical development, which led to the establishment of the Tropical Disease Initiative. There are also a number of not-for-profit "virtual pharmas" such as the Institute for One World Health and the Drugs for Neglected Diseases Initiative.

Science

- Research — The Science Commons was created as an alternative to the expensive legal costs of sharing and reusing scientific works in journals etc.
- Research — The Open Source Science Project was created to increase the ability for students to participate in the research process by providing them access to microfunding — which, in turn, offers non-researchers the opportunity to directly invest, and follow, cutting-edge scientific research. All data and methodology is subsequently published in an openly accessible manner under a Creative Commons fair use license.

MediaWiki logo

MediaWiki
Because ideas want to be free.

Robotics

An open-source robot is a robot whose blueprints, schematics, and/or source code are released under an open source model.

Other

- Open source principles can be applied to technical areas such as digital communication protocols and data storage formats.
- Open design — which involves applying open source methodologies to the design of artifacts and systems in

the physical world. Very nascent but has huge potential.

- Open source appropriate technology (OSAT) refers to technologies that are designed in the same fashion as free and open-source software. These technologies must be "appropriate technology" (AT) — meaning technology that is designed with special consideration to the environmental, ethical, cultural, social, political, and economical aspects of the community it is intended for. An example of this application is the use of open source 3-D printers like the RepRap to manufacture appropriate technology.
- Teaching — which involves applying the concepts of open source to instruction using a shared web space as a platform to improve upon learning, organizational, and management challenges. An example of an Open Source Courseware is the Java Education & Development Initiative (JEDI). Other examples include wikiversity. At the university level, the use of open source appropriate technology classroom projects has been shown to be successful in forging the connection between science/ engineering and social benefit: This approach has the potential to use university students' access to resources and testing equipment in furthering the development of appropriate technology. Similarly OSAT has been used as a tool for improving service learning.
- There are few examples of business information (methodologies, advice, guidance, practices) using the open source model, although this is another case where the potential is enormous. ITIL is close to open source. It uses the Cathedral model (no mechanism exists for user contribution) and the content must be bought for a fee that is small by business consulting standards (hundreds of British pounds). Various checklists are published by government, banks or accounting firms. Possibly the only example of free, bazaar-model open source business information is Core Practice.

Society and Culture

Open source culture is the creative practice of appropriation and free sharing of found and created content. Examples include collage, found footage film, music, and appropriation art. Open source culture is one in which fixations, works entitled to copyright protection, are made generally available. Participants in the culture can modify those products and redistribute them back into the community or other organizations.

Open source culture precedes Richard Stallman's codification of free software with the creation of the Free Software Foundation. As the public began to communicate through Bulletin Board Systems (BBS) like FidoNet, places like Sourcery Systems BBS were dedicated to providing source code to Public Domain, Shareware and Freeware programs.

The rise of open-source culture in the 20th century resulted from a growing tension between creative practices that involve appropriation, and therefore require access to content that is often copyrighted, and increasingly restrictive intellectual property laws and policies governing access to copyrighted content. The two main ways in which intellectual property laws became more restrictive in the 20th century were extensions to the term of copyright (particularly in the United States) and penalties, such as those articulated in the Digital Millennium Copyright Act (DMCA), placed on attempts to circumvent anti-piracy technologies.

Although artistic appropriation is often permitted under fair use doctrines, the complexity and ambiguity of these doctrines creates an atmosphere of uncertainty among cultural practitioners. Also, the protective actions of copyright owners create what some call a "chilling effect" among cultural practitioners.

Few decades back, cultural practitioners began to adopt the intellectual property licensing techniques of free software and open-source software to make their work more freely available to others, including the Creative Commons. The idea of an "open source" culture runs parallel to "Free Culture," but is substantively different. Free culture is a term derived from the free software movement, and in contrast to that vision of culture, proponents of Open Source Culture (OSC) maintain that some intellectual property law needs to exist to protect cultural producers. Yet they propose a more nuanced position than corporations have traditionally sought. Instead of seeing intellectual property law as an expression of instrumental rules intended to uphold either natural rights or desirable outcomes, an argument for OSC takes into account diverse goods (as in "the Good life") and ends.

One way of achieving the goal of making the fixations of cultural work generally available is to maximally utilize technology and digital media. In keeping with Moore's law's prediction about processors, the cost of digital media and storage plummeted in the late 20th Century. Consequently, the marginal cost of digitally duplicating anything capable of being transmitted via digital media dropped to near zero. Combined with an explosive growth in personal computer and technology ownership, the result is an increase in general population's access to digital media. This phenomenon facilitated growth in open source culture because it allowed for rapid and inexpensive duplication and distribution of culture. Where the access to the majority of culture produced prior to the advent of digital media was limited by other constraints of proprietary and potentially "open" mediums, digital media is the latest technology with the potential to increase access to cultural products. Artists and users who choose to distribute their work digitally face none of the physical limitations that traditional cultural producers have been typically faced with. Accordingly, the audience of an open source culture faces little physical cost in acquiring digital media.

Essentially born out of a desire for increased general access to digital media, the Internet is open source culture's most valuable asset. It is questionable whether the goals of an open source culture could be achieved without the Internet. The global network not only fosters an environment where culture can be generally accessible, but also allows for easy and inexpensive redistribution of culture back into various communities. Some reasons for this are given below:

First, the Internet allows even greater access to inexpensive digital media and storage. Instead of users being limited to their own facilities and resources, they are granted access to a vast network of facilities and resources, some free. Sites such as Archive.org offer up free web space for anyone willing to license their work under a Creative Commons license. The resulting cultural product is then available to download free (generally accessible) to anyone with an Internet connection.

Second, users are granted unprecedented access to each other. Older analog technologies such as the telephone or television have limitations on the kind of interaction users can have. In the case of television there is little, if any interaction between users participating on the network. And in the case of the telephone, users rarely interact with any more than a couple of their known peers.

On the Internet, however, users have the potential to access and meet millions of their peers. This aspect of the Internet facilitates the modification of culture as users are able to collaborate and communicate with each other across international and cultural boundaries. The speed in which digital media travels on the Internet in turn facilitates the redistribution of culture.

Through various technologies such as peer-to-peer networks and blogs, cultural producers can take advantage of vast social networks in order to distribute their products. As opposed to traditional media distribution, redistributing digital media on the Internet can be virtually costless. Technologies such as BitTorrent and Gnutella take advantage of various characteristics of the Internet protocol (TCP/IP) in an attempt to totally decentralize file distribution.

Government

- Open politics (sometimes known as Open source politics) — is a term used to describe a political process that uses Internet technologies such as blogs, email and polling to provide for a rapid feedback mechanism between political organizations and their supporters. There is also an alternative conception of the term Open source politics which relates to the development of public policy under a set of rules and processes similar to the Open Source Software movement.

- Open source governance — is similar to open source politics, but it applies more to the democratic process and promotes the freedom of information.

Ethics

It's divide in 2 trands :

- Open Source Ethics as an Ethical School — Charles Ess and David Berry are researching whether ethics can learn anything from an open source approach. Ess famously even defined the AoIR Research Guidelines as an example of open source ethics.
- Open Source Ethics as a Professional Body of Rules — This is based principally on the computer ethics school, studying the questions of ethics and professionalism in the computer industry in general and software development in particular.

Media

This is the age of online journalism where readers canread news of their taste on newspaper's websites. Every leading newspapers have their own website, and they update it regularly at certain intervals. That day is not too far when media industry becomes paperless. Open source journalism — referred to the standard journalistic techniques of news gathering and fact checking, and reflected a similar term that was in use from 1992 in military intelligence circles, open source intelligence. It is now commonly used to describe forms of innovative publishing of online journalism, rather than the sourcing of news stories by a professional journalist.

Weblogs, or blogs, are another significant platform for open source culture. Blogs consist of periodic, reverse chronologically ordered posts, using a technology that makes webpages easily updatable with no understanding of design, code, or file transfer required. While corporations, political campaigns and other formal institutions have begun using these tools to distribute information, many blogs are used by individuals for personal expression, political organizing, and socializing. Some, such as LiveJournal or WordPress, utilize open source software that is open to the public and can be modified by users to fit their own tastes. Whether the code is open or not, this format represents a nimble tool for people to borrow and re-present culture; whereas traditional websites made the illegal reproduction of culture difficult to regulate, the mutability of blogs makes "open sourcing" even more uncontrollable since it allows a larger portion of the population to replicate material more quickly in the public sphere.

Messageboards are another platform for open source culture. Messageboards (also known as discussion boards or forums), are places online where people with similar interests can congregate and post messages for the community to read and respond to. Messageboards sometimes have moderators who enforce community standards of etiquette such as banning users who are spammers. Other common board features are private messages (where users can send messages to one another) as well as chat (a way to have a real time conversation online) and image uploading. Some messageboards use phpBB, which is a free open source package. Where blogs are more about individual expression and tend to revolve around their authors, messageboards are about creating a conversation amongst its users where information can be shared freely and quickly. Messageboards are a way to remove intermediaries from everyday life — for instance, instead of relying on commercials and other forms of advertising, one can ask other users for frank reviews of a product, movie or CD. By removing the cultural middlemen, messageboards help speed the flow of information and exchange of ideas.

Open Document is an open document file format for saving and exchanging editable office documents such as text documents (including memos, reports, and books), spreadsheets, charts, and presentations. Organizations and individuals that store their data in an open format such as OpenDocument avoid being locked in to a single software vendor, leaving them free to switch software if their current vendor goes out of business, raises their prices, changes their software, or changes their licensing terms to something less favorable.

Open source movie production is either an open call system in which a changing crew and cast collaborate in movie production, a system in which the end result is made available for re-use by others or in which exclusively open source products are used in the production. The 2006 movie Elephants Dream is said to be the "world's first open movie", created entirely using open source technology.

An open source documentary film has a production process allowing the open contributions of archival material, footage, and other filmic elements, both in unedited and edited form. By doing so, on-line contributors become part of the process of creating the film, helping to influence the editorial and visual material to be used in the documentary, as well as its thematic development. The first open source documentary film is the non-profit "The American Revolution," which went into production in 2005, and will examine the role media played in the cultural, social and political changes from 1968 to 1974 through the story of radio station WBCN-FM in Boston. The film is being produced by Lichtenstein Creative Media and the non-profit Filmmakers Collaborative. Open Source Cinema is a website to create Basement Tapes, a feature documentary about copyright in the digital age, co-produced by the National Film Board of Canada. Open Source Filmmaking refers to a form of filmmaking that takes a method of idea formation from open source software, but in this case the 'source' for a film maker is raw unedited footage rather than programming code. It can also refer to a method of filmmaking where the process of creation is 'open' i.e. a disparate group of contributors, at different times contribute to the final piece.

Open-IPTV is IPTV that is not limited to one recording studio, production studio, or cast. Open-IPTV uses the Internet or other means to pool efforts and resources together to create an online community that all contributes to a show.

Intellectual Commons

Within the academic community, there is discussion about expanding what could be called the "intellectual commons" (analogous to the Creative Commons). Proponents of this view have hailed the Connexions Project at Rice University, OpenCourseWare project at MIT, Eugene Thacker's article on "Open Source DNA", the "Open Source Cultural Database" and Wikipedia as examples of applying open source outside the realm of computer software. Open source curricula are instructional resources whose digital source can be freely used, distributed and modified.

Many funded research projects produce software as part of their work. There is an increasing interest in making the outputs of such projects available under an open source license. In the UK, which the Joint Information Systems Committee (JISC) has developed a policy on open source software. It also funds a development service called OSS Watch which acts as an advisory service for higher and further education institutions wishing to use, contribute to and develop open source software.

Innovation Communities

The principle of sharing predates the open source movement; for example, the free sharing of information has been institutionalized in the scientific enterprise since at least the 19th century. Open source principles have always been part of the scientific community. There is also a tradition of publishing research results to the scientific community instead of keeping all such knowledge proprietary. One of the recent initiatives in scientific publishing has been open access — The idea that research should be published in such a way that it is free and available to the public. For the dissemination of knowledge to maximum readers, there are currently many open access journals where the information is available free online, however most journals do charge a fee (either to users or libraries for access). The Budapest Open Access Initiative is an international effort with the goal of making all research articles available free on the Internet. The National Institutes of Health has recently proposed a policy on "Enhanced Public Access to NIH Research Information." This policy would provide a free, searchable resource of NIH-funded results to the public and with other international repositories six months after its initial publication. The NIH's move is an important one because there is significant amount of public funding in scientific research. Many of the questions have yet to be answered — the balancing of profit vs. public access, and ensuring that desirable standards and incentives do not diminish with a shift to open access.

The sociologist Robert K. Merton described the four basic elements of the community — (i) universalism (an international perspective), (ii) communalism (sharing information), (iii) disinterestedness (removing one's personal views from the scientific inquiry) and (iv) organized skepticism (requirements of proof and review) that accurately describe the scientific community today. These principles are, in part, complemented by US law's focus on protecting expression and method but not the ideas themselves.

Farmavita.Net — Community of Pharmaceuticals Executives have recently proposed new business model of Open Source Pharmaceuticals. The project is targeted to development and sharing of know-how for manufacture of essential and life saving medicines. It is mainly dedicated to the countries with less developed economies where local pharmaceutical research and development resources are insufficient for national needs.

It will be limited to generic (off-patent) medicines with established use. By the definition, medicinal product have a "well-established use" if is used for at least 15 years, with recognized efficacy and an acceptable level of safety. In that event, the expensive clinical test and trial results could be replaced by appropriate scientific literature.

Benjamin Franklin was an early contributor eventually donating all his inventions including the Franklin stove, bifocals, and the lightning rod to the public domain.

Upcoming non-government ogranisations (NGOs) are initiating to use the open source technology as a tool. One example is the Open Source Youth Network started in 2007 in Lisboa by ISCA members. Open innovation is also a new emerging concept which advocate putting R&D in a common pool. The Eclipse platform is openly presenting itself as an Open innovation network.

Arts and Recreation

Copyright protection is used in the performing arts and even in athletic activities. Some groups have attempted to remove copyright from such practices.

References

1. Andrews, J. 1998. Bacteria as modular organisms. Annual Review of Microbiology, 52:105–126.
2. Bolker, J. A. 2000. Modularity in development and why it matters to Evo-Devo. American Zoologist, 40: 770–776
3. http://publib.boulder.ibm.com/infocenter/iicdoc/v1r4m0/index.jsp?topic=/com.ibm.iic.doc_1.4.0/plan/environment.html
4. Raff, R. A. 1996. The shape of life. Chicago University Press, Chicago.
5. Raff, R. A. 1996. The shape of life. Chicago University Press, Chicago, pg. 326)
6. Hull, D. L. 1980. Individuality and selection. Annual Review of Ecological Systems, 11:311–332
7. Roth, V. L. 1991. Homology and hierarchies: Problems solved and unresolved. Journal of Evolutionary Biology, 4:167–194

8. Wagner, G. 1996. Homologues, natural kinds and the evolution of modularity. American Zoologist, 36:36–43.

9. The concept expands upon a statement found in the Free Software Definition: "Free software is a matter of liberty, not price. To understand the concept, you should think of 'free' as in 'free speech' not as in 'free beer.'"

10. Stallman, Richard M. The Free Software Definition. Free Software Foundation. 2005.

11. Cohn, David. "Free Beer for Geeks". Wired News. 18 July 2005.

12. http://www.adciv.org/Open_collaborative_design

13. A. J. Buitenhuis, I. Zelenika and J. M. Pearce, "Open Design-Based Strategies to Enhance Appropriate Technology Development", Proceedings of the 14th Annual National Collegiate Inventors and Innovators Alliance Conference : Open, March 25-27th 2010, pp. 1-12.

Bibliography

- Applegate, Rachel. "Whose Decline? Which Academic Libraries are "Deserted" in Terms of Reference Transactions?" Reference & User Services Quarterly 2nd ser. 48 (2008): 176-89. Print.
- Britishmuseum.org "Assurbanipal Library Phase 1", British Museum One
- Cohen, L.B. (2007). "A Manifesto for our time". American Libraries 38: 47–9.
- Dana, John Cotton, and Henry W. Kent, eds. Literature of Libraries in the Seventeenth and Eighteenth Centuries. Chicago: A. C. McClure, 1906-07; reissued Metuchen: The Scarecrow Reprint Corporation, 1967. No. 1: The duties & qualifications of a librarian: a discourse ... in the Sorbonne, 1780; by Jean-Baptiste Cotton des Houssayes.—No. 2: The reformed librarie-keeper ... concerning the place and office of a librarie-keeper; by John Dury (1596-1680).—No. 3: The life of Sir Thomas Bodley written by himself together with the first draft of the statutes of the public library at Oxon.—No. 4: Two tracts on the founding and maintaining of parochial libraries in Scotland; by James Kirkwood (d. 1708).—No. 5: A brief outline of the history of libraries; by Justus Lipsius; transl. from 2nd ed, 1607 ...—No. 6: News from France or a description of the library of Cardinal Mazarin

preceded by The surrender of the library ... two tracts written by Gabriel Naude (1600-1653).

- de Goeje(ed.) (1906). AL-Muqaddasi: Ahsan al-Taqasim. BGA, III.
- Epic of Creation in Dalley, Stephanie. Myths from Mesopotamia. Oxford, 1989: pg.233-81
- Epic of Gilgamesh in Dalley, Stephanie. Myths from Mesopotamia. Oxford, 1989: pg.50-135
- Hanson, James C. M. Catalog rules; author and title entries (Chicago: American Library Association. 1908)
- Harris, Michael H. (1984). The History of Libraries in the Western World. Scarecrow Press. ISBN 0810816660.
- John L. Esposito (ed.) (1995). The Oxford Encyclopedia of the Modern Islamic World. Oxford University Press. ISBN 0-19-506613-8.
- McCook, Kathleen de la Peña (2011). Introduction to Public Librarianship, pp. 75-99. ISBN 978-1-55570-697-5.
- Micheau, Francoise. "The Scientific Institutions in the Medieval Near East". pp. 988–991 in Morelon, Régis; Rashed, Roshdi (1996). Encyclopedia of the History of Arabic Science. 3. Routledge. pp. 985–1007. ISBN 0415124107
- Morelon, Régis; Rashed, Roshdi (1996), Encyclopedia of the History of Arabic Science, 3, Routledge, ISBN 0415124107
- Paula D. Watson, "Founding Mothers: The Contribution of Woman's Organizations to Public Library Development in the United States", Library Quarterly, Vol. 64, Issue 3, 1994, p.236
- Phillips, Heather A., "The Great Library of Alexandria?". Library Philosophy and Practice, August 2010

- Prieto Gutiérrez, Juan José (2009) Security Library Seguridad en bibliotecas. Seguritecnia, revista decana independiente de seguridad , julio-agosto (355). pp. 60-64. ISSN 0210-8747.
- Sibai M. (1987). Mosque libraries: An Historical Study. Mansell Publishing Limited. ISBN 0720118964.
- Stockwell, Foster (2000). A History of Information and Storage Retrieval. ISBN 0786408405.
- Striphas, Ted. "Books: "An Outdated Technology?" Weblog post. The Late Age of Print. 4 September 2009. Web. 19 Nov. 2009. Thelateageofprint.org
- Striphas, Ted. The Late Age of Print: Everday Book Culture From Consumerism to Control. New York City: Columbia University Press, 2009. Print.
- Svenonius, Elaine. The Intellectual Foundation of Information Organization. Cambridge, Mass: MIT Press, 2000.
- Taylor, Archer (1986) Book Catalogues: their varieties and uses; 2nd ed., introductions, corrections and additions by W. P. Barlow, Jr. Winchester: St Paul's Bibliographies (Previous ed.: Chicago: Newberry Library, 1957)
- Teva Scheer, "The "Praxis" Side of the Equation: Club Women and American Public Administration", Administrative Theory & Praxis, Vol. 24, Issue 3, 2002, p.525
- The American International Encyclopedia, J. J. Little & Ives, New York 1954, Volume IX
- This section on Roman Renaissance libraries follows Kenneth M. Setton, "From Medieval to Modern Library" Proceedings of the American Philosophical Society 104.4, Dedication of the APS Library Hall, Autumn General Meeting, November, 1959 (August 1960:371-390) p372ff.

- Troll, Denise A. "How and Why are Libraries Changing?" Digital Library Federation. Library Information Technology- Carnegie Melon, 9 January 2001. Web. 29 November 2009. Diglib.org
- University of California Library Statistics 1990–91, University-wide Library Planning, University of California Office of the President (July 1991): 12; University of California Library Statistics July 2001, 7, Ucop.edu, accessed July 17, 2005; University of California Library Statistics July 2004, 7, Ucop.edu. Retrieved July 17, 2005.
- Van De Mieroop, Marc. A History of the Ancient Near East ca. 3000-323 BC. Oxford, UK: Blackwell Publishing, 2007: pg. 263
- Zurndorfer, Harriet Thelma (1995). China bibliography: a research guide ... - Google Books. ISBN 9789004102781. Retrieved 30 April 2010.

INDEX